THIS IS PHILOSOPHY

Series editor: Steven D. Hales

Reading philosophy can be like trying to ride a bucking bronco—you hold on for dear life while "transcendental deduction" twists you to one side, "causa sui" throws you to the other, and a 300-word, 300-year-old sentence comes down on you like an iron-shod hoof the size of a dinner plate. *This is Philosophy* is the riding academy that solves these problems. Each book in the series is written by an expert who knows how to gently guide students into the subject regardless of the reader's ability or previous level of knowledge. Their reader-friendly prose is designed to help students find their way into the fascinating, challenging ideas that compose philosophy without simply sticking the hapless novice on the back of the bronco, as so many texts do. All the books in the series provide ample pedagogical aids, including links to free online primary sources. When students are ready to take the next step in their philosophical education, *This is Philosophy* is right there to help them along the way.

This Is Philosophy: An Introduction
Steven D. Hales

Forthcoming:

This Is Metaphysics: An Introduction
Kristopher McDaniel

This Is Epistemology: An Introduction
Clayton Littlejohn

This Is Philosophy of Religion: An Introduction
Neil Manson

This Is Philosophy of Mind: An Introduction
Pete Mandik

This is Ethics: An Introduction
Jussi Suikkanen

THIS IS PHILOSOPHY

AN INTRODUCTION

STEVEN D. HALES

A John Wiley & Sons, Ltd., Publication

This edition first published 2013

Wiley-Blackwell is an imprint of John Wiley & Sons, formed by the merger of Wiley's global Scientific, Technical and Medical business with Blackwell Publishing.

Registered Office
John Wiley & Sons Ltd, The Atrium, Southern Gate, Chichester, West Sussex, PO19 8SQ, UK

Editorial Offices
350 Main Street, Malden, MA 02148-5020, USA
9600 Garsington Road, Oxford, OX4 2DQ, UK
The Atrium, Southern Gate, Chichester, West Sussex, PO19 8SQ, UK

For details of our global editorial offices, for customer services, and for information about how to apply for permission to reuse the copyright material in this book please see our website at www.wiley.com/wiley-blackwell.

Library of Congress Cataloging-in-Publication Data

Hales, Steven D.
This is philosophy : an introduction / Steven D. Hales.
p. cm. – (This is philosophy)
Includes bibliographical references and index.
ISBN 978-0-470-65882-6 (hardback) – ISBN 978-0-470-65883-3 (paperback) – ISBN 978-1-118-32780-7 (epub) 1. Philosophy–Introductions. I. Title.
BD21.H223 2013
100–dc23
2012026657

A catalogue record for this book is available from the British Library.

Cover Design by www.cyandesign.co.uk

Set in 10.5/13 pt Minion by Toppan Best-set Premedia Limited

V10014700_101119

For Vanessa

Le cœur a ses raisons, que la raison ne connaît point.

CONTENTS

HOW TO USE THIS BOOK

The problems of philosophy are deeply interconnected, and there is no natural or obvious starting point from which to begin. Indeed, plausible arguments might be given for starting with almost any of the central problems in the field. You might think that we should surely start with epistemology; until we understand what knowledge is and settle the matter of whether and how we can gain any knowledge at all, how can we possibly determine whether we can have knowledge of God, or our moral duties, or the nature of the mind? Clearly epistemology is the most fundamental philosophical project. Wait—how can we be sure that knowledge is valuable to have? Or that we ought to care about gaining truth and avoiding error? We'd better start with axiology and sort out duty, obligation, and responsibility first. Normativity and ethics must be foundational. Of course, how can we determine what our epistemic responsibilities are if we don't antecedently know whether we are free to believe one thing rather than another, or if we are truly at liberty to make choices? Let's begin with the issue of free will and figure that out first. If we're not free, that torpedoes a lot of other philosophical agendas. Yet if we don't know what kinds of beings we are, how can we ever determine whether we are free? Maybe personal identity should be the first stop on the road. And so on.

The chapters in the present book are self-contained units on the topics they address. While there are occasional references within them to other chapters, they can be taught or studied in any order. In *Daybreak* (section 454), Nietzsche wrote that, "A book such as this is not for reading straight through or reading aloud but for dipping into, especially when out walking or on a journey; you must be able to stick your head into it and out of it again and again and discover nothing familiar around you." To some extent, the same is true of *This Is Philosophy: An Introduction*, even though it is much more straightforwardly systematic and less aphoristic than Nietzsche's *Daybreak*.

That said, the chapters are not randomly distributed, and are placed in one sensible progression. Most people have views about ethics and God before ever encountering philosophy, and so starting with topics to which they have already given some thought is a natural way to entice students into a deeper investigation. Appeal to human free choice is a venerable move in theodicy, and one with which the chapter on God ends. A chapter on free will then follows. Afterwards is a pair of chapters focusing on what it is to be a thinking, persisting person at all—personal identity and philosophy of mind. The final chapter in the book, on knowledge, ties together the threads of evidence, reason-giving, and rational belief that appear, one way or another, in all of the chapters, and ends with a comprehensive skeptical problem.

The problems of philosophy resemble a **Mandelbrot Set** (see www.youtube.com/watch?v=gEw8xpb1aRA), and the more closely one focuses on the small details, the more complications one finds. Some of the initial hooks and spirals can be found in the annotated bibliographies at the end of each chapter. These bibliographies list primary sources from the great thinkers that one may wish to read in conjunction with the present chapters, as well as some of the more accessible contemporary literature that is the next step for the **Padawan** philosopher (see http://starwars.wikia.com/wiki/Padawan).

PREFACE

If this is the first philosophy book you've ever read, then you probably have no idea what you are in for. You pick up a book on chemistry and you expect diagrams of molecules and talk about "valences," a book on German and there will be long multisyllable words and lots of umlauts. But philosophy? What could that be about?

The word "philosophy" comes from two Greek words: "philia," which was one of the Greek words for love, and "sophia," which means wisdom. Thus philosophy is the love of wisdom. You may think that is not terribly informative, and it isn't. However, you have to remember that, back in ancient Greece, to be a scholar at all meant that one was a philosopher. You might have been a stonemason, a fisherman, a soldier, a physician, or a philosopher, a pursuit that would have included mathematics and science. Over the years, as concrete, definite advances have been made in different areas, philosophy has spawned spin-offs, fields that have become their own disciplines with their own specific methodology and subject matter. Mathematics was one of the first fields to splinter off this way, and then in the Renaissance science became separate from philosophy. In the nineteenth century psychology broke away from philosophy and, most recently, cognitive science, which used to be the scientific end of philosophy of mind, has become its own field. In some ways philosophy proper is left with the hardest questions, the ones that we have made the least definitive progress on.

That does not mean that philosophers have made no progress in 2500 years. We have. Nevertheless, the philosophical issues to be discussed in the present book are tough nuts to crack. Let us hope you do not crack your own coconut in the attempt! In the modern era, philosophy is in the business of giving good reasons for one's nonempirical beliefs. That is, philosophers try to give arguments for believing claims about the nature of the self, or the existence of God, or moral duty, or the value of knowledge. These are topics that the scientific method of performing laboratory experiments and giving mathematical explanations does poorly in addressing. Philosophers take seriously the findings of experts in other disciplines, but we still have our own puzzles to solve.

Some philosophical topics stir great passions, and people find it threatening to ask questions about those issues. Philosophers are proud that one of the greatest philosophers in ancient times, **Socrates**, was executed by the state because he refused to stop questioning authority (see http://classics.mit.edu/Plato/apology.html). Socrates claimed to know nothing, but he was willing to go down for the *pursuit* of truth, fearless inquiry, and the life of the mind. If you are to find something of value in this book, you too need to be prepared to question your long-standing beliefs, to honestly ask yourself if the things you may have believed your entire life are actually true. All of us believe some things for poor reasons, and to be a philosopher is to try to ferret out those beliefs and either justify them or discard them as unworthy of your intellect. It is a difficult and often painful process to become an athlete of the mind, but there is great joy and thrilling discoveries to be had as well.

Just beneath the surface of your everyday life are chasms of mystery. We will not descend into the furthest reaches of the labyrinth in the present book, but there are wonders aplenty in the beginning passages. **Plato** wrote that philosophy begins in wonder (http://classics.mit.edu/Plato/theatu.html)—so let us begin!

ACKNOWLEDGMENTS

Thanks to Jeff Dean at Wiley-Blackwell for encouraging this book and the This Is Philosophy series. He is the *ne plus ultra* of editors. Thanks also to my colleagues at Bloomsburg University for their support, and to my many Introduction to Philosophy students who have participated in the joint enterprise of learning.

1

ETHICS
PRELIMINARY THEORIES

The Normative Universe

Life's just filled with all sorts of things you're supposed to do. You should be nice to your sister, brush between meals, never mix beer and wine, get your car inspected, tithe to the poor, wear clean underwear, avoid consumer debt, love thy neighbor as thyself, buy low and sell high, read good books, exercise, tell the truth, have evidence-based beliefs, come to a complete stop at a red light, eat your vegetables, call your mom once in a while. The list goes on and on. All these things you should do, various obligations, duties, and responsibilities, form the *normative universe.* Shoulds, oughts, duties, rights, the permissible and the impermissible populate the normative universe. Not all these shoulds and oughts are ethical in nature, however. There are many dimensions to the normative universe, not just the moral dimension. Here are a few examples: 1.1

- Jim is deciding whether he should invest his money in gold bullion, mutual funds, or government bonds.
- Vanessa wonders whether it is permissible for her to turn right on red in this state.
- Todd is debating whether he ought to put more cinnamon in his ginger snaps.
- Holly is considering whether she filled out her taxes right.

The first case is about what Jim should *practically or prudentially* invest in; the second example concerns the *legal* permissibility of turning right on

This Is Philosophy: An Introduction, First Edition. Steven D. Hales.

red; the third offers an *aesthetic* case regarding what Todd ought to do when baking cookies; and the fourth case is about the *reasonableness* of Holly's believing that her tax form is correct. In these cases, "should," "permissible," "ought," and "right" have nothing to do with morality, even though they are still normative expressions. When exactly those words concern morality is not an easy matter to describe with any precision. But confusion will ensue if we aren't sensitive to the fact that what we ought to do practically or legally is not the same as what we ought to do morally. We will see more of this later.

1.2 Everyone is faced with making ethical choices—decisions about what they should do in some circumstance. We must each decide for ourselves whether a potential action is right or wrong, and contemplate the nature of honor, duty, and virtue. There are standards of correct action that aren't moral standards. Still, it is clear that the following are cases of moral deliberation.

- Your best friend's girlfriend has had one beer too many and is coming on to you at the party. If you can get away with it, should you hook up with her?
- Your friend Shawna knows how to pirate new-release movies, and wants to show you how. Should you go with her and get some flicks?
- Your grandmother is dying of terminal pancreatic cancer and has only a few, painful, days to live. She is begging you to give her a lethal overdose of morphine, which will depress her respiration and allow her to die peacefully. Should you give her the overdose?
- You are a pregnant, unmarried student. Testing has shown that your fetus has **Down Syndrome.**[1] Should you abort?

- You didn't study enough for your chem exam, and don't have all those formulas you need memorized. One of your friends tells you to get a water bottle and carefully peel off the label. Then write the formulas down on the inside of the label and stick it back on the bottle. Take the bottle of water to the exam; the prof will never know you're cheating every time you take a swig. You should do whatever you can to get ahead in this world, right?

These aren't far-fetched cases; at least a few of them should fit your own experience. Well, how do you decide what to do? If you're like most people, you might reflect on whatever values your parents taught you growing up; or think about what your religion or holy book has to say on the topic; or go with your gut instinct about what to do; or consider the consequences if you do the action; or imagine how it would make you feel later if you did it; or think about whether the proposed action is compatible with some moral rule you believe, like do unto others as they would do unto you. If you look at this list, you'll see that it naturally divides into two main approaches: (1) base your action on some rule, principle, or code, and (2) base your action on some intuition, feeling, or instinct.

Is Morality Just Acting on Principles?

You might think that moral action means sticking to your principles, 1.3
holding fast to your beliefs and respecting how you were raised. Or perhaps morality is acting as you think God intends, by strictly following your holy book. Acting on the basis of your instincts and sympathies is to abandon genuine morality for transient emotions. One person who subscribed to the view that moral action requires strict adherence to principles and tradition was **Osama bin Laden.**[2]

Osama bin Laden was, of course, the notorious terrorist mastermind of 1.4
the 9/11 attacks. Bin Laden was not a madman or a lunatic, though, and if you read his writings you'll see that he was an articulate, educated spokesman for his views. Bin Laden believed that the Western nations are engaged in a Crusader war against Islam, and that God demands that the **Islamic Caliphate**[3] (the theocratic rule of all Muslims under an official successor to the Prophet Muhammad) be restored to power, and that all nations follow Islamic religious law (sharia). In an interview in October 2001, Bin Laden responded to the criticism that he sanctions the killing of women, children, and innocents.

> The scholars and people of the knowledge, amongst them Sahib al-Ikhtiyarat [ibn Taymiyya] and ibn al-Qayyim, and Shawanni, and many others, and Qutubi—may God bless him—in his Qur'an commentary, say that if the disbelievers were to kill our children and women, then we should not feel ashamed to do the same to them, mainly to deter them from trying to kill our women and children again. And that is from a religious perspective . . .
>
> As for the World Trade Center, the ones who were attacked and who died in it were part of a financial power. It wasn't a children's school! Neither was it a residence. And the general consensus is that most of the people who were in the towers were men that backed the biggest financial force in the world, which spreads mischief throughout the world. And those individuals should

> stand before God, and rethink and redo their calculations. We treat others like they treat us. Those who kill our women and our innocent, we kill their women and innocent, until they stop doing so. (quoted in Lawrence, 2005, pp. 118–119)

Bin Laden is clearly concerned with the morality of killing "women and innocents"; he takes pains to note that al-Qaeda attacked the World Trade Center, a financial building that—in his view—contained supporters of an materialist, imperialist nation of unbelievers. WTC was not a school or a home. Moreover, Bin Laden cites religious scholars and interpreters of the Qur'an to support his belief that killing noncombatants as a form of deterrence is a morally permissible act, sanctioned by his religion. Bin Laden was a devout and pious man who scrupulously adhered to his moral principles. If you think that he was a wicked, mass-murdering evildoer, it is not because he failed to be principled. It is because you find his principles to be bad ones.

1.5 What proof is there that Bin Laden's moral principles are the wrong ones? None, really, other than an appeal to our common ethical intuitions that the intentional murder of innocents to further some idiosyncratic political or religious goal is morally heinous. If you disagree, it may be that your moral compass points in such an opposite direction that you don't have enough in common with ordinary folks to engage in meaningful moral discussion. Even Bin Laden worried that it is wrong to kill children and women, which is why he was careful to justify his actions.

1.6 Just because you base your actions on some rule, principle, or moral code that you've adopted or created is no guarantee that you'll do the right thing. You could have a bad moral code—just look at Bin Laden. Well, is it better to base your actions on your intuitions, on the feelings you have about whatever situation is at hand? Not necessarily. Feelings are immediate and case-specific, and the situation right in front of us is always the most vivid and pressing. Your gut instincts may lead you to choose short-term benefits over what's best in the long term. For example, imagine a mother who has taken a toddler in for a vaccination. The child is crying, not wanting to feel the pain of the needle. Surely the mother's instincts are to whisk the child away from the doctor advancing with his sharp pointy stick. Yet sometimes the right action is to set our feelings aside to see the larger picture. The mother has a moral obligation to care for her child, and so must hold back her protective sympathies and force the child to get the shot.

1.7 If we can't trust our moral principles and rules (because we might have bad principles and rules), and we can't trust our moral intuitions (because our sympathies might be shortsighted and narrow), then what should we do? The most prominent approach is to use the best of both worlds. We should use our most fundamental moral intuitions to constrain and craft moral theories and principles. This approach does not mean that we just capitulate to our gut instincts. Sometimes our principles should override those instincts. But, at the same time, when our principles or theories tell us to perform actions that are in conflict with our deepest feelings and intuitions, that is a reason to reexamine those principles and perhaps revise them or even reject them outright. Such a procedure apparently never occurred to Bin Laden, who was unflinchingly convinced of the righteousness of his cause.

1.8 The idea that moral rules be tested against our intuitions is analogous to the scientific method by which scientific theories are tested against experiments and direct observations. Sometimes a really fine and widely repeated experiment convinces everyone that a scientific theory cannot be right, and sometimes experimental results or observations are dismissed as faulty because they come into conflict with an otherwise well-confirmed and excellent theory. There is no hard-and-fast way to decide how to go. But how would all this play out in the case of ethics?

1.9 Here is a simple example to illustrate the procedure, before we move on to taking a look at the more prominent moral theories. Consider the so-called **Golden Rule**,[4] a moral rule dating from antiquity that appears in various forms in a variety of different ancient authors and traditions. It states *do unto others as you would have them do unto you*. What intuitions could be used as evidence against this rule? Put another way, what's counterintuitive about it, if anything? Well, the Golden Rule implicitly assumes that everyone has the same preferences. That assumption seems a bit questionable. Suppose that you like backrubs. In fact, you'd like a backrub from pretty much anyone. The Golden Rule advises you to treat other people the way you would like to be treated. Since you'd like other people to give you unsolicited backrubs, you should, according to the Golden Rule, give everyone else a backrub, even if they didn't ask for one. But some people don't like backrubs, or don't care for strangers touching them. Intuitively, it would be wrong to give backrubs to those people without their consent, or against their will. Since this intuition conflicts with the Golden Rule's implication to administer unsolicited backrubs, we should conclude that maybe the Golden Rule is really iron pyrite after all.

1.10 You might respond that we should revise the Golden Rule to avoid the unwanted implication, or we should replace it with a more precise moral rule. Perhaps *do unto others as they would have be done unto them*, or some such. But then we would have to give others whatever they ask of us, which is surely more than we should have to provide. That's just how moral philosophy proceeds—we modify our moral views in light of compelling arguments and counterexamples, or sometimes go back to the drawing board altogether to come up with better theories.

Divine Command Theory (Is Morality Just What God Tells Me to Do?)

1.11 Morality could be like the law in this sense: an authority is needed to tell us what our moral duties are, and to enforce the rules. Without a lawgiver, a ruler to lay down the moral law, we are adrift with no deeper connection to right and wrong than our own transient preferences. Traditionally, God has been considered to be this moral authority. You might think that if God does not exist, then everything is permitted. The need for God as a source of morality is often cited as a motivation—maybe *the* motivation—to be religious; that the ethical life is possible only within a religious context. It is endorsed, as we saw above, by Osama bin Laden, and promoted by no end of Christian ministers, pundits, and politicians. It is well worth thinking through.

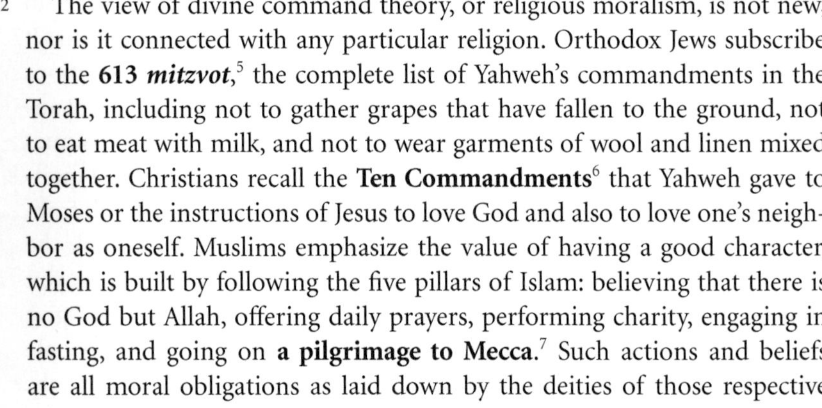

1.12 The view of divine command theory, or religious moralism, is not new, nor is it connected with any particular religion. Orthodox Jews subscribe  to the **613 *mitzvot*,**[5] the complete list of Yahweh's commandments in the Torah, including not to gather grapes that have fallen to the ground, not to eat meat with milk, and not to wear garments of wool and linen mixed  together. Christians recall the **Ten Commandments**[6] that Yahweh gave to Moses or the instructions of Jesus to love God and also to love one's neighbor as oneself. Muslims emphasize the value of having a good character, which is built by following the five pillars of Islam: believing that there is no God but Allah, offering daily prayers, performing charity, engaging in  fasting, and going on **a pilgrimage to Mecca**.[7] Such actions and beliefs are all moral obligations as laid down by the deities of those respective religions.

1.13 The proposal that morality is essentially connected to religion has two chief components:

1. God loves (endorses, recommends, advocates) all good actions and hates (forbids, abjures, prohibits) all evil actions.

2. We can figure out which is which; that is, we can know what God loves and what he hates.

Let's consider these in turn. Grant for the sake of argument that there is a morally perfect God, that is, there is a God who loves everything good and hates everything evil (for more on the attributes of God, see Chapter 3). For the purposes of this discussion, it doesn't matter whether goodness/badness is primarily a quality of persons, actions, characters, or what have you. The notion of a perfectly good God is that his attitudes are in perfect sync with morality.

Plato discussed the idea that morality and religion are inseparable 2500 1.14
years ago in his dialogue ***Euthyphro***.[8] Plato was no atheist—by all accounts he, like his mentor Socrates, respected and accepted the official **Greek gods**.[9] Nevertheless, Plato thought that, even if the gods are perfectly good, that fact is not enough to explain morality. In *Euthyphro* he raises this very subtle and interesting question, here phrased for a monotheistic audience:

> Are things good because God loves them, or does he love them because they are good?

The question presents two very different options about **God's love**.[10]

Option A. Things are good because God loves them. This means that it is God's love that *makes* things good, and his dislike that *makes* things bad. Prior to, or considered independently of, God's judgment, things don't have moral qualities at all. If it weren't for God, nothing would be right or wrong, good or bad. Moral properties are the result of God's decisions, like candy sprinkles he casts over the vanilla ice cream of the material world.

Option B. God loves good things because they are good. On this option, things are good (or bad) antecedently to, and independently of, God. In other words, things already have their moral properties, and God, who is an infallible judge of such matters, always loves the good things and hates the bad things. Morality is an independent objective standard apart from God. God always responds appropriately to this standard (loving all the good stuff and hating the bad), but morality is separate from, and unaffected by, his judgments.

So which is it? Option A, where God creates the moral qualities of things, or Option B, where God is the perfect ethical thermometer, whose opinions accurately reflect the moral temperature of whatever he judges? Following Plato, here are some interrelated reasons to prefer Option B.

1.15 Think about something you love. You love your mom? The Philadelphia Eagles? The Dave Matthews Band? Bacon cheeseburgers? Your pet dog? French-roast coffee? All good choices. Now, reflect on why you love them. You can give reasons, right? You love your mom, but not everyone's mom, because she raised you, cares for you, is kind to you, etc. Other moms didn't do that. You love the Dave Matthews Band because of their jam-band grooves, jazz syncopation and instrumentation, and catchy hooks. You love French-roast coffee over milder roasts because you really like the pungent, smoky, bitter brew it produces. You get the idea. In other words, your love is grounded in reasons for loving. In fact, it would be downright bizarre if someone asked you why you love one brand of pizza over another and your response were "no reason." It might not always be easy to come up with the reasons why you love one thing over another, but if you literally had no reasons whatsoever, it would be perplexingly mysterious why you love that thing. Your love of that pizza would be arbitrary.

1.16 Our emotions and feelings are in part judgments that respond to the world around us. If you are angry, you are angry for a reason—you believe that someone insulted you, or cut you off in traffic, or whatever. When emotions do not have this component of judgment, we generally think that something has gone wrong. For example, if someone is depressed because they lost their job and their spouse died, then depression is a reasonable reaction—it is a rational response to real-world events. On the other hand, if someone is depressed but has no good reason to feel blue, then we naturally look for a different kind of explanation of their depression. We may look for a causal explanation involving brain chemistry; perhaps they have serotonin deficiency, say. Irrational depression is a medical problem. Similarly, if someone is angry all the time for no apparent reason, we are liable to say that they have an anger problem, and should seek therapy. In other words, irrational emotions unconnected to facts about the world are a sign of mental stress or illness.

1.17 Under Option A God has no reasons at all for loving one thing over another. As soon as he loves something, then it *becomes* good, pious, and right. So there is no *moral reason* for God to declare murder wrong instead of right. This means that morality is completely arbitrary; the fact that rape and murder are immoral is random. God could have just as easily made rape and murder your moral duty. What's to stop him? He's God after all, and he decides what's right and wrong. You can't very well insist that God would not have made murder your positive moral duty, because murder is immoral—that's to assume that morality is an objective standard apart from God's decisions, which is Option B. We're here assuming Option A is true.

What's more, God could change his mind at any minute. He might show 1.18
up and declare that he's gotten bored with all those old commandments and instructions, and that he's issuing some new moral laws. Covet thy neighbor's wife. Do unto others before they do unto you. Eat bacon sandwiches on the Sabbath. Carve graven images of Muhammad. Thou shalt kill. If he were to declare these new rules the moral law, then they would in fact become your moral duties. Perhaps you think that God would never do such a thing. Well, why not? If you think that he is obliged to be consistent in his moral dictates, then you are setting up consistency as an objective external normative standard that God must respect. Yet the whole idea of Option A is that God's opinions *establish* the normative universe, not that they abide by it.

To sum up, under Option A morality is random and arbitrary. God 1.19
chooses some things to be good and others to be bad without any reasons whatsoever for his choice. His preferences are based on nothing at all, and he might as well be rolling dice to decide what to love and what to hate. Indeed, such random emotional judgments, unconstrained by external facts, are more indicative of mental illness or a loss of control than a divinely omniscient mind. Moreover, literally any action could be your moral duty, and will be the minute God declares that he loves it. The cherry on top is that there's no reason God wouldn't or couldn't reverse all his previous opinions and turn morality upside down. Expect the unexpected.

If you think that those results are a bunch of crazy talk—as Plato did— 1.20
then you should conclude that God's love does not make things good. Instead, vote for Option B: God loves things because they are good. That is, God's judgments flawlessly track moral reality; he invariably loves the good and hates the wicked. God may be a perfect judge, but he does not make the moral law. In other words, morality and religion are logically separate, which means that whether God exists has nothing to do with whether there are moral facts or what those facts are.

Now, you might suggest at this point that even if God not does make 1.21
morality, nevertheless the smart move is to pay attention to his moral advice. God is supposedly morally perfect, so as an ethical role model, there's no one better. Since morality is a hard thing to figure out, if

God's got it all solved for us, we should listen up—scripture's just *Ethics for Dummies.*

1.22 While this is certainly an approach we might try, as a practical matter it is not exactly smooth sailing. Here's what we'll need to do. Step one: prove that a perfectly good God exists. Step two: prove that there are no other Gods whose moral opinions we must also consult. That is, not only is your religion right but also everyone else's is wrong. Step three: show how we can know what God's moral views are. If you think that the Qur'an, the Bible, the Torah, the Upanishads, or whatever, are the word of the Lord, you'll need to prove that. Or if you believe you have God's cell phone number, and he's letting you know what he thinks, you'll need to show why you're not just delusional instead. Step four: offer a clear and unequivocal interpretation of God's moral views. We might be able to pull off all these things. But each of the steps is mighty heavy lifting. If Plato is right, and morality and religion are logically independent, then we *can* investigate ethics without debating religion. Perhaps the smart practical move is to do that very thing.

Egoism (Is Morality Just My Own Personal Code?)

1.23 Maybe morality is just a matter of each individual's personal ethical views, along the lines of the following sentiments:

- Morality is just whatever you believe it is.
- Everyone has his or her own morality.
- Real morality is just "look out for #1."
- Here's the real Golden Rule: he who has the gold makes the rules.
- "What is moral is what you feel good after and what is immoral is what you feel bad after."—**Ernest Hemingway**[11]

- "Man's greatest good fortune is to chase and defeat his enemy, seize his total possessions, leave his married women weeping and wailing, ride his gelding, use the bodies of his women as a nightshirt and a support, gazing upon and kissing their rosy breasts, sucking their lips which are sweet as the berries of their breasts."—Genghis Khan
- "What is best in life is to crush your enemies, see them driven before you, and to hear the lamentation of their women."—**Conan the Barbarian**[12]

- "The achievement of his own happiness is man's highest moral purpose."— **Ayn Rand**[13]

Psychological and ethical egoism

There are a couple of different ideas expressed by these slogans, and we should pry them apart. One is a purely descriptive thesis about human psychology, namely: 1.24

Psychological egoism: everyone always acts in his or her own self-interest.

The other idea is a normative thesis about morality, namely:

Ethical egoism: everyone *should* always act in his or her own self-interest.

Both of these theses could be true. Obviously, if psychological egoism is true, then fulfilling one's moral duties according to ethical egoism is a piece of cake. It's easy to do what you can't avoid doing anyway. Or it could be that psychological egoism is true and ethical egoism is false, in which case everyone acts selfishly, but that's just evidence of flawed human beings who must struggle against their nature to do the right thing. Or perhaps ethical egoism is true but psychological egoism is false, in which case everyone ought to just look out for themselves, but misguided social pressure forces us to sacrifice for others. Or perhaps both psychological and ethical egoism are false.

Let's take a look at these two in turn. First up is a popular argument for psychological egoism, namely that altruism is always merely superficial and the authentic springs of actions are invariably self-interested ones. Thus even people who sacrifice for others, donate to charity, feed the poor, etcetera, only do so because it makes them feel good about themselves, or impresses others. Nobody would help other people if they didn't get something in return—self-satisfaction, self-esteem, community respect, higher social standing, better choice of mates. On the surface charity looks like altruism, but when we dig a little deeper we can see that it is self-interest after all. Sometimes "altruism" is obviously selfish, as in the case of someone who tithes to the church or gives alms to the poor in order to get a shinier halo in heaven. No matter what you do, you get something out of it, or you wouldn't be doing it. Which is just to say that everyone always acts in his or her self-interest; we just can't help it. 1.25

What would count as evidence against this argument for psychological egoism? Consider an act of putative self-sacrifice, in which Generous George gives away a considerable amount of money to a needy stranger. The psychological egoist is committed not only to the view that George 1.26

stands to benefit in some way (for example, by feeling good about himself) but his benefit outweighs the cost of getting it. Otherwise, it is a net loss for George. Put another way, one can't reasonably argue that Saleswoman Sarah is a smart car dealer if she keeps selling cars for less than the dealership paid for them. Losing money is not self-interested behavior. She acts in her self-interest only if she's making a profit and selling cars for more than her company paid for them. Likewise Generous George isn't acting in his self-interest if what he's getting out of his charity is less valuable than the money he's giving away. So here's a test for egoistic action: an action is egoistic only if the benefits to the giver exceed the cost of the giving. Put conversely, if the benefits to the giver are less than the value of the gift, then the action is not egoistic. Now that we know in principle how to refute psychological egoism, are there any real-life, actual cases of non-egoistic behavior? The answer is yes.

1.27 Ross McGinnis was a 19-year-old army private from Pennsylvania serving in the Iraq War. On December 4, 2006, he was manning an M2.50-caliber machine gun in the turret of a Humvee patrolling Baghdad's Adhamiyah district. A rooftop enemy insurgent lobbed a fragmentation grenade at the Humvee, which fell through the gunner's hatch and landed near McGinnis. He immediately yelled, "the grenade is in the truck," and threw himself on it. His quick action allowed all four members of his crew to prepare for the blast. According to the Army, "**McGinnis** absorbed all lethal fragments and the concussive effects of the grenade with his own body."[14] He was killed instantly. His platoon sergeant later stated that McGinnis could have jumped from the Humvee to safety; instead he chose to save the lives of four other men at the sacrifice of his own. For his bravery McGinnis was posthumously awarded the Medal of Honor.

1.28 McGinnis certainly did not act in his own self-interest. He received no benefit at all from his heroism, and even the Medal of Honor is cold comfort to his grieving family, who would have much preferred the safe return of their son. It is an understatement to observe that the value of his gift—saving the lives of four fellow soldiers—was greater than what he got in return, which was merely death.

1.29 You might be inclined to argue that McGinnis is a rare exception, and that heroic self-sacrifice is far from the norm. Maybe psychological egoism isn't true of every human being ever to live, but it could still be true of the vast majority. You might think that *nearly* everyone always acts in his or her own self-interest. Yet even this modified claim of predominant egoism is apparently false.

Consider child rearing. One of the most pervasive beliefs around the 1.30
world is that having children will make people happy. Childless couples imagine a future filled with beautiful, successful, loving children, of cheerful holiday dinners and birthday parties at the park. Parents whose children are grown look back fondly on family traditions, vacations taken, and funny episodes of life. So parents encourage their childless friends and adult children to have kids of their own, they tell them that kids are wonderful, a blessing not to be missed. Everyone is happier with a brood. Sure, there are diapers to be changed, homework to monitor, and orthodontists to be paid, but all in all, the hard work of parenting pays back big dividends.

Recent studies have shown, however, that "children will make you 1.31
happy" is a myth. In fact, children make you less happy. The family life of an average person will be a lot less happy with children than without them. Psychologists who study happiness with sophisticated surveys and tests have discovered that couples tend to start out quite happy in their marriages, but grow increasingly less happy over the course of their lives together until the children leave home. It is not until they reach "empty nest" that the parents' marital happiness levels return to what they were pre-children. The Harvard psychologist Daniel Gilbert plotted the results from four different happiness studies (Figure 1.1), all of which tell the same story.

Given the evidence that children make our home lives less happy, why 1.32
does everyone insist on the opposite? In Gilbert's view, we are all wired by evolution to deceive ourselves—and others—about how much having kids decreases our happiness. Even though studies repeatedly show that women (historically the primary caregivers) are less happy taking care of their children than when eating, exercising, shopping, napping, or watching TV (Gilbert, 2005, p. 243), our subconscious minds ignore the evidence and tell us the opposite. Imagine a world in which everyone believed the truth that having kids will, on the whole, only add to your misery. Apart from accidents, people would stop having them. Failing to reproduce is the fastest way for a species to go extinct, so evolution builds in some safeguards, including blindness about what actually makes us happy.

If the happiness researchers are right, then having and raising children 1.33
is a genuine act of altruism. The benefits to the giver, in this case the parents, are less than the value of the gift, namely the gift of life and the resources to survive until adulthood. Having children is one of the most common human activities, and not a rare act of courage like that of Private

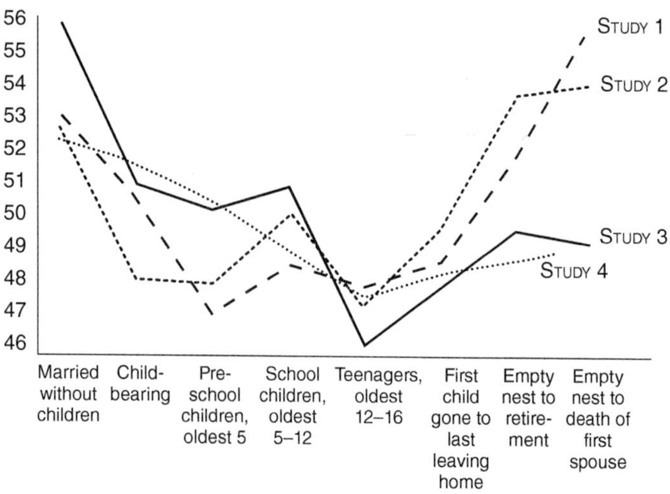

Figure 1.1 Marital satisfaction. In C. Walker, "Some Variations in Marital Satisfaction," *Equalities and Inequalities in Family Life: Proceedings of the Thirteenth Symposium of the Eugenics Society London 1976* (Academic Press, 1977). As the four separate studies in this graph show, marital satisfaction decreases dramatically after the birth of the first child and increases only when the last child leaves home

McGinnis. When you decide to ignore the happiness findings and go on to have children (as most of the readers of this book will), you will be intentionally performing a pure act of altruism, in the full knowledge that you will be giving benefits to others with a net loss to your own happiness. The evidence is thus that psychological egoism is false. People routinely do not act in their own self-interest.

1.34 But what about ethical egoism? Perhaps we *should* all be acting in our own self-interest. Earlier we argued that we should test proposed ethical theories against our most basic and ingrained intuitions about permissible actions. What are the intuitive pros and cons of ethical egoism?

1.35 On the plus side, egoism captures the idea that each human life has intrinsic merit. It allows each person to view his or her own life as being of ultimate value, thereby taking the importance of the human individual seriously. Any moral philosophy that requires sacrifices for others compels individuals to set their own interests aside in order to promote the welfare of others whom they may not care about. That suggests that an individual's life is something at the disposal of others, not something to be valued for its own sake.

More concretely, suppose that you have a hamburger. It's legitimately 1.36 yours—you bought it fairly with money you legally earned though your own labor. Now, imagine that as you leave Harry's Hamburger Haven with your lunch you see a hungry beggar. You could give him your burger, or you could keep walking and enjoy it yourself. Let's suppose that he would get much more out of the burger than you would; he hasn't eaten in two days whereas you haven't eaten for two hours. Nevertheless, there is an intuition that it is *your* hamburger to do with as you please. If you choose to give it to the beggar then of course you may, but if you eat it yourself, then that's your prerogative too. Egoism effortlessly explains why there's nothing wrong with you keeping and eating your own lunch, even when it would benefit others even more. As we will see later, other moral theories, such as utilitarianism, can't easily allow such a simple thing.

Another argument is that we are each best suited to figure out what our 1.37 own wants and needs are. Maybe the kinds of things you want out of life aren't the things your parents want. There are many different visions of the good life—a yurt in the desert, living off the grid, communing with nature and smoking homegrown cannabis; a condo on the upper East Side in Manhattan with a Porsche in the parking garage; a cloistered monastery in the Italian Alps with prayers and silence. People ought to each pursue their own vision of the best life for themselves and be free to do so. If we interfere in each other's lives, even out of a sense of beneficence, we are more likely to make a botch job of it. We'll just wind up imposing our own values on each other, when it is far better for each of us to pursue our own interests.

Now, you might think that if ethical egoism were widely adopted that it 1.38 would result in a bunch of uncooperative, self-absorbed loners. However, that's not true. Ethical egoism is entirely compatible with collective action based on reciprocity. You may decide to help your neighbor work on his roof because you know that later on he'll help you with your deck. Or you might decide to pool your money with your friends and get a keg of beer, knowing that you'll get a better price for such a bulk purchase. Everyone profits by having more beer for less money, including you. In these cases each person acts to promote his or her own self-interest, but other people benefit as well. The image of ethical egoism is the wolfpack—hunting together the pack can take down a moose, but each wolf is out to benefit itself.

Objections to ethical egoism

1.39 What's the downside of ethical egoism? There are three main objections to egoism.

1.40 *Objection 1: Horrible consequences* There are many intuitively heinous actions that, under ethical egoism, are morally permissible. For egoists, nothing that people do to each other in the name of his or her own self-interest is immoral. Consider the following. In 1991 Phillip and Nancy Garrido of Antioch, California kidnapped a blond, pony-tailed 11-year-old little girl named **Jaycee Lee Dugard**.[15] For the next 18 years they kept her prisoner in their backyard while they raped her. Phillip Garrido fathered two children with Jaycee, the first when she was only 14 years old, and kept the children isolated, uneducated, and captive. The children had never been to a doctor. In 2009 the Garridos were discovered and arrested. Or consider the case of **Kristen Diane Parker**,[16] a surgery technician at Denver's Rose Medical Center and Colorado Springs' Audubon Surgery Center. A heroin addict, she routinely stole Fentanyl, a powerful painkiller, from cancer patients, whom she left in pain as she replaced their drugs with saline. As she carelessly switched her used syringes for fresh ones, Parker infected three dozen people with hepatitis C. In 2010 she was sentenced to 20 years in prison.

1.41 Every day newspaper headlines tell of cases just like these, where people are acting in their own self-interest without regard for others. If you think that Parker and the Garridos are moral monsters, brutal narcissists who have no place in a civilized society, then you should doubt that ethical egoism is the correct theory of morality. After all, under ethical egoism their actions were not merely permissible, but, since they served to advance their own interests, their positive moral duty. Remember, the thesis of ethical egoism is that everyone *should* always act in his or her own self-interest, which the Garridos and Parker apparently did. When the kidnapping and sexual enslavement of children and the theft of painkillers from cancer victims turn out to be anyone's moral duty, one might reasonably question the moral theory at hand.

1.42 A defender of ethical egoism might argue that in fact the Garridos and Parker failed to act in their own self-interest, on the grounds that they were caught, convicted, and sent to prison. Surely imprisonment was not in their self-interest. That's why their actions were wrong; they led to negative consequences for themselves down the road. However, such a defense means that kidnapping, rape, and theft are morally heinous only if you are caught—if you get away with your crimes, then you did nothing wrong after all. Such a defense goes against the intuition that it would have been far worse for Phillip Garrido to continue child rape and enslavement, far worse for Kristen Diane Parker to have continued to infect people with Hepatitis C and steal pain meds from cancer patients. If the world was made better by their capture, then the egoist defense does not work.

Objection 2: Subjectivity The second objection to ethical egoism is that it 1.43
makes morality wholly subjective, in just the same manner as matters of taste. Many people think that if anything is purely subjective, then taste is. Thus there is no objective fact of the matter about whether broccoli tastes delicious, or whether roses smell better than lilacs. There is simply personal preference; some like roses better, others lilacs. It is hardly a matter over which we might have violent disagreement, or, really, any meaningful disagreement at all. You like one and your friend likes the other. You acknowledge each other's preferences and move on. How exercised can one really get about Coke vs. Pepsi, or what your favorite color is?

If ethical egoism is correct, then morality is just as subjective as matters 1.44
of taste. Suppose Joe thinks eating babies is morally wrong and Jane thinks eating babies is not only morally permissible, but delicious to boot. As in the cases of taste, there is no true disagreement between Joe and Jane—they are doing no more than expressing the preferences they have, in light of the goals and desires they each possess. Joe advances his interests by not eating babies, and Jane advances her (presumably culinary) interests though cannibalism. Joe is doing the morally right thing (for Joe) and Jane is doing the morally right thing (for Jane). Therefore they are in no position to criticize each other. The most each could say is "I wouldn't do what you're doing—but by all means, carry on." The ethical egoist credo is live and let live, or, perhaps *de gustibus non est disputandum* (in matters of taste, there is no disputing). But each is acting to pursue his or her own self-interest, which is exactly what ethical egoism says they ought to do. If you think that it is entirely reasonable and morally fair to criticize Jane for her cannibalism, then ethical egoism is not the correct moral theory.

Objection 3: Equal treatment The third objection to ethical egoism is that 1.45
it violates an intuitively plausible constraint on moral theories, namely the principle of equal treatment.

Principle of equal treatment: Two people should be treated in the same way unless there is a relevant difference between them.

The principle of equal treatment does not require that everyone be treated alike; it allows variable treatment. Discrimination gets a bad name because people tend to conflate reasonable discrimination with unreasonable discrimination. If you were choosing up sides for a basketball team, no one would expect you to pick an overweight 4'11" senior citizen over a 6'11" college athlete. Fitness, age, and height are all relevant criteria for basketball performance. Likewise, if you're hiring for a managerial job, it's fair to grant interviews to candidates who have college degrees, previous management experience, and good letters of reference over applicants who have none of those things. These are cases of discrimination—treating people differently—but there are relevant differences that make the varying treatment permissible and expected.

1.46 The cases in the preceding paragraph are judicial discrimination. There is also prejudicial discrimination, which is more pernicious. If one picks basketball players on the basis of skin color, or hires for a managerial position on the basis of religious beliefs, then that is treating people differently when there is no difference among them relevant to basketball or job performance. It is because those cases violate the principle of equal treatment that we tend to regard them as cases of immoral treatment.

1.47 The problem for ethical egoism is that egoism counsels each person to treat everyone differently than they treat themselves, irrespective of whether there is any relevant difference. So, as an ethical egoist you will act to advance your own interests regardless of how that may affect the interests of others. But the principle of equal treatment states that you should treat two people the same unless there is some relevant difference between them. What, then, is the relevant difference between you and everyone else that you should give no weight whatsoever to their preferences? Ethical egoism implies that you are such a unique snowflake that you ought to treat every other person differently than you treat yourself, since you should care only about promoting your own interests. You're you; that's true. But what makes you so special? In fact, runs the objection, none of us is so special that we should each treat ourselves completely differently from how we treat every other living creature. In short, ethical egoism is just a form of prejudicial discrimination, and for that reason should be discarded.

1.48 If you think the costs of ethical egoism are too high for its benefits, then you should consider other moral theories before making a purchase. Here's another popular contender.

Moral Relativism (Is Morality Just How Society Says We Should Act?)

According to ethical egoism, morality is no more than your own code of 1.49
behavior, designed to advance your own goals. Perhaps morality should be understood not on the personal level but on the social level. Here are some representative slogans of this idea, the idea of *moral relativism*.

- **When in Rome, do as the Romans do.**[17]
- **What happens in Vegas stays in Vegas.**[18]
- "Each man calls barbarism whatever is not his own practice; for indeed it seems we have no other test of truth and reason than the example and pattern of the opinions and customs of the country we live in." (Michel de Montaigne, 1580)

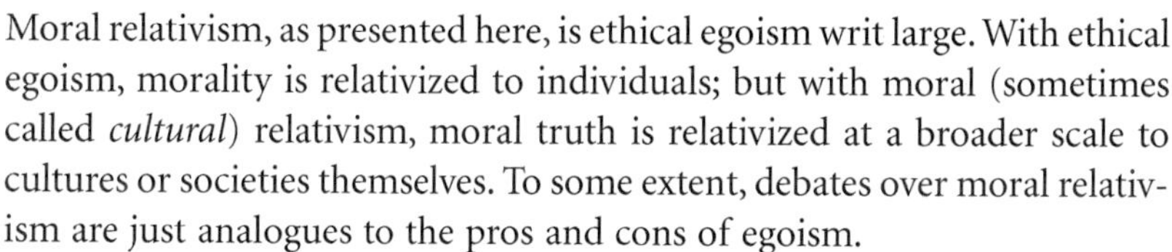

Moral relativism, as presented here, is ethical egoism writ large. With ethical egoism, morality is relativized to individuals; but with moral (sometimes called *cultural*) relativism, moral truth is relativized at a broader scale to cultures or societies themselves. To some extent, debates over moral relativism are just analogues to the pros and cons of egoism.

Descriptive and moral relativism

To start with, notice that there is a difference between descriptive relativism 1.50
and moral relativism, as follows:

Descriptive relativism: beliefs about morality and the values people possess vary across cultures divided by times and places.

Moral relativism: the truth of moral claims and which values people should adopt vary across cultures divided by times and places. What is morally permissible in one culture may be morally wrong in another culture.

Moral relativism is attractive in lots of ways. For one, it serves to counterbalance the provincialism of assuming that the moral principles and codes that you've grown up with must be the best ones for everyone in the world. You probably know people who have never gone more than 20 miles away from the same small town in which they were born, and think that their little corner of the world has everything one could want— the best barbecue, as solid citizens as you'll meet anywhere, fine schools, good-looking children, devout churchgoers, sincere patriots, and first-rate scholars. But if you've traveled a bit, or moved in from another part of the world, you are probably aghast at such insularity and ignorance. People all over the world have found different forms of the good life, with views about purity, authority, respect, and piety that may be wholly alien to one's own. A young woman from Saudi Arabia may consider American college students in miniskirts to be no better than immodest whores who conveniently label themselves with tramp stamps, and American coeds may think that Saudi women are living under the false consciousness of repressive patriarchy, yet both groups manage to raise their children and find ways to lead satisfying lives.

1.51 Worse than provincialism is imperialism. When practitioners of a religion decide that they have discovered the one true way that everyone ought to live, the results tend to be the Spanish Inquisition and people flying airplanes into skyscrapers. When countries decide that their form of political economy alone will lead to human flourishing, then we get wars to force others to accept democracy, or become communists, or Roman subjects, or whatever it will take to remake foreigners into people Just Like Us. Moral relativism is offered as a corrective to such arrogant and aggressive moral absolutism, one that respects cultural diversity and allows for more than one decent way to live.

1.52 The preceding reflections give rise to a popular argument for moral relativism, which goes as follows. Moral beliefs vary all over the world, from place to place and from time to time. The values crafted by a tribe or a nation fit their specific circumstances and may be completely at odds with the moral codes of other societies—codes that they developed given their own idiosyncratic situation. The harsh morality of **Sparta**,[19] beset by warring enemies in a dry and rocky terrain, is hardly suited for the laid-back free-love natives of the tropical **Trobriand Islands**.[20] Insisting that every culture must have the same morality is like telling a chef that every dish he prepares must have the same spicing. The results will range from excellent, to palatable, to execrable. Moralities grow organically, and what works in one culture is inappropriate for another. Not only do moral beliefs and values vary across societies, but they should. In other words, the fact of descriptive relativism provides an excellent reason to adopt moral relativism.

1.53 The argument just provided assumes that descriptive relativism is true, assumes that if it is true then moral relativism is true, and validly infers from those premises that moral relativism is true. Let's examine the very first claim: is descriptive moral relativism really true? There can be little doubt that moral practices, customs, and beliefs vary considerably from one society to the next. For Muslims, it is immoral to drink alcohol, yet for most Christians it is a sacramental imperative to drink alcohol. Western European societies consider the death penalty immoral, whereas China does not. In the United States, polygamous marriages are considered unethical, but in Islamic countries and the indigenous cultures of sub-Saharan Africa, they are expected. The ancient Spartans considered it their moral duty to leave weak or defective infants alone to die from the elements, and perhaps no modern society condones such a practice.

On the face of it, then, it seems that moral beliefs are quite variable from 1.54
one society to another. However, it would be hasty to conclude that descriptive relativism is definitely right. The anthropologist **Donald E. Brown** has identified 373 traits as human universals[21]—characteristics present in every human society that has so far been identified and studied (Brown, 1991, ch. 6). Some of these traits are facts about language use, patterns of inferential reasoning, symbolic gesturing, and the structure of social groups. However, the majority of human universals involve moral or proto-moral judgment and behavior. For example, human societies universally judge that it is good to help others, that incest and indiscriminate killing are wrong, and that one has familial duties of piety towards one's parents and obligations of care towards one's children.

Some philosophers have argued that the moral norms universally adopted 1.55
are very general and open-ended, therefore allowing for local interpretation and variation. So we might have two societies agree that incest is immoral, but the first society condones kissing cousins (cousins don't count for the incest taboo), whereas in the second society cousins might as well be siblings (kissing cousins are forbidden). It doesn't matter for our purposes here. As a purely descriptive matter, relativism turns out to be partly true and partly false. There are moral beliefs present in some societies/cultures, but not in all, and other moral attitudes that do seem to be in all societies. But the fact that there are at least some moral universals stops any simple inference from descriptive relativism to moral relativism.

A second reason to reject the argument that descriptive relativism leads 1.56
to moral relativism is as follows. Descriptive relativism, if true, is something that anthropologists ought to discover. Moral relativism, on the other hand, is not a matter for anthropology. Consider an analogy. Anthropologists and historians have provided convincing evidence that human societies throughout history have had a great variety of scientific and medical beliefs.

For instance, commonplace beliefs in some societies have been that Earth is the center of the universe, that the motion of the sun is due to the gods' pulling a fiery chariot, that insanity is caused by demonic possession, that base metals can be turned into gold through chemical manipulation, and that sickness is caused by an imbalance in the four bodily humors.

1.57 As a matter of mere description, there is no problem noting that these empirical claims were widely believed in assorted societies throughout history. Nevertheless, modern science and scientific medicine have now shown that all of those beliefs are false. Thus we may say that descriptive scientific relativism is true, even though Earth is not the center of the universe, the sun doesn't really move across the sky, demons aren't behind insanity, alchemy is a failure, and humorism has been completely discredited. But that's just to say that people have had many false scientific beliefs. Perhaps people have had lots of false moral beliefs as well. Knowing what people in fact believe very rarely tells us what they ought to believe. Therefore the second premise of the relativist's argument, that if descriptive relativism is true then moral relativism is true, is also false.

Criticism objection

1.58 A chief complaint against moral relativism is the *criticism objection*: if moral relativism is true, then meaningful criticism of either other societies, or one's own, is impossible. Here's why. Under moral relativism, the moral truth itself varies from one society or culture to the next. An act might be morally wrong in one society but morally permissible or even obligatory in another—not simply *believed* to be permissible or obligatory, but in *fact* permissible or obligatory. It would therefore make no sense whatsoever for people in the first society to criticize the members of the second society for their moral views since those views are, by hypothesis, true (in that society). To criticize them is to criticize the truth, which is surely misguided. Here is an illustration.

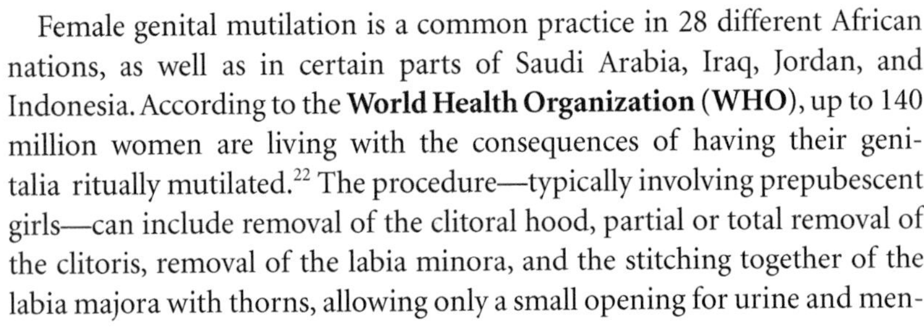

1.59 Female genital mutilation is a common practice in 28 different African nations, as well as in certain parts of Saudi Arabia, Iraq, Jordan, and Indonesia. According to the **World Health Organization** (**WHO**), up to 140 million women are living with the consequences of having their genitalia ritually mutilated.[22] The procedure—typically involving prepubescent girls—can include removal of the clitoral hood, partial or total removal of the clitoris, removal of the labia minora, and the stitching together of the labia majora with thorns, allowing only a small opening for urine and menstrual blood to pass through. Their legs are tied together for weeks afterwards to allow the scar tissue to form. Village elders carry out these operations typically without sterilization or anesthesia. Medical consequences include loss of sexual pleasure, infertility, reproductive and urinary tract infections, and various risks concerning childbirth. Girls have also died from shock, blood loss, and infection as the result of female genital mutilation.

According to WHO, there is no medical benefit to these surgeries. So 1.60
why are they performed? The answer is because of social mores. Social groups that practice female genital mutilation often do so because of their ethical views about proper sexual behavior, coupled with the idea that only by crippling women's' libidos can they resist the temptations of illicit sex. There are also aesthetic beliefs regarding modesty and femininity, and the proper way that women should look. Finally, practitioners often believe that there are religious reasons for female genital mutilation, although no major religion condones it.

If we accept ethical relativism, then it seems that mutilating the genitals 1.61
of young girls without their consent is morally acceptable—at least in places like Somalia and Egypt where it is done to over 95 percent of their females. Again, not only do Somalians and Egyptians *believe* that it is morally acceptable, but it really *is* morally acceptable. Of course, it is immoral to maim children in other places, like the United States. Under ethical relativism, here are two true propositions:

Pro-FGM: There is nothing wrong with female genital mutilation (in central Africa).
Anti-FGM: Female genital mutilation is immoral (in the United States).

While it is consistent to hold both pro-FGM and anti-FGM views, the objection to moral relativism is that one should not hold them both, because it is entirely reasonable to criticize female genital mutilation as cruel and wicked butchery. This is not ethnocentrism; in fact it takes the beliefs and practices of foreign cultures more seriously than does moral relativism. Moral relativism presumes that different cultures are so estranged that they cannot sensibly have a dialogue together about morality; instead each must go their own way. Yet allowing the possibility of criticism means that people from differing cultural traditions can reason together, criticizing each others' views, to discover the moral truth. Somalians are just as entitled to criticize Americans for *failing* to practice female genital mutilation. Moral relativism precludes substantive ethical dialogue among differing cultures, but rejecting moral relativism allows potentially fruitful debate. In this way all cultures are treated as equal partners in the practice of reason. In other words, despite cultural relativism's pretensions to promoting tolerance and equality, in fact it does the opposite. True respect for the views of others comes from taking those views seriously through critical engagement.

1.62 Not only does the criticism objection apply to the criticism of foreign cultures, but also to one's own culture. For example, in 1830 slavery was widely accepted in the United States as morally permissible. There had been an abolitionist movement in North America since colonial times, but in 1830 it was still a minority voice. If we accept moral relativism, then both of these propositions are true:

Pro-slavery: There is nothing wrong with US slavery (in 1830).
Anti-slavery: There is something wrong with US slavery (now).

Given the truth of pro-slavery, it must have been the case that in 1830 the abolitionists were just all mistaken. They were wrong for wanting to abolish slavery, and misguided in condemning slave-owners. Why? Because owning slaves was entirely morally permissible. If you think that in 1830 the abolitionists were on the side of the right and the good, despite being a minority, then pro-slavery is false. Since moral relativism implies that Pro-slavery is true, just as it implies that anti-slavery is true, moral relativism must also be false. Moral relativism prevents the coherent criticism of the failings of one's own society every bit as much as it disallows the coherent criticism of the practices of other cultures. If you think that we ought to review the popular morality of our culture, and aim for its improvement, then you have a reason to doubt that moral relativism is correct.

Annotated Bibliography

Brown, Donald E. (1991) *Human Universals* (New York: McGraw-Hill). A work of anthropology in which the author argues for an extensive list of universal human traits.

Gilbert, Daniel (2005) *Stumbling on Happiness* (New York: Random House). This is a book by a psychologist aimed at a popular audience. In it Gilbert addresses the question of why people are so lousy at predicting what will make themselves happy in the future.

Hobbes, Thomas (1647) *Philosophical Rudiments Concerning Government and Society*, full text available at www.constitution.org/th/decive.htm, accessed May 4, 2012. Originally published in Latin as *Elementa Philosophica de Cive*, here Hobbes presents his view that by nature humans are selfish and motivated by survival instincts. This natural egoism in the state of nature leads to a war of all against all, a situation that demands a social contract and the formation of a state.

Lawrence, Bruce (ed.) (2005) *Messages to the World: The Statements of Osama bin Laden* (New York: Verso). The only extant work in English translation of the speeches, interviews, and letters of Osama bin Laden.

Montaigne, Michel de (1580) *The Essays*, full text available at www.gutenberg.org/ebooks/3600, accessed May 4, 2012. While there is no professional engagement with moral relativism prior to the twentieth century, Montaigne's chapter "Of Cannibals," www.gutenberg.org/files/3600/3600-h/3600-h.htm#2HCH0030, accessed May 4, 2012, is a valuable precursor that treats shocking behavior in other societies with respect and seriousness.

Plato (380 BCE) *Euthyphro*, full text available at http://classics.mit.edu/Plato/euthyfro.html, accessed May 4, 2012. The dialogue in which Socrates and Euthyphro discuss the nature of morality, and whether things are good because they are loved by the gods, or whether the gods love them because they are good.

Online Resources

1. A clinical description of Down Syndrome, from the US National Library of Medicine: www.ncbi.nlm.nih.gov/pubmedhealth/PMH0001992/
2. A brief biography of Osama bin Laden: http://en.wikipedia.org/wiki/Osama_bin_Laden
3. A discussion of the concept and history of the Islamic Caliphate: http://en.wikipedia.org/wiki/Caliphate
4. Versions of the Golden Rule from various religions: www.religioustolerance.org/reciproc2.htm
5. A list of the 613 commandments in the Torah, with textual citations: www.jewfaq.org/613.htm
6. A discussion of the meaning and history of the Ten Commandments: http://en.wikipedia.org/wiki/Ten_Commandments
7. An explanation of the the five pillars of Islam—the fundamental obligations of every Muslim: www.islam101.com/dawah/pillars.html
8. The complete text of Plato's dialogue *Euthyphro*: http://classics.mit.edu/Plato/euthyfro.html

9 A graphical representation of the ancient Greek gods and their relationships to each other: http://en.wikipedia.org/wiki/Family_tree_of_the_Greek_gods
10 An entertaining dialogue between a philosopher and "Mr. Deity" on the *Euthyphro* question: www.youtube.com/watch?v=pwf6QD-REMY&lr=1
11 Famous quotations from Hemingway, including his line in *Death in the Afternoon* (1932, chapter 1) "About morals, I know only that what is moral is what you feel good after and what is immoral is what you feel bad after.": http://en.wikiquote.org/wiki/Ernest_Hemingway
12 A clip from the film *Conan the Barbarian*, in which Conan declares what is best in life: www.youtube.com/watch?v=6PQ6335puOc
13 Ayn Rand's thoughts on egoism, happiness, and the virtue of selfishness: http://aynrandlexicon.com/lexicon/happiness.html
14 The official US Army profile of Medal of Honor winner Ross McGinnis: www.army.mil/medalofhonor/mcginnis/profile/index.html
15 A summary of the kidnapping and rescue of Jaycee Lee Dugard: http://en.wikipedia.org/wiki/Kidnapping_of_Jaycee_Lee_Dugard
16 A newspaper account of the crimes of Kristen Diane Parker: www.huffingtonpost.com/2009/07/11/kristen-diane-parker-scru_n_230042.html
17 The meaning and origin of the expression "when in Rome, do as the Romans do": www.phrases.org.uk/meanings/when-in-rome-do-as-the-romans-do.html
18 The Urban Dictionary's take on the expression "what happens in Vegas stays in Vegas": www.urbandictionary.com/define.php?term=what%20happens%20in%20Vegas%20stays%20in%20Vegas
19 The history of the ancient Greek city-state of Sparta: http://en.wikipedia.org/wiki/Sparta
20 A discussion of the people of the Trobriand Islands in the South Pacific: www.newworldencyclopedia.org/entry/Trobriander
21 A list of cross-cultural human universals as compiled by anthropologist Donald E. Brown: http://condor.depaul.edu/mfiddler/hyphen/humunivers.htm
22 The World Health Organization's fact sheet on female genital mutilation: www.who.int/mediacentre/factsheets/fs241/en/index.html

2

ETHICS
THE BIG THREE THEORIES

In the last chapter we examined divine command theory, ethical egoism, and moral relativism. All of these theories have been historically influential, and each continues to have modern supporters who try to answer (or at least swallow the pain of) the objections presented. Nevertheless, they aren't really the big players in contemporary ethics. In this chapter we will examine the three 800-pound gorillas of ethical theory. 2.1

Utilitarianism (Is Morality Doing What I Can to Make This the Best World Possible?)

One of the criticisms of ethical egoism in the preceding chapter was that egoism meant that each person treated himself or herself differently than everyone else in the world, even if there was nothing that merited this differential treatment. That is, egoism violated the principle of equal treatment. A related problem cropped up in the case of moral relativism, in that if morality is restricted to cultures or societies, then how you should treat members of your own culture may be wildly different from how you should treat people in other cultures. The duties you have to fellow Roman citizens are completely unlike your duties to outsiders; in fact you might have no obligations to the barbarians at all. Here too there is a sort of equal treatment problem—the in-group/out-group distinction doesn't seem to be a relevant distinction for a difference in how you treat people, as moral relativism demands. 2.2

This Is Philosophy: An Introduction, First Edition. Steven D. Hales.

2.3 A moral theory that does treat everyone equally, without prejudice to personal standing, is utilitarianism. Utilitarianism is an enormously influential ethical theory. The basic idea is that moral action is all about producing good in the world; the more good your action produces, the better it is. Your moral duty is to perform whatever actions are the best ones in this sense. Utilitarianism is focused on the outcomes of action—will a possible action create happiness, produce pleasure, and improve the lives of those it will affect, or will it cause pain, harm, and make people worse off? There is a fundamental tie to what morality is intuitively all about, namely the improvement of our lot by increasing our well-being and easing our burdens.

2.4 In addition utilitarianism is able to provide, in principle, an answer to every moral question or ethical dilemma. Should we legalize drugs? Well, will doing so lead to net gain in our collective happiness (because people are freer to do as they wish, fewer people will be in prison, and we will have tax revenues from drug dealers) or will it lead to a decrease in our net happiness (because there will be more addicts, less productivity, and more DUIs)? All we need to do is settle the question about potential consequences and we automatically get an answer about the morally correct course of action. Should abortion remain legal? Should you steal music? Should we kill animals for food? Even if the answers to these questions are not obvious, utilitarianism still provides the means to answer them. In this way it is an incredibly powerful, flexible moral theory.

Consequentialism and hedonism

2.5 Utilitarianism is made of two parts: (1) a theory about the structure of morality, and (2) a theory about the object or end of morality—that is, what morality is aiming at. Let's look at the first idea. Utilitarians hold that the only thing that matters for morality is the consequences of what you do. So part of the utilitarian creed is that consequentialism is the correct structure of morality. We can put it like this:

> *Consequentialism*: All that morally matters is the consequences of action.

It doesn't matter what you say, what you plan, what you intend, or what you tried to do. From the perspective of morality, all that matters is what you actually did. To find out whether you did the right thing or the wrong thing, all we need to do is look at the consequences of your action. In fact, what you should do is produce the best consequences you possibly can. For utilitarians, the bar is set high: you are always obligated to do the best that you can. Here are the principles that lay out obligation, permissibility, and impermissibility under classical utilitarianism.

- If an action X has better consequences than any other action you could perform instead, then your duty (moral obligation) is to do X.
- If an action X has better consequences than any other action you could perform instead, then you are morally forbidden from doing any action other than X. Doing something else is the wrong thing to do.
- If actions X and Y have better consequences than any other action you could perform instead, and X does not have better consequences than Y, but Y does not have better consequences than X either, you are obligated to perform one of the actions, but it is morally permissible for you to pick either one.

The idea is this. At any given time you are faced with a range of possible actions that you might perform. You could keep reading this chapter, go for a walk, take a nap, get a coffee to help you make it to the end, all kinds of things. Which thing you decide to do should be whatever has the best consequences. What you should *not* do is something suboptimal, something that doesn't have the best results. Suppose there is a tie at the top—you could donate $10 to UNICEF or to Oxfam but not both; those choices are tied with each other and both are superior to all other options. In that case it is morally indifferent which you do. Just pick one.

Obviously, there are many questions that immediately arise. One is *consequences for whom*? When you're contemplating the possible outcomes of various choices, who should you be thinking about? Should you only care about consequences for yourself, or do other people count too? What about future people, or nonhuman animals? Only short-term consequences, or do you have to weigh the long-term as well? The utilitarian answer is simple: *you have to consider the consequences for everyone affected by your action, not just now, but indefinitely into the future.* Morality is not all about you. If you only had to be concerned with the consequences for you, then utilitarianism would devolve to egoism. One of the big differences with egoism is that, for utilitarians, everyone is on equal footing. You count for moral assessment, but you don't count extra. 2.6

You may be asking *what about motives and intent*? Surely that matters too; if one intentionally does something immoral, isn't it worse than someone who does the wrong thing by accident? Doing the wrong thing in the 2.7

heat of the moment, or just messing up, well, that may be bad, but planning to do evil, intending to do so with malicious motives and a wicked heart, that's just so much worse. So consequentialism can't be correct—there must be more to morality than just consequences alone.

2.8 The standard utilitarian response is to make a sharp division between blameworthiness/praiseworthiness and right action/wrong action. The rightness and wrongness of actions, utilitarians continue to insist, just has to do with consequences. But whether someone is blameworthy or praiseworthy for his or her action, that has a good deal to do with motive and intent. For example, suppose Johnny Missalot tries to shoot you. Fortunately for you, Johnny's such a lousy shot that he couldn't hit the ground with his hat. Now, clearly he did the right thing by missing. Missing his shot had better consequences than other actions he might have taken, like aiming a little to the left and actually shooting you. But he's certainly not praiseworthy for what he did, since he tried to shoot you, even though in one sense he did the right thing.

2.9 Or, to take another example, imagine you try really hard to do the right thing in some situation. You think things through, and make every possible attempt to do right. But suppose that you screw things up anyway and do the wrong thing. An example would be a case of "**friendly fire**":[1] a soldier who carefully follows orders to bomb a target and scrupulously aims his missiles, but still kills his comrades, who he did not know were in the target zone. A utilitarian would say that you still did the wrong thing (an action with suboptimal consequences compared with other actions you might have performed), but you might not be blameworthy for it. In fact, you might even deserve praise for having tried your best to do the right thing.

2.10 The next obvious question is what are good consequences and what are bad ones? In answering this question we come to the other key component of utilitarianism: a theory of the highest good (the ***summum bonum***)[2] or what the aim of morality really is. Utilitarianism as such isn't committed to any particular theory of the good, and we'll get different versions of the theory depending on what is named as the highest good. For example, some contemporary proponents of the view argue that preference satisfaction is the *summum bonum*. Classical utilitarianism is *hedonistic utilitarianism*, according to which the highest good is pleasure. We'll focus on this traditional view. Thus,

Consequentialism + the highest good is pleasure = hedonistic utilitarianism

What does it mean to say that the highest good is pleasure? Well, it means that pleasure is intrinsically valuable. It is an important, valuable thing to possess in its own right, and not because of something it will produce or provide for us later on. Moreover, nothing is more valuable than pleasure. So the point of morality is for each person to produce the greatest amount of pleasure in the world with each action they perform. That sounds a bit daunting, or excessively lofty, but the idea is modest: you should always do the best you can. And the best you can do in any situation is whatever action will produce the best balance of pleasure over pain for everyone your action affects (including you).

You might wonder what you should do when you're in a lousy situation 2.11
and there aren't any pleasure-producing options available to you. Your car is hydroplaning in a storm and you could bring it to a stop either by rear-ending the motorcycle in front of you or steering it into the guardrail on your right and grinding along until friction slows you down. Neither choice is one that is going to be producing much pleasure. However, one is definitely worse: hitting the motorcycle. Turning into the guardrail will tear up your car, but hitting the motorcycle will kill its driver. The utilitarian judgment is to choose the lesser of two evils: hit the guardrail. The total amount of happiness in the world will be higher with that choice than it would be with the choice to hit the motorcycle.

Measuring pains and pleasures

You might think that all this sounds fine, but rather abstract. How are we 2.12
supposed to measure the prospective pains and pleasures of our actions, so that we know which things to do and which to avoid? The utilitarian will first note that most of the time you don't need to spend a lot of thought on this issue. Mostly it will be rather obvious—you should use your hammer to hit the nail instead of hit yourself in the head. Did you really need to sit down with pen and paper and calculate the relative values of the prospective pains and pleasures for those choices? Of course, there are complicated questions. Should the death penalty be abolished? Is it morally proper to legalize marijuana? Is there anything wrong with assisted suicide? In these cases, we need to think things through.

In the eighteenth century, Jeremy Bentham, an early and influential 2.13
utilitarian, proposed a way to figure out what the consequences of our actions will be, that is, how we can measure the future pains and pleasures

our actions might cause. Bentham's proposal was the *felicific calculus.* He claimed a pleasure or a pain may be measured by its

1. Intensity

   How powerful or intense is the pleasure or pain? Some pleasures are mild, like a tasty apple. Some are great, like the joy of graduation, or a wedding. Some pains are mild, like a papercut, others are strong, like a migraine headache.

2. Duration

   How long will the pain or pleasure last? Obviously, you want pains to be brief and pleasures to be long lasting.

3. Certainty or uncertainty

   How likely is it that the possible pain or pleasure that we're considering really will occur? An action with a high likelihood of pleasure to follow and a very low risk of pain looks like a better choice, all other things being equal, than an action with a low chance of pleasure and a high risk of pain. When you're playing cards, bet high on good hands.

4. Propinquity or remoteness

   How soon is the pain or pleasure? Is it going to happen right away, or is it years in the distance? The pleasures of education may be a long time coming—learning to play guitar is a slow process, and the joy of mastery is remote in time. The pleasure of an afternoon nap is imminent. The further away a sensation is, the more intervening factors there may be that prevent it, and so the less likely it is that it will ever happen.

5. Fecundity

   A sensation is fecund just in case it tends to be followed by the same type of sensation. For example, the pleasure of learning to read tends to lead to other pleasures, such as reading a good book. So the pleasure of learning to read is fecund. The pain of food poisoning often follows the unpleasantness of eating bad seafood, so the latter is a fecund pain. Clearly you would prefer your pleasures to be fecund and your pains not.

6. Purity

   A sensation is impure just in case it tends to be followed by the opposite type of sensation, otherwise it is pure. For example, drinking a lot of alcohol is an impure pleasure, since it tends to be followed by the pain of a hangover. Working out at the gym is an impure pain since it tends to be followed by the pleasure of fitness. So you should want your pleasures to be pure and your pains impure.

7. Extent

   How many people will be affected by your action? To what extent will the pains or pleasures produced by your behavior spread out to other people? Those have to be taken into account and added up too.

Again, you needn't work through the felicific calculus every time you act. But it is there, waiting in the wings, for those problematic cases in which it's not obvious what the right action and the optimal consequences really are.

Quality and quantity

The root notion of utilitarianism is that we should act in such way as to 2.14
maximize the quantity of pleasure in the world. You might be concerned that utilitarians make no mention of the *quality* of pleasures and pains. Indeed, Bentham was quite clear about that, writing, "Prejudice apart, the game of push-pin is of equal value with the arts and sciences of music and poetry. If the game of push-pin furnish more pleasure, it is more valuable than either" (Bentham, 1825, bk. III, ch. 1). Push-pin was a child's game much like tiddlywinks. For Bentham, it was mere snobbery to suppose that the pleasures of art museums, classical music, and fine literature are any better than cheap beer, horror movies, and NASCAR. The quantity of pleasure is all that matters, and it is just pompous moralizing to declaim that this or that pleasure is somehow superior in any way other than its amount.

Not all utilitarians have agreed with Bentham. Later, in the nineteenth 2.15
century, John Stuart Mill tried to develop a way for utilitarianism to accommodate the idea that some pleasures are of higher quality than others, in a way that just measuring their quantity could not capture. Pleasures might be better or worse in some way besides mere amount. It may initially seem that one can't aim to maximize pleasure in general while at the same time maximizing high quality pleasures in particular. However, even under the fundamental position of hedonistic utilitarianism that our moral duty is to produce as much pleasure in the world as is possible by our actions, there is still room for promoting quality as well. Suppose that you could perform either an action X or an action Y, and both are superior to any other action you might do, but are tied with each other. Commonly utilitarians say that it is then morally indifferent which you do; as long as you do either X or

Y, you should just pick one. However, if quality matters too, then when there is a tie in quantity of pleasure produced, we ought to choose the action that produces the higher quality pleasure. The promotion of quality is far from innocuous. In fact, the idea that we should promote and appreciate higher quality pleasures is a substantive and radical proposal about how we ought to live.

2.16 Let us understand quality as the *density of pleasure per unit of delivery*. Consider two fishing trips. On fishing trip A you fish all day, pulling up one modest fish after the next. There is always something on the line, so you never get bored and there is always a little thrill. But at the same time you don't really catch anything particularly noteworthy. On fishing trip B you fish all day and only catch one fish—but it is a monster. It takes all your skill and cunning to boat the giant lunker, but you eventually do. It does not take much imagination to suppose that the total amount of pleasure attached to both fishing trips is the same; we can even suppose that the total weight of edible meat is identical. The quantity of pleasure associated with the string of fish from trip A is identical with the quantity of pleasure represented by the string of fish from trip B; it is just that there is only one fish on the string in the latter case. Other things being equal, A and B are equally good choices as far as the *quantity* of pleasure is concerned.

2.17 Trip B has one key thing going for it: the giant lunker. This is a higher quality fish than any of the ones caught on trip A, in fact that single fish is as good as the entire string from trip A. How should we understand this higher quality? Precisely as the density of pleasure: there is more pleasure concentrated in the lunker than in any of the other fish. This interpretation of quality well accords with our ordinary intuitions and once we start thinking about quality in this way, we can see that it is ubiquitous. However, the pursuit of high quality pleasures has its risks.

2.18 Suppose that Jane has $30 to spend on beer. Jane is debating whether to spend her $30 on two cases of Coors Extra Gold pilsener or one case of Pilsener Urquell. According to *The Beer Lover's Rating Guide* (Klein, 2000, p. 102), Coors Extra Gold is "sharp, light, and tasteless . . . it quickly subsides into a typical pedestrian brew, even on a summer picnic with cold cuts and salads. Touted as a 'full-bodied beer'—yes, in comparison to Coors' regular pilsener." On a scale of 0 to 5, Klein rates Coors Extra Gold 1.8, which means it is below average and suitable only for the extremely thirsty. Pilsener Urquell, on the other hand, Klein describes as "crisp, fresh, and mustily hoppy pleasant, understated aroma; intensely carbonated; floral mouthfeel contains some bitterness, but it is subtle and well-calibrated; admirable textural strength; slides into tempered sweetness with spicy foods; a first-class beer to be enjoyed in multiples" (p. 242). Klein rates it 3.5, which is the middle of the above average range. If we assume that taste is objective, Klein is a competent judge of beer, and that Klein's rating system is linear, then Pilsener Urquell is about twice as good as Coors Extra Gold. Under these assumptions, Jane's choice is to buy two cases of Coors or half as much Pilsener Urquell, which tastes twice as good. The cost is the same, and the total quantity of pleasure to be produced is the same. How is Pilsener Urquell a higher quality beer than Coors? There is twice as much pleasure per bottle.

Let's stick with the beer example for a moment. As one becomes more 2.19 informed and more expert about any subject—food, antiques, literature, tennis racquets, movies, travel, romantic trysts, jazz, or Platonic dialogues—one gains a finer appreciation for the high end while losing the ability to be satisfied with the low end. The recognition of quality comes at a cost. In the case of beer, a casual beer drinker will be more willing to knock back a corporate brew, and more likely to get a little pleasure out of it, than someone who consumes only cask-conditioned ales pulled from an English beer engine.

Suppose that Jane Pivo, a beer enthusiast, and Joe Sixpack, who is just 2.20 enthusiastic, decide to drink beer together every night for a month. Their financial resources are limited, so they cannot afford artisanal craft beer every night. Most nights they will be forced to drink mass-produced beer, but once in awhile they splurge and drink the top-shelf stuff. Jane gets very little pleasure on the nights when they drink Rolling Rock Light and very great pleasure the evenings they share a **Brooklyn Black Ops** Imperial Russian stout[3] aged in bourbon barrels. Joe likes Rolling Rock just fine, although he is not a complete idiot and enjoys the Brooklyn a bit more. Their month of tasting can be presented graphically in Figure 2.1.

For the month, Jane totaled 300 units of pleasure and so did Joe. Thus, 2.21 from a purely quantitative standpoint, it is no better to be informed and knowledgeable about beer than not. Jane received no more pleasure than did Joe over the course of the month. Joe's pleasure was more frequent and more evenly spread out, whereas Jane's beer-induced pleasure was rarer and more concentrated. The Millian view on quality is that we should live our lives like Jane Pivo—we should become knowledgeable about various pleasures, pursuing and promoting them. When confronted with two courses of action that produce the same quantity of pleasure, we ought to

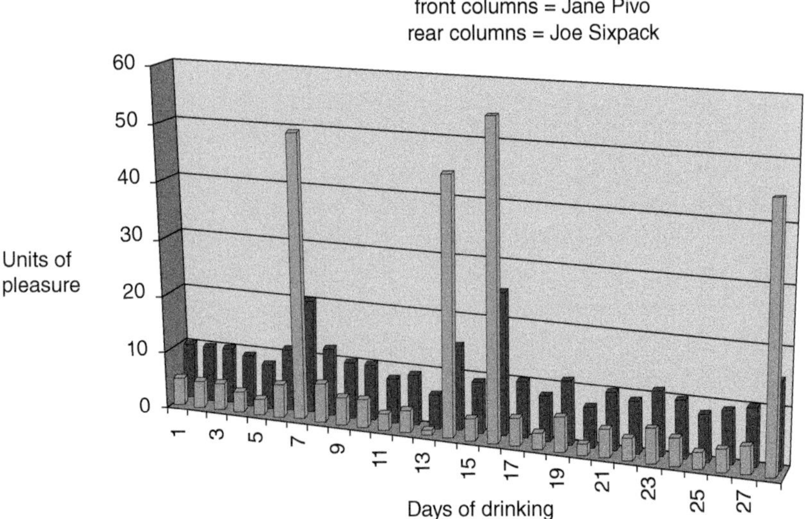

Figure 2.1 Two ways to experience the same total pleasure over a month of drinking beer

pursue the one with the higher quality, concentrated pleasures, even knowing that it is at the expense of enjoying lower-quality ones.

2.22 Mill's recommendation here should be tremendously controversial; it is not some innocuous, modest view that every utilitarian should obviously hold. Consider Jane. She might well wonder whether becoming a beer aficionado was worth it; after all she and Joe Sixpack drank all the same beers and on most nights Joe had a better time. Why isn't it perfectly reasonable for her to wish, as she sips an Old Milwaukee, that she could enjoy it as much as Joe?

2.23 One lesson here is that the appreciation of high quality pleasures is certainly worthwhile when the cost of gaining those pleasures is low. If Jane and Joe both had unlimited resources and could afford to drink only the finest beers every night, then clearly Jane is better off. She will get more pleasure out of each beer, and since she will never drink a low grade beer again, will end up with more total pleasure than Joe. Some pleasures are like this, even for the poor. Fine literature, for example, is in great abundance at public libraries and is available for low or no cost. There is no concomitant downside to learning to appreciate great literature, since it is free for the taking and in a supply greater than anyone could read in a lifetime. With the advent of digital music files that are easily shared, music is becoming like literature, where the abundance of inexpensive music is so considerable that we are well advised to seek out and grasp the higher quality. Music and literature are a vast prix fixe buffet—there is no point in loading up on the Jell-O with mini marshmallows when one could have the lobster instead. In these contexts, the pursuit of high quality pleasures will lead to greater overall quantity, and the fundamental tenet of hedonistic utilitarianism is that we should perform those actions that produce as much pleasure as possible.

The controversy is in cases where either (1) the high quality pleasures 2.24
are in short supply, or (2) they are expensive or difficult to obtain. In such instances one might prefer to remain in ignorance and not become sensitive to and appreciative of the subtle nuances that make for fine art, desirable first editions, Highland single malts, or super sports cars.

Objections to utilitarianism

There are six primary objections to utilitarianism, which will be addressed 2.25
in roughly ascending order of seriousness.

Objection 1: Practicality The first objection is that one of the things we 2.26
want out of morality is real guidance about what we should do and how we ought to act. Utilitarianism, though, is not a very practical ethical theory, since there is no way that we can perform the requisite calculations. We could make an educated guess or a decent calculation for the short term, but there is no way that we can predict all of the outcomes of our actions to the end of time, which is what the theory demands. If we don't know the ultimate result of a butterfly flapping its wings on the opposite side of the world, how can you possibly know whether some action will eventually lead to more pleasure than pain, or vice versa?

Utilitarians respond that no one said that doing the right thing was easy. 2.27
Recall the discussion of praiseworthiness and blameworthiness earlier. You might select one college over another, there meet your eventual spouse, and go on to have children with that spouse. There is no way to tell in advance if one of your children will become a serial killer or the winner of the Nobel Peace Prize. But if your son becomes a killer, then you could reasonably judge that you should have gone to a different college, thus leading to a different spouse and children. You might have done the wrong thing, but you're not blameworthy for it. All we can do is the best we can; we have no

control over the final consequences of our actions. Utilitarianism tells us that tells us that *in fact* the right thing to do is whichever act maximizes the good in the world, and even if we are not sure how to hit that target, it is still what we should aim for.

2.28 *Objection 2: Invasiveness* The second objection is that, under utilitarianism, morality is just too invasive. Now every single aspect of our lives has moral weight. Whether you take out the garbage before or after dinner is now a moral issue. What you have for breakfast is laden with moral choices. You probably have a moral duty to get out on one side of the bed rather than the other. If getting out on the left side of the bed puts you that much closer to the bathroom, or your closet, or wherever you first go when you get up, then that's the side you *should* get up on. There's just a tiny bit less hassle in your life getting up on the left side of the bed, just a little bit less pain. So now it is your positive moral duty to get up on the left side of the bed. If someone gets up on the wrong side of the bed, well, that's no longer a figure of speech. Then might have gotten up on the morally wrong side. But that's crazy, goes the objection, morality has no business telling me how to get out of bed. Morality should be about the big issues—how we treat others, things like that.

2.29 Utilitarians reply that, yes, maybe you should take the garbage out after dinner and get up on the left side of the bed. But that's nothing to get too excited about; those are small potatoes sorts of actions. Every action has moral properties like every object has mass. Feathers aren't as likely to have much impact as bowling balls, but technically they have mass too. Utilitarianism shouldn't be seen as invasive, but merely comprehensive.

2.30 *Objection 3: Supererogation* The third objection is that under utilitarianism there is no such thing as supererogation. "Supererogation" refers to actions that are good actions, but greater than what duty requires. Recall the case of Private McGinnis, who threw himself on an Iraqi grenade to save his fellow soldiers. You may think that what he did was the very epitome of heroic, noble self-sacrifice, above and beyond the call of duty. Not utilitarians. If jumping on a grenade produced better consequences for everyone involved than any other action Pvt. McGinnis might have taken, then doing so was no more than his moral duty.

2.31 Utilitarians don't deny that, strictly speaking, there are no supererogatory acts. You are always obligated to perform the best action you possibly can. In some circumstances, like those of Pvt. McGinnis, doing the best thing may be very difficult, or come with great personal sacrifice. In those cases it is quite reasonable to regard those who did the right thing as especially praiseworthy or admirable. Utilitarianism may mean that there are no supererogatory actions, but that does not mean that there are no morally heroic actions. There might be situations in which you're a hero just for doing your duty.

Objection 4: ***Simpson's Paradox***[4] The fourth objection is deeply puzzling, 2.32

and some regard it as a showstopper for utilitarianism. The problem arises out of a statistical oddity called Simpson's Paradox. Simpson's Paradox is when a set can be partitioned into subsets that each have a property opposite to that of the superset. That sounds a little technical, but there are familiar examples. In the **2009 Wimbledon finals**,[5] Roger Federer beat Andy Roddick by a score of 5–7, 7–6 (8–6), 7–6 (7–5), 3–6, 16–14. Even though Roddick won most of the games (39 versus Federer's 38), he still lost the match. In 2003 the New York Yankees finished the regular season with 10 more wins than the Florida Marlins. The two teams met in the World Series and the Yankees outscored the Marlins 21–17 over the course of the series. Nevertheless, the Marlins won the World Series by four games to two. These cases are examples of Simpson's Paradox. The problem for utilitarianism is that we may be obligated to make every person alive less happy, because it will increase the total global amount of happiness. Consider the following two scenarios (Figures 2.2 and 2.3).

In Scenario 1, imagine that there are two people alone on a desert 2.33
island. It isn't a paradise; there's limited food, water, and shelter, and the two people have to struggle for survival. But suppose that nonetheless they are reasonably happy. Let's say that each person has a total of 100 units of

Figure 2.2 Two people on a desert island

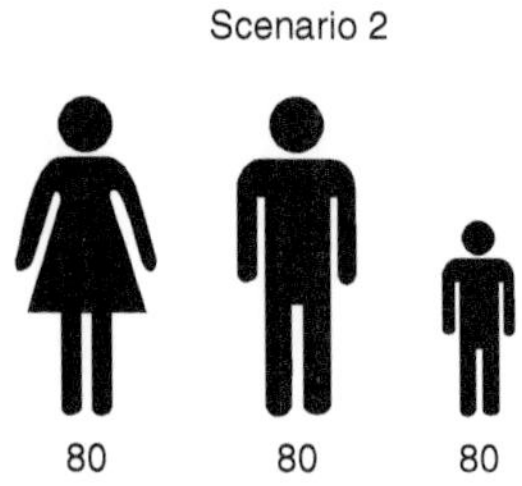

Figure 2.3 Three people on a desert island

happiness at the end of their life. The numbers don't matter; they're just placeholders to indicate relative values. Now, suppose that the couple is considering having a child, and creating Scenario 2. In this condition each adult is a bit less happy (remember that children make parents less happy), and they have to work that much harder to provide for their child. But the child has a fairly happy life, and the parents, while less happy, are still in the positive numbers for lifetime happiness.

2.34 Which is the morally preferable world according to utilitarianism? The answer is Scenario 2, because it is an overall happier world than Scenario 1, totaling 240 happiness units to 200. In this case, the couple on the desert island is morally obligated to create more people, even though it makes everyone there less happy. The desert island scenarios, while somewhat abstract, are not that far removed from reality. It is not hard to imagine that the entire planet is like the desert island, and that we might under utilitarianism be obligated to keep increasing the human population until we reach a tipping point, even if by doing so we make every living person less happy. This very counterintuitive result is a reason to reject utilitarianism.

2.35 *Objection 5: Agent-relative intuitions* The fifth objection to utilitarianism concerns, surprisingly, one of the initially attractive features of the theory, namely its respect for the principle of equal treatment. Utilitarianism is an agent-neutral moral theory, that is, one according to which everyone has the same duties and moral aims, no matter what their personal interests or interpersonal relationships. Theories like egoism are agent-relative, meaning that your moral obligations and goals may be completely different from mine. Consider the following two cases, which are designed to cut against agent-neutral intuitions.

Drowning swimmers. You can save one of two drowning swimmers but not both. You are the only means of rescue. One of the drowning swimmers is your child and the other is a stranger, but still a child with equal life prospects and a comparable network of family and friends. From the perspective of total happiness in the world it is morally indifferent which child you save. You may have a preference to save your own child, but in addition do you think you have a special duty to your own child. Are you obligated to save your own child?

A friend in need. Your best friend is down on her luck. Her husband left her and she is looking for work. She is having trouble making ends meet and you are considering buying some groceries for her to tide her over. As you enter the grocery store, you see a charity collecting outside to send money to aid famine victims in a distant land you have never visited. The charity claims that you will save lives through the donation of a few dollars. Not being terribly flush yourself, you can either buy groceries for your best friend or donate to the charity, but not both. Even though donating to the charity will produce more global happiness, do you think you have a duty to help your friend instead?

A utilitarian faced with the drowning swimmers case might choose his or her own child, but would have no obligation to do so. Or perhaps the utilitarian might decide that flipping a coin is the fairest way to decide who gets to live and who dies in that instance. The friend in need would just plain be out of luck. The distant charity should get the money. If you're inclined to think that those actions are not what you should do, then you might doubt that utilitarianism is the correct moral theory.

Objection 6: Nothing is absolutely wrong The final objection is that under 2.36
utilitarianism there is no act so heinous, so terrible, that it is utterly unconscionable. In fact, think of the worst possible action you can, and there is an imaginable scenario under which it is your utilitarian moral duty to perform that very action. Think that no one should ever own slaves? Knowingly convict an innocent person of a crime? Kill the innocent? Torture political enemies? For utilitarians, all of those actions might be your moral duty, given the right set of circumstances. For instance, see what you think about this case.

The organ-robber. Imagine you are an attending physician in a busy emergency room. You're particularly worried this evening, because there has been

> a train wreck, and not only are all ten victims your patients, but each of them needs an organ transplant—kidneys, livers, hearts, lungs, they each need something different. You've seen the wait list for new organs, and you know they're not going to make it. As you ponder this sad situation, Joe Klutz walks into the ER. Joe has fallen off of his ladder and has broken his arm. You set Joe's arm, and decide to run a couple of routine tests while he is there. You look at the test results and realize that, incredibly, Joe is a perfect donor match for all ten of your patients. You start thinking it over, and realize that if you just slipped Joe some chloroform, well, you could harvest his organs and save the lives of all ten of your patients.
>
> Joe might live another 50 years without your intervention, but each of those patients would easily survive at least 20 years apiece with Joe's organs. 200 years of life versus 50: it's a utilitarian no-brainer, right? Sure, there would be family grieving for Joe, but there would be ten times as many people grieving for your other patients, should you not harvest Joe's organs. All in all, the world will be a much better place if you piecemeal Joe to save the lives of ten other people.

If you think that murdering an innocent person in order to cut them up and steal their body parts is wrong, no matter what good may come of it, then that is a reason to reject utilitarianism. Let's move on to consider the second major player among ethical theories, namely deontology, or Kantian ethics.

Deontology, or Kantianism (Is There an Absolute Moral Law?)

2.37 The last complaint against utilitarianism was that there are no actions that are absolutely morally forbidden. Every possible action—killing the innocent, rape, torture—could be your moral duty if the stakes are high enough. This goes against the intuition that some things are so terrible that it is always wrong to do them, no matter what the practical results. The German philosopher **Immanuel Kant** (1724–1804)[6] agreed, and maintained that the morality of actions does not vary from circumstance to circumstance, but instead there is an absolute moral law which applies to everyone at all times. The behavior that we owe to each other does not vary, and it is this idea that is behind the notion of moral rights. Of all the moral theories discussed so far, it is Kantianism alone that underwrites the possibility of you possessing moral rights.

Imperatives and good motives

Kant thought that utilitarians had things backwards. For utilitarians, things like intent and motive are completely divorced from what makes an action a right action. Kant, on the other hand, argued that good intention, or a good will, is the only thing that is good without any qualification. In contrast, lots of character traits like courage, resolution, and constancy of purpose are not good or bad in themselves. Same thing for the gifts of fortune like power, fame, and wealth. It all depends what you use those talents and gifts to do. If you use your wealth and forceful personality to establish a religious cult whose sacraments are crack cocaine and kinky acts with the deacons, then maybe those weren't good personal traits to have. But noble motives and intentions, the desire to do the right thing, that's invariably good. Of course, we all know what road is paved with good intentions. Having a good will does not guarantee that one will do the right thing. Often our attempts to do the right thing are thwarted, or we're unlucky, or we act on bad information, or we just don't understand what the right thing to do really is. So exactly how can we distinguish having good intentions from having bad ones? 2.38

Kant's answer is that you have a good will if you try to do what's right, if you try to follow the moral law. Unlike utilitarians, who think that you could accidentally do the right thing by bringing about the best overall consequences, for Kant you do the right thing only if you do it out of a sense of duty. Having a good will is the only thing good in itself. Good motives are part of what it is to do right; the other part is the successful following of the moral law. Thus: 2.39

You have good motives + you follow the moral law = you do the right thing

What exactly is this moral law idea? It is a certain kind of imperative about what you should do. Of course, there are lots of imperatives, for example:

- If you want to pass the test, then you should study.
- If you're going to drink, then don't drive.
- If you can't make our meeting, then be sure to call.
- If you're planning to read Kant, then drink plenty of coffee.
- If you're the last one out, then you should turn off the lights.

Notice that all of these imperatives have a conditional structure, that is, an if . . . then . . . form. None of them tell you what you should do, come what may. You're not instructed to study, give up your keys, call, guzzle some coffee, or leave. These instructions tell you to do those things under certain conditions: if you want to pass, if you're going to drink, if you can't make our meeting, if you're going to read Kant, if you're the last one out. But maybe you're not going to do any of those things, in which case the imperatives don't have any force. They just don't apply to you. These if . . . then . . . instructions are *hypothetical imperatives*. Hypothetical as in "hypothetically speaking, if you were to scratch Sara's new car, then she would be very angry with you." None of that means that Sara is in fact angry with you.

2.40 All those hypothetical imperatives may be true of everyone, but for most people they are trivially true. Even for teetotalers it is true that "if you're going to drink, then don't drive"; it's just not a rule that affects their behavior. The moral law can't be one of these hypothetical imperatives, since it governs everyone's behavior, no matter what their own plans or personal situation may be. The moral law is therefore a *categorical imperative*—it tells you what you should do irrespective of idiosyncratic facts about you.

2.41 Kant gives a couple of different formulations of the categorical imperative, which he believed to be in some sense equivalent. Working out what Kant really meant is a task for Kant scholars. Here let's just take a look at the principles he gives.

Categorical imperative (version 1)

> The *categorical imperative* (version 1, universalizability): Act only according to those principles of action that you could will to be a universal law of nature.

2.42 The basic notion isn't as complicated as it first appears. When you were a kid, and wanted to do something your parents disapproved of, did they ever tell you, "what if everybody did that!?" If so, then your parents were closet Kantians.

2.43 Every time you do something, we can describe your reasons for acting in terms of a general principle, or maxim, of action. For example, suppose you're driving down the road, and you've just polished off a Big Mac, fries, and a Diet Coke from Mickey D's. You wad up your garbage and toss it out of the window. In this case, your principle of action is something like *whenever there is garbage in the car, get rid of it in the easiest way possible.* This, of course, is when your mom pipes up with "what if everybody did that!?" She obviously doesn't mean to suggest that everyone could perform the exact action you just did since, well, you've already done it, and your car is free of trash. What she means is what if everyone acted in the same way for the same reasons you just did—what if your principle of action was made into a law that everyone followed, and everyone was chucking their garbage out of the window? You wouldn't want that. Kant is after the same idea as your mom; he just spells it out it more detail.

There are two ways that a principle of action can violate the categorical imperative and thereby be a morally wrong principle to act upon. 2.44

Inconsistency Suppose that you have a serious gambling problem, and you've already blown all of your money at the racetrack. But you're absolutely sure that Plato's Beard is going to win in the seventh race. So you go up to one of your friends and say, "Bob, can I borrow $50? I promise to pay you back." But in fact your plan is to go gamble with Bob's money. Actually, even if Plato's Beard does win, you know that you'll stay at the racetrack, betting on everything in sight, until you're broke again. You have no intention of paying Bob back. You probably find deceitful promise-making to be intuitively wrong. But just how does it come into conflict with the categorical imperative? 2.45

In this case, your principle of action is something like "promise to achieve your own advantage, even when you know that you will not keep the promise." Let's universalize that. Now everyone acts on exactly the same principle. What will happen to promising? It will become meaningless; everyone will know that promises aren't worth spit. Which means that your false promise to Bob will get you nothing. Bob's not about to give you $50, knowing that promising is just some empty convention. In this case, universalizing makes your act of promising worthless. False promising is effective only against a backdrop of general honesty; if everyone is dishonest, then deceit won't work. In sum, 2.46

1. If your principle of action were universalized, then it would make your own action an impossible or fruitless one.
2. Thus your act could not be the result of a principle of action that you could will to be a universal law of nature.
3. Thus your act violates the categorical imperative.
4. Thus your act is immoral.

It is because false promising violates the categorical imperative that it is morally wrong.

2.47 *Inconsistent willing* Here's the second case. Suppose that no matter what, you always look out for yourself. If some politician wants to raise your taxes to provide health care to poor people, you'll vote them out of office. Whenever there's a food drive, the only canned goods you'll contribute are that tin of pickled beets that has been in the back of your pantry for two years. If somebody is poor, or sick, or uneducated, it's either his or her own fault or just bad luck. Either way it's not your problem. Everyone in this world has to take care of himself or herself, that's just the way it is.

2.48 We can characterize your principle of action in this case as "act selfishly." How does it stack up against the categorical imperative? Unlike the false promising case, act selfishly is a principle of action that is consistently universalizable. It could be the case that everyone always acts solely in his or her self-interest. However, "act selfishly" is not a principle that you can consistently *want*. It's easy to advocate selfish action when everything is going well for you, when you're young, healthy, strong, and have money in your pocket. But suppose that your car breaks down in the middle of a blizzard out in the boonies someplace and your cell phone's dead. If "act selfishly" is a universal law of nature, then no one is going to stop and help you. Then you'll be extremely sorry that everybody only cares about themselves. In other words, you can't consistently want that "act selfishly" be universalized. Here's the argument:

1. You could not consistently will that your principle of action be universalized.
2. Thus your act could not be the result of a principle of action that you could will to be a universal law of nature.
3. Thus your act violates the categorical imperative.
4. Thus your act is immoral.

Relentlessly selfish action is immoral because it violates the categorical imperative, as just discussed. It's another way to understand the violation of equal treatment complaint against ethical egoism—egoism is incompatible with the categorical imperative because it can't be universalized. Selfish action is appealing when you are on top of the world, otherwise, not so much.

Categorical imperative (version 2)

As mentioned, Kant gives another formulation of the categorical imperative too. Here it is. 2.49

> The *categorical imperative* (version 2, treating others): Treat other people as ends in themselves and never merely as means to your own ends.

What is this business about ends, or ends in themselves? The basic idea is pretty simple: treat other people with respect for their own goals, values, and interests; recognize the inherent dignity in others. In other words, don't just use people to get what you want. Immoral action comes from treating others as merely there for your use, just objects to be manipulated to your advantage, bodies to be stepped on as you climb the corporate ladder.

Sometimes people get the categorical imperative confused with the 2.50
Golden Rule, which says to treat others as you would like to be treated. They are not quite the same principle, though, and differ in this important aspect: the Golden Rule assumes that everyone has the same aims and preferences. Your goals are those of your neighbor's too, so you should act in a way to further her achievement of those goals (because that's how you would like your neighbor to treat you). But, as was noted at the beginning of this chapter, people don't have the same preferences. The categorical imperative does not assume that everyone has the same values and interests, in fact it demands that we treat others with respect for *their own* goals, ones which may turn out to be radically different from or even dramatically opposed to ours.

Actions that we ordinarily take to be immoral are easily shown to be 2.51
wrong under the categorical imperative. Consider theft, rape, killing, and fraud. All of these actions treat other people as merely as means to one's own ends. If you knock over a liquor store, you treat the store's owner and employees as just bodies who stock the shelves and fill the till. When you steal, you fail to treat them with respect for their own goals, values, and interests, which surely include the interests they have in retaining their property and remaining in business. Thus the categorical imperative offers a theoretical explanation of why those actions are wrong.

Here's a possible concern. Suppose you go into Wal-Mart to buy some 2.52
tennis balls. You go up the cashier, hand her some money, get your receipt, and leave with a can of tennis balls. Presumably you just used the cashier

to get what you want, namely some tennis balls. She used you too; by servicing customers she gets to keep her job. Since the categorical imperative tells us that using people is wrong, purchasing tennis balls is immoral. It is a short step to showing that every kind of transaction must be morally wrong. A result that counterintuitive shows that the categorical imperative must be mistaken.

2.53 The proper response is to note the little word "merely" that appears in the categorical imperative. It is wrong to treat other people *merely* as a means to your own ends. But you and the cashier, while you do indeed use each other to further your own ends (getting tennis balls and getting a paycheck, respectively), do not use each other *merely* as a means to your own ends. After all, you did pay her for the balls, and she did give them to you. If you had stolen the balls, that would have been to treat the cashier without respect for her own goals and interests and would therefore have violated the categorical imperative and have been the wrong thing to do.

2.54 You might claim that a shopkeeper has a *right* not to have his or her goods stolen. In fact, the very idea of moral rights comes from Kantian ethics. None of the moral theories so far considered in this chapter—religious moralism, ethical egoism, moral relativism, or utilitarianism have any truck with the idea of moral rights. Utilitarians, for example, think that whatever situation one is in, the morally correct action is the one that produces the greatest amount of pleasure in the world. No one has a right to anything. In fact, that was one of the objections to utilitarianism, that no action, no matter how intuitively horrible, is ever absolutely forbidden.

2.55 Recall the organ-robber case. Under utilitarianism, it looked like the morally correct thing to do was to butcher Joe Klutz and redistribute his organs. If you thought that result was completely mistaken, it is likely that you thought that Joe had a right not to be a killed, and a right not to have his bodily organs stolen, no matter how noble the purpose. Under Kantianism, the moral law is universally applicable and exceptionless, and the organ-robber case treats Joe merely as a means, and not as an end-in-himself. Precious little respect for Joe's interests is shown by carving him up against his will, which is why it is wrong to do so. Kantianism thereby gives the intuitively correct answer in the organ-robber case.

2.56 The categorical imperative sets out a claim against the behavior of other people, that is, others are obliged to treat you in a certain way— they should treat you with respect for your own dignity and interests. Rights too are claims against the behavior of others. For example, you have a right not to be killed, which means that you have a claim on the behavior of others that they refrain from killing you. This is a right that would hold against everyone at large. Other kinds of rights may only hold against specific individuals. For example, you may have a right that your priest keep the confidence of the confessional, even though you have no claim against others that they keep your secrets. The priest, however, promised confidentiality. We saw earlier how false promising violated the first formulation of the categorical imperative, which explains why the priest owes you silence. While a detailed discussion of different kinds of rights and how to understand them is beyond the scope of this chapter, it is worth noticing that the origin of the contemporary conception of rights is in the categorical imperative. If you think that people have moral rights that others must respect, then you might wish to side with the Kantians.

Objections to deontology

Objection 1: Generality The first objection to Kantianism focuses on the 2.57
first formulation of the categorical imperative, the idea that our principles of action must be consistently generalizable. The problem has to do with the right way to describe one's principle of action. Consider the organ-robber case again. All of the following are plausible candidates for being the operant principle of action.

1. If you want someone's bodily organs, just kill them and help yourself.
2. If you are a physician, you should save the lives of as many of your patients as possible.
3. You should act in such as way as to produce as much pleasure in the world as you can.

Number (1) fails the test of the categorical imperative. You couldn't consistently want everyone to act on that principle, not when needy patients start to stare hungrily at your young and healthy heart, liver, and lungs. Since the principle of action in (1) fails the categorical imperative, organ-robbing is immoral.

However, (2) apparently conforms to the categorical imperative. It does 2.58
not generate any inconsistencies to will that it be a universal law for physicians to save the lives of as many of their patients as possible. Nor does it

seem implausible that you could consistently will such a principle to be a universal law. In fact, some principle like this one underwrites the idea of triage—battlefield and ER doctors tend first to the patients most likely to survive only with immediate treatment at the expense of the less injured. While principle of action (2) leads to organ-robbing in unusual circumstances, it is seemingly compatible with the categorical imperative. Therefore organ-robbing is morally permissible.

2.59 Principle of action (3) is just the fundamental utilitarian directive. Is this principle of action something that can be universalized in accordance with the categorical imperative? Perhaps it can. Kantians will certainly reject the idea that morality is all about you, or all about me. Remember that earlier Kant explicitly argued that the egoist position of "act selfishly" violated the categorical imperative and was thus an immoral principle of action. So Kantians must be prepared to make some personal sacrifices in order to do the right thing, something obviously believed by utilitarians as well. One can't reasonably argue that (3) can't be universalized because you couldn't consistently will it to be a universal law when the time comes for you to sacrifice for the greater good. To do so is to slide towards egoism. But if (3) can be universalized, then organ-robbing in the case described is the right thing to do.

2.60 The objection to Kantianism is that each of three principles of action just listed can be cited as the principle of action in the organ-robber case. But (1) violates the categorical imperative, whereas (2) and (3) apparently do not. Therefore the categorical imperative leads to inconsistent moral judgments.

2.61 *Objection 2: Agent-neutral intuitions* One of the objections to utilitarianism was that it was incompatible with agent-relative intuitions. One of the selling points of Kantianism is that it *is* an agent-relative theory. All well and good. However, there are agent-neutral intuitions too, and those cut against Kantianism. Consider this case. You're a manager at a large company, and you're hiring for a new entry-level position. You know that your niece Sylvia is looking for a work, so you blithely decide that you'll give the job to her. There are other applicants for the job, equally as qualified as Sylvia.

2.62 Kantianism is an agent-relative moral theory according to which our interpersonal relationships can impose particular moral obligations that we do not have to others. Promising is an obvious example: you're obliged to give Tim a cup of coffee because you promised him one, although you're not obliged to give a cup of coffee to everyone who wants one. In the nepotism case you may judge that it is wrong to dismiss the other qualified applicants for the position. Sylvia's hire was a foregone conclusion; the other applicants never really had a chance at all and suffer unfair opportunity costs by applying. If nepotism is wrong, then the morally correct thing to do would be to treat all of the candidates equally, without prejudice, so that any of them have a fair shot at being hired. Agent neutrality is the morally correct stance.

The drowning swimmers case prompted agent-relative intuitions (you 2.63
should save your own child from drowning), and so was an objection against utilitarianism. Yet the nepotism case motivates agent-neutral intuitions (you should give all applicants an equal chance at the job) and so counts against Kantianism.

Objection 3: Horrible consequences The Kantian bumper sticker is damn 2.64
the consequences, abide by the categorical imperative! Like false promising, Kantians think that lying fails the categorical imperative and is for that reason always wrong. But how about this case? You're at home watching the Cubs break your heart again when there is a frantic pounding on your door. You open it to find your friend Maria. She tells you that her crazy boyfriend is trying to kill her and begs you to hide her. You tell her to go hide in the bedroom, and you lock the door. A few minutes later there is more frantic knocking on the door. You open it and there is Dangerous Dan, holding a 10-inch combat knife with a tanto point and a serrated recurve. He has bloodlust in his eyes. He asks you if you've seen Maria. Do you say:

1. "Why, yes. She's in the bedroom."

or

2. "No, I have no idea where she is."

If you choose (2) and decide to lie, then you are using Dangerous Dan merely as a means to your own ends, in this case the end of protecting Maria. You are not demonstrating any respect for Dan's own values and goals (murderous though they are). Kantianism does not allow violations of the categorical imperative in order to prevent other violations of the categorical imperative. To do so would mean that the moral law is not truly categorical after all; instead it is just another hypothetical imperative, along the lines of "treat others as ends in themselves and not merely as means unless by doing so you enable others to treat others merely as means." Not only does this move give up the absolute, categorical nature of the moral law, but it looks suspiciously utilitarian. If Kantianism just capitulates to utilitarianism when the going gets tough, then it's not really offering an alternative moral theory.

2.65 Thus according to Kantianism, your moral duty is to tell the truth. So in accordance with the categorical imperative, you tell Dangerous Dan that Maria's in the bedroom. If you're inclined to think that's completely absurd, and that clearly you should lie to protect Maria, then that's a reason to reject Kantianism. One could only wonder what would have happened to the Jews who worked at **Oskar Schindler's munitions factory** if Schindler had been a good Kantian and never lied to his Nazi bosses.[7] A stern and inflexible absolute moral law is difficult to square with the lavish and unforeseeable variety of human situations.

Virtue Ethics (Is Morality All about Having a Virtuous Character?)

2.66 The final ethical theory on deck is also the most ancient, endorsed by religions such as Islam and with a pedigree going back to Aristotle's discussion in *Nicomachean Ethics*. It is the idea that morality isn't about outcomes (like utilitarians think), or rule following (like Kant and Christians think), but about being a certain type of person. Instead of obsessing about good *actions*, we ought to focus on what it is to be a good *person*. This is the idea of virtue ethics. Virtue is an appealing way to understand morality. Instead of a daunting calculus that must take every actual and future person into account, or some rigid and abstract moral law, virtue is within the grasp of everyone. We can become the people we ought to be though the development of our own characters, without needing some God's eye perspective on the human condition. Morality ceases to be another imposition or just a bunch of rules you're supposed to follow, but instead naturally arises out of your emotional motivations working in harmony with rational reasons for acting. A virtuous person does good in the world because she wants to.

2.67 There are two central components of virtue ethics: the concept of virtue, and the concept of character. A good person is a virtuous person, one with a certain sort of character.

What is virtue?

Virtues are good qualities or characteristics. Some virtues are narrow ones, specific to particular tasks or professions. For example, a good trait for football linemen is to be big, with bulging muscles and excellent short-term speed and power. Someone weighing 140 pounds with thin arms and a scrawny chest would get broken in two in the NFL. However, professional cyclists need the opposite qualities. Weighing 300 pounds with a muscular upper body is a serious vice for a cyclist, who would lose badly trying to cart all that weight up a mountain. Nor do cyclists need brief explosive speed nearly as much as they need steady endurance, which is largely unimportant for football players. 2.68

Moral virtues are those qualities of personality that are valuable for everyone to have, whether they are an offensive tackle, cyclist, or anyone else. Possessing and acting on the virtues amounts to living a morally worthwhile and flourishing life for a human being. Moral virtue does not guarantee that your life will go well in the sense that you will be immune to bad luck, or you will never make mistakes. Messing up and suffering ill fortune is the stuff of tragedy. Yet being a virtuous person assures that you are doing the best that you can and that you are living the best life possible given whatever situation you are in. 2.69

Here is a partial list of typical moral virtues: loyalty, honesty, fairness, kindness, courage, considerateness, civility, compassion, friendliness, patience, self-reliance, generosity, and dependability. The opposite of virtue is vice. According to Aristotle, many virtues are the midpoint, or "**golden mean**"[8] between related vices of deficiency or excess. Virtue is a sort of Goldilocks zone. Here are some examples. 2.70

Too little	*Just right*	*Too much*
Stingy	Generous	Wasteful
Cowardly	Courageous	Reckless
Cranky	Friendly	Sucking up/brown-nosing
False modesty	Honesty about oneself	Bragging
Anorexia	Moderate consumption	Gluttony
Sloth	Ambition	Workaholism

It is courageous to defend your country from an invading army, and cowardly to run from the battle. But it is also reckless or foolhardy for a soldier with a pistol to singlehandedly attack a platoon armed with machine guns.

It is good to be ambitious and bad to be lazy or slothful. Yet it is also a bad thing to be a workaholic who ignores all other valuable things in life to take as much overtime as possible and work seven days a week.

2.71 When the Roman statesman **Marcus Tullius Cicero** (106–43 BCE)[9] wrote that, "Extremism in the defense of liberty is no vice; moderation in the pursuit of justice is no virtue," this would have been startling to his audience. It would have been startling because Cicero was explicitly rejecting the Aristotelian idea that virtue is (generally) to be located at the golden mean, a traditional view that would have been well known among the Romans.

What is character?

2.72 For virtue theory, the virtues are not specific behaviors or actions so much as they are habits of character. No single action demonstrates much, if anything, about one's character. Rather, character is a tendency to act in certain sorts of ways. Someone with an honest character will routinely tell the truth, even when it may be unpopular or difficult to do so. That doesn't mean that an honest person absolutely never lies, but to do so is uncharacteristic of them, or goes against their native feelings. Character reflects a kind of steadiness of behavior.

2.73 Character is the sort of thing that comes in degrees. So someone with a strong character is dependable, steady, unflinching, unwavering, steadfast, and reliable. Someone with a weak character is fickle, weak, faithless, irresolute, erratic, capricious, and incontinent. Strength of character does not alone guarantee that a person is virtuous or honorable. A vicious person might be dependably wicked—the schoolyard bully is reliably cruel. To lead the morally good life you need to cultivate a character that is both strong and virtuous. Moreover, it is not enough to be a loyal friend but also stingy and cheap, or to be compassionate but a workaholic. A genuinely flourishing life requires *personal integrity*: a unity of the virtues, made habitual, and leading to action.

Objections to virtue ethics

2.74 *Objection 1: Virtue is compatible with evil* The first objection to virtue theory is that it seems entirely possible to cultivate and endorse the classic moral virtues and still participate in considerable wickedness. Consider Cosa Nostra, also known as the Mafia. When Salvatore Lo Piccolo, the capo of the **Sicilian Mafia**, was arrested in 2007, the police found a written code of behavior for the mob.[10] Here's the Mafia's "**ten commandments**."

1. No one can present himself directly to another of our friends. There must be a third person to do it.
2. Never look at the wives of friends.
3. Never be seen with cops.
4. Don't go to pubs and clubs.
5. Always being available for Cosa Nostra is a duty—even if your wife is about to give birth.
6. Appointments must absolutely be respected.
7. Wives must be treated with respect.
8. When asked for any information, the answer must be the truth.
9. Money cannot be appropriated if it belongs to others or to other families.
10. People who can't be part of Cosa Nostra: anyone who has a close relative in the police, anyone with a two-timing relative in the family, anyone who behaves badly and doesn't hold to moral values.

Lo Piccolo's list emphasizes honesty, respect, duty, and moral values. Traditional Mafia morality also includes absolute loyalty to the family, the **omertà code of silence**,[11] and the prohibition on harming a made man. (Remember: a friend will help you move, but a true friend will help you move a body.) Despite the Mafia's promotion of such traditional virtues among its members, nevertheless it is a criminal organization that also engages in extortion and murder. You may think that a Mafioso who is scrupulous about never speaking to the police and is completely loyal to his bosses is doing the wrong thing. It would be better if he were a stool pigeon who ratted out his fellow criminals to the cops. Genovese family soldier **Joseph Valachi**,[12] who broke the code of omertà and squealed to the FBI and the US Senate on the inner workings of the Mafia, was a disloyal man who violated his own blood oath. Still, you might reasonably hold that doing so made him morally superior to his mob bosses.

The problem for virtue theory is that it looks like less "virtue" might 2.75
result in better behavior in the Mafia case. A virtue theorist may rejoin that mafiosos only have some of the virtues, but clearly lack some major virtues as well. The good life consists in possessing all the virtues and

having an integrated, unified moral character. Having some virtues and some vices might lead to worse consequences than not having those virtues at all.

2.76 Unfortunately, if having virtues and vices is to be evaluated in terms of the behavioral consequences they lead to, then virtue ethics seems to devolve into just a cumbersome utilitarianism. When is loyalty good? When it leads to good consequences. When is remaining loyal bad? When it leads to bad consequences. Or you might see it as a form of Kantianism. Having a virtue is a good thing if it leads to respecting the categorical imperative, but a bad thing if it leads to rights violations. No trait of character is virtuous in itself—you always need to look at consequences to tell. But if the very same trait can be either virtuous or vicious, then it does not look like virtue ethics is bringing anything new to the table.

2.77 If virtue theory is to remain a distinctively different moral theory, it needs to prevent assimilation into either utilitarianism or Kantianism, while at the same time explaining how it is possible that having some good character traits might lead to a worse life or worse results for others than lacking those qualities.

2.78 *Objection 2: Clashing virtues* Virtue ethics advises that the good life consists in cultivating *all* the virtues. It is a good thing to be honest, but it is even better if you are a kind person too. The present objection is that some virtues apparently conflict with each other. For example, suppose that your girlfriend is showing off her new hairstyle. She asks, "How do you like my new haircut?" In truth, it's awful. You say,

1. Babe, that looks great!
2. Whoa! Did you use a weed whacker on that?

Option (1) is a much kinder and considerate response. But (2) is more honest. Which wins out, kindness or honesty? Here's another example. Imagine that your favorite indie band is now donating all of their profits to charity. That's pretty virtuous, right? Since they want to give as much to charity as possible, the band starts writing radio-friendly pop drivel and commercial jingles which earn a lot of money. In other words, **the band just sells out.**[13] Should you be disappointed? Selling out is surely a vice of rock bands. On the other hand they are giving piles of money to save baby seals. One more example: workaholism is a vice of excess, as discussed earlier. Suppose, though, that you're a workaholic to support your large and

otherwise impoverished family. Taking care of your family is a virtue. So are you doing the right thing or the wrong thing?

If the virtues can conflict with each other, as in these examples, then 2.79 virtue theory is offering no guidance about how we should live or what we should do. Should you be an honest person or a kind one? Should your band sell out or be true to your muse? There is no broader, overarching guidance other than the familiar "just be virtuous," which is no help in these conflict cases. It's like telling someone to just do the right thing when they are confronted with a moral dilemma and have no idea what the right thing is.

Objection 3: Relativism about virtues The third objection is that what 2.80 qualities of character count as virtues and which count as vices seems to be heavily dependent on the culture in which you are raised. For example, consider the Amish. The Amish are a religious sect that rejects modernity in order to live lives much like their eighteenth-century forebears. They emphasize humility, modesty, and plainness as cardinal virtues. In order to avoid their clothing from drawing attention to themselves, the Amish shun ostentation such as buttons, zippers, or even Velcro, fastening their clothes with straight pins and snaps. The clothing itself includes bonnets, long dresses, and capes in dark colors and body-covering styles.

Now contrast the Amish with the participants in **the World Naked** 2.81 **Bike Ride (WNBR)**.[14] The WNBR is a series of organized bicycle rides held in major cities in countries all over the world. The participants ride nude in order to draw media attention to their cause, which is protesting oil dependency and promoting cycling as an environmentally friendly alterative to automobiles. The riders in the WNBR celebrate freedom, body confidence, healthy lifestyles, and environmental awareness as important virtues.

It is inconceivable for an Amish man or woman to ride in the World 2.82 Naked Bike Ride, just as it is impossible for a WNBR rider to endorse the virtues held by the Amish. So which are the right virtues to live by? Is it better to be modest, plain, and humble before God, or better to flamboyantly reject an uptight society that's addicted to oil?

Aristotle argued that **human beings have a function**,[15] and perhaps if 2.83 we understood the nature of this function that we could decide which virtues are best to adopt. Just as the function of the opposable thumb is to grasp, and the function of the eyes is to see, Aristotle thought that there must be a function, or a right way of functioning, for human beings. It

can't simply be to take in nutrition or to grow, since we share those traits with plants. Nor can it be merely having sense perceptions, or gratifying our base desires, since we share those urges with nonhuman animals. There must be some unique function for human beings that we alone have. Aristotle argued that reason and rational action are alone the province of humans. Canine happiness may come from answering the perennial question that dogs face: "Do I eat it, pee on it, or roll in it?" But human happiness, he thought, consists in the use of reason to guide our lives. Happiness is not the result of rational decision-making, but the process of it in accordance with virtue. Happiness is a journey, not a destination.

2.84 Whatever the merits of Aristotle's function argument, it is rather nonspecific about exactly which virtues contribute to the good human life. You can agree with him that the rational life is the proper function of a human being, but still aver that this does not yield much in the way of contentful virtues. So we are still stuck with the relativism problem.

2.85 The present objection is similar to the problem of clashing virtues, but with a twist—one might simply relativize virtues and vices to cultures. Thus humility and modesty are vices in the culture of WNBR cyclists while being virtues for the Amish, and vice versa. The problem with endorsing relativism about virtue is that virtue ethics is supposed to tell us those qualities of personality that are valuable for *everyone* to have. There may be different sporting virtues for offensive linemen than there are for riders in the Tour de France, but the traits that make for the good life, for being an honorable human being, are the same. At least, that's the promise of virtue ethics. Yet allowing relativism about virtue reneges on that promise. What's more, a relativized virtue ethics would then have to deal with all the objections to cultural relativism that were discussed earlier in the last chapter.

2.86 *Objection 4: There is no such thing as character* The final objection to virtue ethics comes from experimental psychology, and is perhaps the most powerful complaint. Essential to virtue ethics is the notion of character, the idea that each person has a tendency to act in certain sorts of ways given the appropriate situation. Thus an honest person will refrain from cheating or stealing, even in a situation when they could clearly get away with it. A gentle person won't harm others, even when they are told to do so, or when annoyed or made angry by another. Tendencies to behave in certain ways are *explained* by the fact that a person is honest, gentle, or has other character traits. Furthermore, those personality characteristics are *predictive*—knowing that a person is caring allows us to predict that she will help others who need a hand.

According to the experimental psychologists, "character" is just a story 2.87
that we tell about people after they act in certain ways. If someone demonstrates bravery in battle, we say that it was due to his or her courageous character. When participants in a prison simulation descend into barbarity we tell ourselves that their true natures were revealed. But the experimental evidence from psychology is that these categories are no more than convenient pigeonholes. People aren't "jerks" or "losers" or "alpha males" or "nature's nobility." Appeal to character is a tidy plotline to understand the behavior of others (and ourselves), but isn't nearly as predictive as the general facts of human nature that the experimentalists are uncovering.

What are these experimental results? John Doris, a prominent contem- 2.88
porary critic of virtue ethics, summarizes the argument as follows.

> Numerous studies have demonstrated that minor situational variations have powerful effects on helping **behavior**: hurried passersby step over a stricken person in their path, while unhurried passersby stop to help;[16] passersby who find a bit of change stop to help a woman who has dropped her papers, while passersby who are not similarly fortunate do not. Situations have also been shown to have a potent influence on harming: ordinary people are willing to torture a screaming victim at the polite request of an experimenter, or perpetuate all manner of imaginative cruelties while serving as guards in a **prison** simulation.[17] The experimental record suggests that situational factors are often better predictors of behavior than personal factors, and this impression is reinforced by careful examination of behavior outside the confines of the laboratory. In very many situations, it looks as though personality is less than robustly determinative of behavior. To put things crudely, people typically lack character. (Doris, 2002, p. 2)

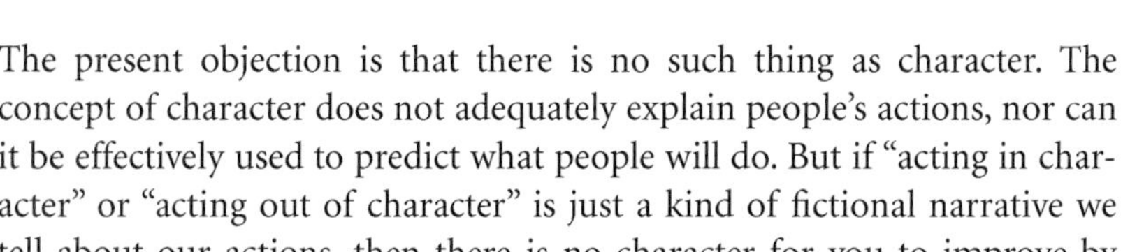

The present objection is that there is no such thing as character. The concept of character does not adequately explain people's actions, nor can it be effectively used to predict what people will do. But if "acting in character" or "acting out of character" is just a kind of fictional narrative we tell about our actions, then there is no character for you to improve by trying to make virtues habitual. There is nothing for virtue ethics to be *about*.

Conclusion

2.89 Some moral theories enjoy currency among the general public, especially religious moralism, ethical egoism, and moral relativism. These were discussed in Chapter 1. Others are taken more seriously by professional philosophers, particularly utilitarianism, Kantianism, and virtue ethics. These were addressed in the present chapter. Contemporary philosophers have developed sophisticated versions of those theories in an attempt to address the criticisms of the basic models canvassed above. The two ethics chapters in this book have not discussed every ethical theory, but hopefully you see how moral theories are crafted and debated, and what the pros and cons are of the theories that have been presented. Moral reasoning is quite a bit more than just registering one's opinion on the hot-button topic of the day.

2.90 Many issues in moral philosophy are unexplored here, and are beyond the scope of a general introduction to philosophy. For example, what is the meaning of moral propositions? Is there some kind of objective moral reality to which they correspond? Or do such propositions do no more than express the approval or disapproval of the speaker towards certain sorts of actions? How are human ethical intuitions related to the moral or proto-moral instinctive actions of nonhuman animals? Can evolutionary psychology provide a unified account of these intuitive responses, and what would this mean for moral theory, or for the idea that there is a moral reality?

2.91 Finally, and this may be the hardest question to answer satisfactorily, why be moral? Clearly the response "because you should" misses the point. Such an answer presupposes that paying attention to morality matters and you ought to care about it, which is the very issue at hand. Perhaps you should only care about *appearing* to be a morally upright person, displaying public virtue yet preserving private, secret vice. The real question here is "Why should I adopt the moral point of view, why should I enter into the game of morality at all?" That question is a difficult one indeed.

Annotated Bibliography

Aristotle (350 BCE) *Nicomachean Ethics*, full text available at http://classics.mit.edu/Aristotle/nicomachaen.html, accessed May 8, 2012. Here Aristotle presents his seminal defense of virtue ethics. It remains the touchstone for virtue ethicists after nearly two and a half millennia.

Bentham, Jeremy (1789) *An Introduction to the Principles of Morals and Legislation* (Oxford: Clarendon Press, 1907), full text available at www.econlib.org/library/Bentham/bnthPML.html, accessed May 8, 2012. Bentham's classic presentation and defense of utilitarianism, including the felicific calculus.

Bentham, Jeremy (1825) *The Rationale of Reward* (London: John and H.L. Hunt), full text available at www.archive.org/stream/rationaleofrewar00bent/rationaleofrewar00bent_djvu.txt, accessed May 8, 2012. Contains Bentham's defense of the view that only the quantity of pleasure matters. He derides the self-appointed arbiters of good taste in defense of his claim that push-pin is as good as poetry.

Doris, John (2002) *Lack of Character: Personality and Moral Behavior* (Cambridge: Cambridge University Press). Doris argues against virtue ethics on the basis of "situationist" evidence from experimental psychology.

Kant, Immanuel (1785) *Groundwork for the Metaphysics of Morals* (Cambridge: Cambridge University Press, 1998), full text available at www.earlymoderntexts.com/pdf/kantgrou.pdf. 415 editions of this book were published in 20 languages between 1785 and 2008. It contains Kant's most famous presentation of deontology, including the categorical imperative.

Klein, Robert (2000) *The Beer Lover's Rating Guide*, 2nd edn (New York: Workman Publishing). Somewhat dated and eccentric, nevertheless a useful guide to good beer.

Mill, John Stuart (1863) *Utilitarianism* (London: Parker, Son, and Bourn), full text available at www.earlymoderntexts.com/pdf/millutil.pdf, accessed May 8, 2012. Like Bentham, Mill was interested in penal reform, and this is his presentation of utilitarian theory, including the idea of higher and lower pleasures.

Sidgwick, Henry (1874) *Methods of Ethics*, full text available at http://archive.org/details/methodsethics03sidggoog, accessed May 8, 2012. Sidgwick was, along with Bentham and Mill, the third great classical utilitarian. *Methods of Ethics* is the most systematic treatment of the theory prior to the twentieth century.

Suikkanen, Jussi (forthcoming) *This is Ethics: An Introduction* (Oxford: Wiley-Blackwell). A comprehensive introduction to ethics. It covers such topics as pleasure and happiness, well-being and the meaning of life, egoism and altruism, ethical theories and principles, moral motivation and reasoning, and how to apply ethics in ordinary life.

Online Resources

1 The definition and causes of friendly fire, along with historical examples: http://en.wikipedia.org/wiki/Friendly_fire

2 A dictionary entry on "summum bonum": http://en.wiktionary.org/wiki/summum_bonum
3 Beer Advocate's description and assessment of Brooklyn Brewery's Black Ops imperial stout: http://beeradvocate.com/beer/profile/45/40149
4 A sophisticated discussion of the mathematics underlying Simpson's Paradox: http://plato.stanford.edu/entries/paradox-simpson/
5 Highlights from the 2009 Wimbledon men's final: www.youtube.com/watch?v=rAu_woONfUs
6 A substantive overview of Kant's moral philosophy: http://plato.stanford.edu/entries/kant-moral/
7 The entry on Oskar Schindler at the United States Holocaust Memorial Museum: www.ushmm.org/museum/exhibit/focus/schindler/
8 A review of the concept of the golden mean in classical philosophy: http://en.wikipedia.org/wiki/Golden_mean_(philosophy)
9 The life, times, and philosophy of Cicero, the greatest orator of ancient Rome: http://plato.stanford.edu/entries/ancient-political/#CicRomRep
10 A news report on the arrest of Sicilian mob capo Salvatore Lo Piccolo and the Mafia's "ten commandments": http://news.bbc.co.uk/1/hi/world/europe/7086716.stm
11 A discussion of the meaning and origins of omertà, the honor code of silence: http://en.wikipedia.org/wiki/Omert%C3%A0
12 A substantial biography of famed mob informant Joseph Valachi: www.trutv.com/library/crime/gangsters_outlaws/mob_bosses/valachi//index_1.html
13 An overview of The Who's 1967 album *The Who Sell Out*: www.thewho.com/discography/index/album/albumId/62
14 The home page for The World Naked Bike Ride: http://worldnakedbikeride.org/
15 A more in-depth look at Aristotle's function argument and conception of the human good: http://plato.stanford.edu/entries/aristotle-ethics/#HumGooFunArg
16 An overview of the behavioral psychology's good Samaritan experiment: www.experiment-resources.com/helping-behavior.html
17 The Stanford prison experiment is presented and discussed in a video: www.youtube.com/watch?v=sZwfNs1pqG0&feature=related

3

GOD

According to a recent Gallup poll, 92 percent of Americans believe in the 3.1
existence of God.[1] This is a staggering consensus—it is impossible to get so many people agreeing about almost any other topic. To provide some context, only 79 percent of Americans believe that the **Earth revolves around the Sun**,[2] a fact settled by Copernicus and Galileo over 300 years ago. Indeed, the number of people that believe that God is dead is about the same number that believe **Elvis is still alive**.[3] Of all the topics in this book, the one you most likely already have some opinion about is whether God exists.

The matter of God is also unlike other philosophical topics in the level 3.2
of passion it generates. Religious enthusiasm is responsible for some of the most magnificent and sublime art, architecture, and music the world has ever seen. The **Parthenon in Athens**,[4] the **Blue Mosque in Istanbul**,[5] the temples of **Angkor Wat**,[6] **Michelangelo's *Pietà***,[7] the ceiling of the **Sistine Chapel**,[8] J. S. Bach's ***Mass in B Minor***,[9] John Coltrane's ***A Love Supreme***,[10] and George Harrison's ***My Sweet Lord***[11] were all inspired by religious conviction. Very seldom do other philosophical ideas inspire such artistic achievements. (There are rare exceptions, such as Richard Strauss's tone poem ***Also Sprach Zarathustra***,[12] inspired by the philosopher Friedrich Nietzsche's book of the same name, Raphael's ***School of Athens***,[13] and Jacques-Louis David's painting ***The Death of Socrates***.[14]) On the other hand, no one launches a crusade or a jihad over epistemological skepticism, or uses professional torturers to convince others that libertarianism is the correct account of free will, or shuns their neighbors because they are utilitarians. But people have done all those things and more in the name

This Is Philosophy: An Introduction, First Edition. Steven D. Hales.

of religion. Why this one topic stirs such strong emotions is an important issue for psychologists and sociologists to sort out. As philosophers, however, what we want to know is whether, and which, religious claims are true.

Faith

Faith as confidence

3.3 If you believe in God, you may well cite *faith* as the explanation of your belief. In one sense, "faith" means confidence. Suppose your friend Scott tells you that he has faith in the Washington Redskins this year. Surely Scott is not informing you that he believes in the existence of the Redskins, which would be a very odd thing to say, and would elicit some strange looks. Rather, he *presupposes* that the Redskins exist, and his faith in them is simply his confidence that the Redskins are going to have a good season. Similarly, you could have confidence in God, that he will do certain things, or help you in various ways, or whatever. But if that describes your faith in God, then it presupposes that God exists (just as Scott's faith in the Redskins presupposed their existence), and doesn't really say why you think God exists.

Faith as belief without reason

3.4 In another sense, "faith" means believing without evidence or reasons. If that is the sort of faith in God that you have, then it still doesn't do much to justify your belief. In fact it does nothing other than admit that there is no rational basis for your belief in God at all. In other contexts, believing without evidence is a terrible plan. If you're in Las Vegas, plunking down a piece of change on the roulette wheel because of your faith that this time it's going to hit on red 32, well, get ready for the poorhouse. Faith is more like wishful thinking than a path to knowledge. Choosing to believe things when there is no reason to do so is a swift path to being suckered by all sorts of swindlers, con artists, bullshitters, and snake oil salesmen. Chapter 7 on knowledge addresses this problem in much more detail, and explains why evidence matters when deciding what to believe.

3.5 Perhaps religious belief is different. Maybe when it comes to religious matters, faith—belief without reason—is the appropriate way to believe that there is a God. The idea that faith and reason are at odds with each other has a long standing in Christian thought. The third-century theologian **Tertullian** reputedly declared "*credo, qua absurdum est*"; I believe because it is absurd.[15] Even if reason showed his religious beliefs to be absurd, that didn't bother Tertullian in the least. Similarly, **Martin Luther**[16] thought that reason was a fine thing "in comparison with other things of this life, the best and something divine" (*Disputatio de Homine* (1536), section 4), but that it was useless in theological matters. Later he offered the opinions that Aristotle, who represented the pinnacle of philosophical reason for Luther, knows nothing about "theological man" and that it is impious and in opposition to theology to suppose that reason can aspire to the knowledge of God. Luther even embraced the Tertullian enthusiasm for absurdity and contradiction. In responding to an argument that Christ could not be eternal because he was born, and hence had a beginning, Luther wrote, "In philosophy this is true, but not in theology. The Son is born eternal from eternity; this is something incomprehensible. But this belongs to theology" (***Disputation on the Divinity and Humanity of Christ***, section VI).[17]

One may certainly argue that there are limits to human understanding, 3.6
or that there are truths beyond our capacity to know them. However, it's a bit peculiar to argue that there are matters beyond the reach of reason and then turn around and claim to *know* the truth about these very matters. Here's an analogy from a different branch of inquiry. In the 1930s the logician Kurt Gödel proved that there are mathematical facts that are eternally beyond the power of logic to establish as either true or false. More exactly, Gödel proved that there must be mathematical propositions that could not be derived from any logical system with a finite number of mutually consistent axioms. Gödel's finding revolutionized mathematical logic. While Gödel showed that there had to be such unprovable propositions, he never claimed to know exactly what they were, or whether they were true or false. In fact, one way to understand his results is that since there are unprovable mathematical facts, there are logical limits in one area of human knowledge. For believers like Tertullian and Luther, we can know things like "Christ is born eternal from eternity," despite a lack of reasons, despite conceding that it is incomprehensible, by faith alone. Believing it anyway, in the teeth of rational evidence, is supposed to amount to knowledge.

If faith is no more than belief without reasons or evidence, then it is by 3.7
that very fact not within the domain of philosophy (which Luther, for example, would be quick to endorse). Philosophy is very keen on supplying

good reasons to believe things. There is a long tradition within philosophy, however, of using reason to evaluate claims of the divine. This practice is known as ***natural theology***.[18] The existence of God is of course one topic in natural theology, but not the only one. The divinity of other religious figures (Jesus, Buddha, Krishna, etc.), the existence of angels or demons, the reality of Heaven, Hell, or any sort of afterlife, the possibility of resurrection or reincarnation, whether there is a day of judgment, the coherence of the Trinity, and whether there have been genuine miracles have been thoroughly debated by philosophers. Those issues are all beyond the scope of the present chapter (although *This Is Philosophy of Religion: An Introduction* (Manson, forthcoming) provides a much more comprehensive treatment). The remainder of the present chapter will look at one topic within natural theology, namely, the reasons for and against believing that God exists.

The Attributes of God

3.8 Before we can begin examining whether there is a God, we must first have some conception of what God is. If we have no idea who or what God could be, then we'll have no idea if we actually run across him, her, or it. The quest for God would be no more than a **snipe hunt**.[19] Whether God truly exists is independent from the issue of what God's qualities or properties are. Let's say we're looking for unicorns.

3.9 Maybe you think they are mythological, maybe you think that they are real. Either way we have to know what unicorns are supposed to be before we can effectively look for them. Suppose we decide that whatever else unicorns are, at the very least they are horses that have a single horn on their heads. If we find a horse with a horn, we can reasonably claim to have located a unicorn. If we scour the Earth and find no such animal, then we can conclude that there are no unicorns. If we further find no unicorns in the fossil record, no transitional forms, and no suitably empty slots in equine taxonomy, then we can reasonably conclude that there never have been unicorns. A lack of unicorns did not mean that the concept of "unicorn" was empty, though, or that we didn't know what we were searching for.

3.10 What, then, are the attributes of God, so we can start looking around? Loads of qualities have been assigned to God, not all of them consistent with each other. God is reputed to be perfectly just (=always giving people what they deserve) yet also perfectly merciful (=always letting people off the hook). He's supposed to be loving but also vengeful, the lord of peace but still a **bloodthirsty conqueror**.[20] God is said to be omnipresent (=everywhere at once), yet is an immaterial spirit with no spatial location. He is supposed to exist eternally (=present at every moment) while also existing outside of time. Some claim God is infinite, but that alone doesn't mean very much. Is he infinite in quantity? Infinitely large? Infinitely puny? Infinite in duration? Infinitely fat? Infinitely jolly? The historical traditions are convoluted, to say the least.

In the classical tradition of natural theology, God is assumed to have the 3.11
following three properties:

Omnipotence: being all powerful
Omniscience: being all knowing
Omnibenevolence: being morally perfect, or perfectly good

If there is a God, then of course he will have more than just these three properties, just as unicorns, were they real, would have more qualities than just "horse with a horn." The idea is that if we can demonstrate the existence of any being that is omnipotent, omniscient, and omnibenevolent, then we have proven the existence of God. If we are able to show that there is no being that has those three attributes, then we have proven that God does not exist. The remainder of this chapter will be divided into two halves. The first half will present and critique the arguments in favor of God's existence. The second half will present and critique the arguments against God's existence.

Why There Is a God

The argument from scripture

Many people defend their religious beliefs on the grounds that they come 3.12
from some book that they regard as completely accurate, and this book makes religious claims. So you might say that you believe that God exists because it says so in the Bible. It's important to keep in mind from the outset that there are many different religious scriptures, they each promote different deities, and offer only occasionally overlapping religious stories. **The Rig-Veda** is one of the sacred texts of Hinduism,[21] and consists of a

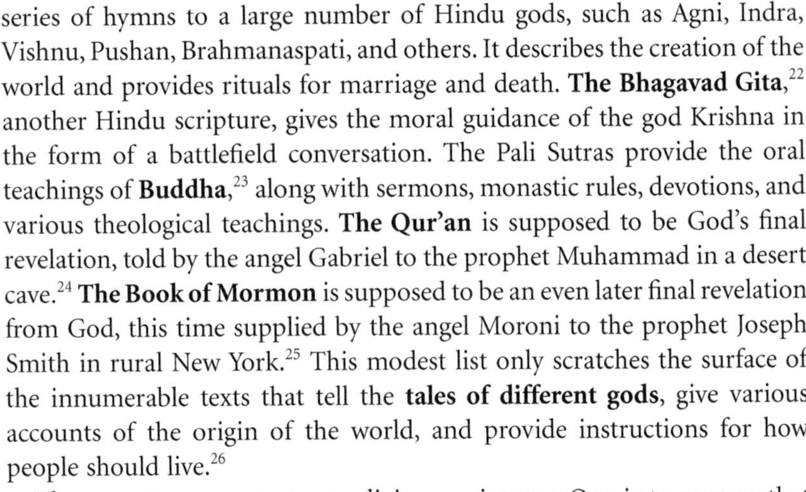

series of hymns to a large number of Hindu gods, such as Agni, Indra, Vishnu, Pushan, Brahmanaspati, and others. It describes the creation of the world and provides rituals for marriage and death. **The Bhagavad Gita**,[22] another Hindu scripture, gives the moral guidance of the god Krishna in the form of a battlefield conversation. The Pali Sutras provide the oral teachings of **Buddha**,[23] along with sermons, monastic rules, devotions, and various theological teachings. **The Qur'an** is supposed to be God's final revelation, told by the angel Gabriel to the prophet Muhammad in a desert cave.[24] **The Book of Mormon** is supposed to be an even later final revelation from God, this time supplied by the angel Moroni to the prophet Joseph Smith in rural New York.[25] This modest list only scratches the surface of the innumerable texts that tell the **tales of different gods**, give various accounts of the origin of the world, and provide instructions for how people should live.[26]

3.13 There are two ways to treat religious scriptures. One is to assume that they are divinely inspired, and so everything they contain is sacred, infallible, and any apparent errors are to be explained away by whatever means available. If your preferred holy book was dictated by flawless holy beings, then it may contain poetry, prayers, or hymns, but it certainly does not contain falsehoods. The problem is that, as a reason to believe in the existence of God, assuming the divine inspiration of scripture is not a good argument. It is essentially this argument:

1. Assume that the Bible (or whatever holy book you prefer) is the divinely inspired word of God.
2. God doesn't lie.
3. The Bible says God exists.
4. Therefore, God exists.

The first premise implicitly assumes that there is a God, namely the very individual who inspired the Bible. In other words, the argument proceeds from assuming that God exists, to the conclusion that God exists. Unfortunately, this assumes the very thing to be proven, and the premises are thereby no more plausible than the conclusion is. Logicians call this "circular reasoning" or "**begging the question**."[27] So if we treat the Bible as divinely inspired, it cannot serve as evidence that God exists, on the grounds that assuming divine inspiration already presupposes that God exists.

3.14 The other way to treat religious texts is to hold them to the same historical standards that we do other old books and documents. Ancient historians like Herodotus, Thucydides, Josephus, and Suetonius are not taken at face value, but their accounts are closely examined in light of other evidence we have about the past. For example, we have imperial and court records, and the writings of other historians of the time. There are also archaeological finds that provide physical evidence about migratory patterns, battles, populations, architecture, kings, and settlements. Moreover, we import what we know about human nature to ask whether an ancient writer is trying to flatter the rulers, curry favor with religious authorities, demonize their enemies, or just write a fabulous tale. All of these things are the raw materials out of which contemporary scholars try to reconstruct the past in the most accurate way they can.

One of the problems with investigating the historical claims made in a 3.15
book like the Bible is that the investigators usually have strong religious convictions which bias their scholarship. It wasn't until the nineteenth century that Biblical scholars treated archaeological digs in the Holy Land as anything more than a means of vindicating what they already believed by faith. Needless to say, such prior convictions colored their interpretations of what they found. If all you have is a hammer, everything looks like a nail. A discussion of what contemporary historians think about the historical accuracy of the **Bible** is a tale best told by them.[28] It's worth noting, however, that mainstream historians tend not to regard the Bible as especially more reliable than other ancient sources. But let's assume that it is—suppose that the Bible's account of ancient history is extremely good. What could be inferred about the existence of God? Here's an argument:

1. Most of the historical claims in the Bible can be proven to be true by modern archaeology and historical study.
2. If the historical claims (dates, places, battles, kings, cities) are true, then the religious claims (gods, demons, spirits, miracles, afterlife) are probably true.
3. Therefore the religious claims are probably true.

The logic of the argument is flawless; if the two premises are true, then the conclusion is most definitely true. Let's even grant the first premise for the sake of argument. The controversial assumption is in premise (2). The problem is that there is no particular reason to think that an accurate account of historical events supports any sort of religious interpretation of those events.

3.16 Consider a nonscriptural historical account that, like religious texts, is chockablock with the doings of divine beings, namely, the ***Iliad***[29] and the ***Odyssey***[30] by Homer. Homer was an eighth-century BCE Greek poet who chronicled the war between Greece and Troy. For millennia after Homer, Troy was thought to be a mythological city, and the war no more than Homer's imagination. Modern historians now think that Troy was a real city and the war described by Homer has at least a core of truth in Bronze Age Greek warfare. Let's take this further. Suppose for the sake of argument that Homer's tale was 100 percent accurate—the beautiful Helen, wife of King Menelaus, was kidnapped and taken to Troy, and to avenge the kidnapping her brother-in-law, Agamemnon, laid siege to Troy for a decade. In fact, let's imagine that Homer was totally precise in his description of the heroes Achilles, Ajax, Odysseus, and Hector, and that we have even found physical remains of the famous wooden Trojan Horse. Let's even assume that there is excellent empirical evidence that Homer was right about the number and composition of the Greek fleet, the commanders and allies, and so on.

3.17 The *Iliad* and the *Odyssey* are woven through with the stories and doings of the Greek gods. The Trojan War had at its root a quarrel among the goddesses Athena, Aphrodite, and Hera about who is the fairest. After Paris judged Aphrodite to be the fairest, she made Helen the most beautiful woman. The god Apollo caused a plague among the Greeks; Helen's father was the god Zeus; and Achilles's mother (a nymph) attempted to make him immortal by dipping him into the river Styx. On his way home from the war Odysseus encountered the witch-goddess Circe, was captured by a Cyclops, was lured by magical Sirens, narrowly avoided the monster Scylla, and managed to tick off the god Helios. There are numerous other encounters and stories of assorted divine beings in Homer as well.

3.18 Here is the question: even if we stipulate the excellence of Homer's history, are you prepared to admit the existence of all the Greek gods and demigods? The question is not whether you agree that *Homer* believed in all those gods, but whether *you* do. If you think that no, Athena, Circe, and all the rest were just fanciful myths that embellished Homer's historical narrative, then you reject premise (2) in the argument above. It is not the case that if the historical claims (dates, places, battles, kings, cities) are true, then the religious claims (gods, demons, spirits, miracles, afterlife) are probably true. Even if we found Noah's Ark on Mount Ararat, we would have no reason at all to believe that God told him to build it. Even if we could DNA-test Jesus's blood from a piece of the cross, that would give no more credence to the claim that he was the son of God than finding the bones of Achilles is evidence that his nymph-mother dunked him in the River Styx to secure a magical protection.

In sum, the argument from scripture faces a dilemma. Assuming that a religious scripture is divinely inspired presupposes that God exists. Presupposing that God exists is not a very convincing, or logically cogent, way to argue that he does. Not assuming that a religious scripture is divinely inspired means that its accuracy is to be assessed in the same way any ancient tale is evaluated, namely by the best techniques of modern historiography that we possess. Yet the best those techniques could yield is a vindication of the properly historical claims of scripture, not its particularly religious claims. The conclusion is that appeal to scripture does not seem to be a very promising way to prove God's existence. 3.19

The ontological argument

The argument from scripture tries to show that God exists because it says so in a special book. The argument to be discussed presently, the **ontological argument**,[31] goes in the complete opposite direction. It attempts to show that God's existence can be demonstrated by pure abstract reason alone. St Anselm of Canterbury, a medieval monk, first devised The ontological argument and presented it in his book *Proslogion* in the year 1078. The basic idea of the argument is that existence is part of the very nature of what it is to be God, and to conceive of God at all is to realize that he must exist. It is a very clever argument, and has captured the attention of philosophers and logicians for nearly 1000 years. Here is a version. 3.20

1. The concept of God is that of the most perfect being imaginable.
2. Either God is purely imaginary or God is real.
3. It is more perfect to exist than not to exist.
4. Therefore a purely imaginary God is less perfect than a real God.
5. Therefore a purely imaginary God does not correspond to the concept of God, which is that of the *most* perfect being.
6. Therefore God is real.

Anselm rightly notes that even nonbelievers will grant that the concept of God is of a most perfect being. While nonbelievers just deny that there is such a being, it looks like they will accept the first premise. The second premise is also hard to deny: either God's real or he isn't. What about the third premise? It certainly has some initial plausibility, anyway—a real, flesh-and-blood rich and handsome boyfriend is better than an imaginary one. The real one is a more perfect boyfriend. So a real God is better and more perfect than a purely imaginary one. The remainder of the argument is supposed to be no more than the implications of the first three premises. There is something about the very concept of God that ensures his existence, and to grasp the idea of God at all is to recognize that he must exist.

3.21 *Objection 1: The fool's response* A contemporary of Anselm's, a monk named Gaunilo, raised the first objection to the ontological argument. Gaunilo raised his objection "on behalf of the fool." He meant that only a fool would doubt **God's existence**[32] or the awesomeness of the ontological argument. Still, Gaunilo thought, some poor misguided soul might argue like this. Let imagine an island, call it the Lost Island, which is the most perfect island imaginable. It is lush with palm trees and tropical flowers, laden with pineapples and breadfruits, it has wide, white sand beaches and turquoise waters, and the weather is always ideal. We can prove that the Lost Island exists using the ontological argument:

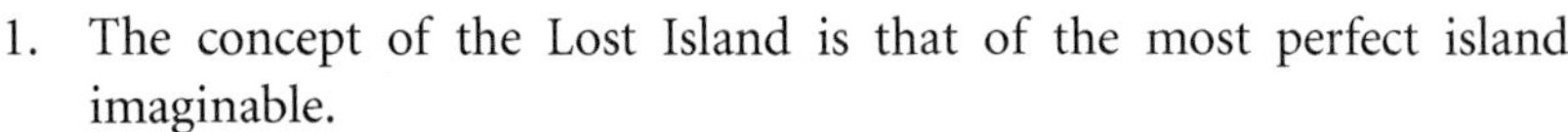

1. The concept of the Lost Island is that of the most perfect island imaginable.
2. Either the Lost Island is purely imaginary or the Lost Island is real.
3. It is more perfect to exist than not to exist.
4. Therefore a purely imaginary Lost Island is less perfect than a real Lost Island.
5. Therefore a purely imaginary Lost Island does not correspond to the concept of the Lost Island, which is that of the *most* perfect island.
6. Therefore the Lost Island is real.

If the ontological argument can prove that the Lost Island is real, then it proves too much. Something has gone wrong somewhere.

3.22 One sort of reply to Gaunilo is to note that no matter how wonderful the description of the Lost Island, it could be even a little bit better—a little more scenic, a bit more colorful. In fact, wouldn't the island be even better if it could spontaneously produce lavish luau feasts every night? Or if it could heal any injuries one might suffer from falling coconuts? Really, the island could be further improved if it were a sentient being, one that wanted to help tourists, give them directions, and so on. Of course, a morally perfect, helpful island would be improved if it knew exactly how to improve the lives of its visitors. The more it knows, the better. You may notice that the description of the island is on its way to being all knowing, all powerful, and perfectly good. In short, if the Lost Island were *truly* perfect in every way, it would be God. Which just means that the ontological argument works after all—it shows the reality of the only perfect thing, which is God.

You might be inclined to rejoin that God is not an island, not even a 3.23
perfect island. "Perfect" modifies all kinds of nouns, and just because a word has "perfect" in front of it, does not mean that the word is just code for "God." You can have a perfect spiral pass, perfect spheres, a perfect argument, a perfect cup of coffee, and a perfect island. Being perfect doesn't require being God, and so Gaunilo's original objection stands.

Objection 2: A reverse parody Another objection to the ontological argu- 3.24
ment is that its reasoning can be flipped on its head. A parody version tries to show that nonexistence is better and more perfect than existence, so God exists only in the imagination.

1. The concept of God is that of the most perfect being imaginable.
2. Either God is purely imaginary or God is real.
3. It is more perfect *not* to exist than to exist.
4. Therefore a purely imaginary God is *more* perfect than a real God.
5. Therefore a real God does not correspond to the concept of God, which is that of the *most* perfect being.
6. Therefore God is purely imaginary.

Why believe the new premise (3)? Here's why. Suppose you were to play tennis with #1 ranked **Rafa Nadal**.[33] He will completely clobber you, because he is an incredible tennis player, and presently the best the world. No surprise there, and really, for him to beat you is not that impressive. But suppose we give him a handicap—instead of a tennis racquet, he has to use a whisk broom. Now when he beats you, that feat *is* rather impressive. The man was using a broom after all. Suppose we handicap him even more, and he has to play right-handed (Nadal is left-handed). Now beating you is even more impressive, right? Now let's make him play while hopping on one leg. If Nadal keeps winning while playing right-handed with a whisk broom and hopping on one leg, the more amazing he is. That is, the more we handicap Nadal, the more awe-inspiring it is when he continues to beat you at tennis. Clearly, the most incredible feat that he could pull off is

beating you *when he doesn't even exist*. Nonexistence is the greatest possible handicap, and if he can still win then, well, he truly is a tennis icon.

3.25 Likewise, God is that much more impressive if he can do everything he is supposed to have done while laboring under a handicap. The greatest conceivable handicap—and thus the one that would make God as awesome as possible—is nonexistence. So the most perfect imaginable being is one that can do anything while not even bothering to exist. A purely imaginary God is therefore more perfect than a real God. Therefore, God only exists in the imagination.

3.26 At this point you may suspect that there is something screwy with how existence and nonexistence are being treated in these ontological-style arguments. Playing tennis with a whisk broom is a hindrance, but nonexistence isn't just some obstacle to performance. Without existence, there's no one to do any performing at all.

3.27 *Objection 3: Existence is not a property* Perhaps the most compelling objection to the ontological argument has to do with the way in which the argument treats existence. Immanuel Kant complained that the ontological argument uses existence as a property that things might or might not have. So God could have the property of existing, or he might lack it. The problem, as Kant saw it, is that existence is *not* a property at all. To see his point, imagine that your friend Jakwon comes up to you and starts telling you all about his new girlfriend. She's tall, has curly dark hair, hazel eyes, skin like café au lait, a swimmer's body . . . he goes on and on about how wonderful she is. You tell Jakwon how much you look forward to meeting her. He says that he would love to introduce you to her, because she's terrific, but she does have one unfortunate quality—she doesn't exist.

3.28 What makes that conversation sound so odd is that existence isn't a property. Jakwon's girlfriend doesn't have a bunch of great qualities (except existence), because there is no girlfriend. Since she doesn't exist, she doesn't have any properties at all. The problem in the ontological argument is in premise (3), which states that it is more perfect to exist than not to exist. Existence isn't a perfection because it isn't a property at all, much less one that comes in degrees or in optimal quantities.

3.29 In modern logic existence is treated as a quantifier: you have to specify what exists first, before you can start saying what properties things have. Otherwise you can wind up in some very strange places.

"What's behind that tree?"

"Nothing."

"Tell me about the nothing. What is it like? Does it noth?"

Nothing isn't a thing, and shouldn't be treated as a noun. The denial of existence (there is not a thing such that . . .) is a quantifier just as much as the assertion of existence (there is a thing such that . . .). Trying to build existence into a property like *being perfect*, as the ontological argument does, makes no logical sense. 3.30

The cosmological argument

The ontological argument tried to prove God's existence from pure rational intellection alone. The argument to be discussed now is empirical at heart. It tries to demonstrate there must be a God because of what we observe, namely the existence of the world around us. 3.31

You may believe that God exists because the universe had to come from somewhere, and this somewhere is a some*one*, namely God. This is the idea of God as creator, and is at the heart of what is known as the cosmological argument. The argument goes back to the ancients, particularly Aristotle, who gives versions of it in book VIII of his *Physics* and book XII of the *Metaphysics*. The cosmological argument was popular in the Middle Ages, both in Christianity and in **Islam**.[34] The best-known medieval defense was by the Catholic theologian and saint Thomas Aquinas in ***Summa Theologica***.[35] The cosmological argument is more than a mere hypothesis that a divine power created everything. Aristotle and Aquinas provide an intriguing argument to support a creator God. 3.32

For Aristotle and Aquinas, the argument part comes from the observation that everything seems to have a cause. There is a reason for everything that happens—not necessarily "a reason" in the sense of "there's a purpose" or "it's reasonable," but a reason in the sense that something was the cause. So if there is thunder, there is a reason for it. There is a reason at least in the sense that there is a cause for the thunder, namely lightning. Since there's a cause for everything, there is a cause for the lightning too: water droplets and ice crystals in clouds collide in the turbulent air and build up an electrical field which at a certain strength discharges a spark known as lightning. The tale doesn't stop there. There are causes for the presence of water vapor, why some is frozen into ice crystals, why there are atmospheric convection currents, and so on. Then there are causes for there being an atmosphere around Earth at all instead of none. The existence of the Earth, too, has a cause, presumably in terms of gravity and space dust. 3.33

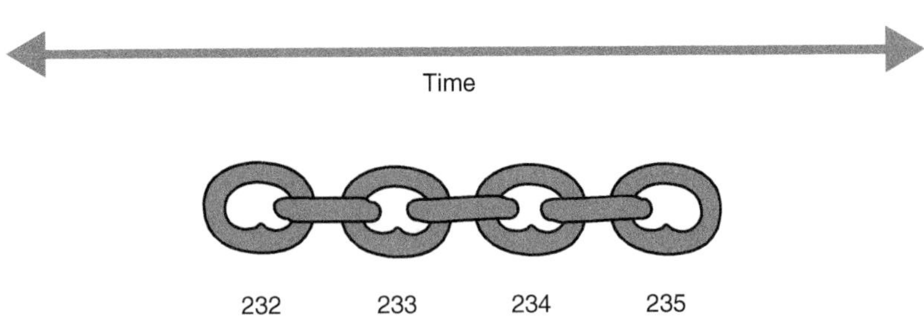

Figure 3.1 The causal chain

3.34 All of these events or facts are (1) caused by something else, and (2) that something else was earlier in time. You might imagine an endless chain, where each link in the chain is an event. The link immediately preceding any given link is its cause, and the link right after is the effect it causes. Granted, the chain image is an oversimplification, since events tend to have complex, multiple causes that work conjointly to produce an effect. There are also complications in understanding exactly what causation is, and how we can isolate "the" cause of an event. But set all that aside. Look at Figure 3.1.

3.35 Consider event 235. Our task is to explain what caused that event. Fortunately, in this simple model we have an answer ready to hand: it's event 234. Now is event 234 also an effect of some kind, or it is uncaused? Well, it too has a cause, namely event 233. We can then raise the same question all over again: what is the cause of 233? Each time we ask for a cause, we move back another link in the chain. So long as every proposed answer to "What is the cause of this event?" is itself an effect of a further prior cause, we are faced with an infinite regress of causes and effects, going back forever in time. Why is this so bad? It's unacceptable because it is a *vicious regress*, meaning that when we try to solve the problem of "What is the cause of this event?" the same problem crops up again in the proposed solution. The identical question arises at each link in the chain, ad infinitum. Therefore no caused event could serve as a satisfactorily general explanation of caused events.

3.36 To solve the vicious regress problem, the cosmological argument posits that there had to have been an event 1, the first thing, an ultimate cause that is the first link in the chain. The chain cannot be infinite both forwards and backwards in time. To get the chain of causation started, there must have been a first cause, or, in Aristotle's terminology, a prime mover. There must be something that shoved everything into motion. Since this first event was itself uncaused, the question "What is the cause of this event?" does not arise, and the vicious regress is escaped. What exactly is the first cause, the prime mover, the big shover? What else could it be but God?

Here is the argument in outline form. 3.37

1. Everything is caused by something prior in the causal chain.
2. It is absurd to think that the chain of causation can go back infinitely.
3. Thus there had to be some uncaused thing at the beginning that started the whole chain of causation.
4. This uncaused thing is God.

There are several objections to the cosmological argument. Here are the more prominent concerns.

Objection 1: Inconsistency The first premise states that everything is caused by something prior in the causal chain. This assumption is a key motivating factor in the cosmological argument, since if some things come into existence for no reason at all (they are uncaused) then there is no especial reason to think that the universe was caused to begin. That is, the beginning of the universe might have been *random*, just a mere cosmic fluke or accident. A random beginning doesn't demand that there be a God to start things off, since literally nothing started things off. So universal causation is an essential element of the argument. 3.38

Unfortunately, premise (3) states that there is some uncaused thing at the beginning, which is in direct contradiction with (1). Either something is uncaused or nothing is—the argument can't have it both ways. Inconsistent premises are a serious logical problem. If you assume a contradiction, you can prove anything whatsoever. So in one sense the existence of God follows validly from the premises. But, then again, so does everything else, including the proposition that there is no God, which is clearly not a happy result for a theist. Rewriting premise (1) so that it is consistent with (3) would yield: some things are caused by something prior in the causal chain. As noted in the preceding paragraph, that's too weak to motivate much of anything beyond a yawn. If some things are caused and some are not, what's the motivation to suppose there must be a first cause? 3.39

Objection 2: Problem of the attributes Let's set aside the inconsistency issue, and assume that the argument is good up to premise (3): there had 3.40

to be some uncaused thing at the beginning that started the whole chain of causation. Why should we leap to the conclusion that this uncaused thing is God? Remember, we have assumed that whatever else God is, he has at least these three qualities: omniscience, omnipotence, and omnibenevolence. The problem of the attributes objection is that the cosmological argument provides no reasons to think that the first cause has even one of these attributes.

3.41 You might be inclined to argue that God is omnipotent—a great power to have if you're in the business of universe-creating. Therefore if there's something that started off the universe, it must be an omnipotent being like God. Unfortunately, that's to reason exactly backwards. The cosmological argument is attempting to use the existence of our causally structured universe to infer the existence of God. You can't go the other way and assume that since there's an omnipotent God, he could have created the universe. That strategy assumes, and does not demonstrate or give evidence for, God's existence.

3.42 Perhaps you can't think of another explanation of what could possibly be the first cause if it isn't God. It doesn't really matter, though. Failure of imagination to think of an alternative to God as the first cause does not show that the step from (3) to (4) is a legitimate move. Even if there is a first cause, the cosmological argument provides no reason to suppose that the first cause is conscious, or a being of any sort. The first cause, for all we know to the contrary, was just some mindless random event. In fact, that is just what contemporary scientists think about the origin of the universe. About 100 years ago scientists were able to develop an alternative explanation to God, one grounded in observations of the universe and tied together by Einstein's Theory of General Relativity.

3.43 *Objection 3: Alternative scientific explanations* Contemporary science agrees with Aristotle, Aquinas, and the other ancient and medieval defenders of the cosmological argument on one very crucial point: the universe does have an origin, and is not eternal. It is no slight on Aquinas and the others that they could not imagine a first cause other than God. Nevertheless, physics gives very different reasons to think that there is a beginning to the universe, and what that beginning consists in. The standard model of cosmology in contemporary physics is the **Big Bang model**.[36] According to this theory, the entire universe was once infinitely dense and very tiny; then it rapidly expanded, and eventually turned into everything there is.

Physicists aren't just making this stuff up; there's very compelling and fascinating empirical evidence for the Big Bang.

Back in the 1920s, astronomers like Edwin Hubble discovered a surprising fact: everything in the universe is moving away from every other thing at a high rate of speed. The universe is like a loaf of raisin bread; as the bread rises in the oven, the raisins all move further away from each other. Another analogy is that polka dots on a balloon uniformly separate from each other as the balloon is inflated. The stars, galaxies, and other celestial bodies are like the raisins or polka dots. Well, once it was realized that the universe is expanding, it didn't take much insight to figure out if you ran the film backwards that in the past things were closer together. Go further and further into the past and the universe is smaller, more compact, denser, until . . . stop: 13.7 billion years ago the entire universe and all its contents were jammed into something smaller than a pinhead. This wasn't some pinhead hanging out in space, that *was* the whole universe, space and all. Since it was infinitely dense and hot, it was not a very stable setup and instantly expanded at a colossal rate. The universe is still expanding—indeed, its expansion is accelerating. 3.44

There are several other physical reasons to accept the Big Bang, but since this is not a physics **primer**,[37] I'll just mention one more. Space is cold, but it is not completely cold. Everywhere in the universe radiates heat at just under 3° Kelvin. This radiation is in the microwave part of the electromagnetic spectrum and is invisible to the naked eye, like X-rays, or ultraviolet light. If this heat radiation were visible, the entire universe would softly glow uniformly in every direction. It is known as the *cosmic microwave background*. There are two reasons that the existence of the cosmic microwave background is evidence for the Big Bang. The first is that its uniformity cannot be explained by local heat sources. Stars, for example, are localized hot spots in the universe, but don't produce the pervasive background heat that is everywhere. The second reason is that the Big Bang does explain the cosmic microwave background, and the mathematics of the theory predict the exact temperature scientists find experimentally. The cosmic microwave background is the residual leftover heat of the Big Bang. 3.45

What all this means for the cosmological argument is that, as far as the origin of the universe is concerned, God isn't the only game in town. There's also a sophisticated, evidence-based competing scientific explanation, which means that some strong reasons will be needed to prefer the God explanation to the scientific one. 3.46

3.47 You might be tempted to insist that the Big Bang didn't just come from nowhere—there had to be something that caused it, and *that's* God. Well, fine. But then you're on the hook to explain what caused God. The view of physicists is that there is nothing that caused the Big Bang. If you're dissatisfied with an uncaused Big Bang, why are you more satisfied with an uncaused God? What makes him a better explanation? The German philosopher **Arthur Schopenhauer** wrote that in the cosmological argument the principle of universal causation is "used like a hired cab, which we dismiss when we have reached our destination."[38] The destination in the cosmological argument is God; once we've gotten there, everyone out of the cab. We don't need to press on to ask about where God came from, in classic **pay-no-attention-to-that-man-behind-the-curtain** fashion.[39] Yet it's no more than special pleading to reject an uncaused Big Bang as insufferably bizarre but then turn around and embrace an uncaused God as a completely reasonable alternative.

3.48 It is worth mentioning that the second premise of the cosmological argument declares that an infinite chain of causes is absurd, but the solution to the problem is an infinitely existing God. That's not flatly contradictory, but, like Schopenhauer's cab, it's arbitrary. In short: if eternal existence is ridiculous, then it applies to God too. If everything needs a beginning, then so does God. The cosmological argument is an attempt to offer God as an explanation of the origins of the universe, but it isn't going to work if it only replaces one mystery with something more mysterious.

The teleological argument or the argument from design

3.49 The teleological argument for God's existence, more commonly known as the argument from design, or intelligent design, has enjoyed a recent resurgence of popularity outside of professional philosophy. But it is not a new argument at all—Thomas Aquinas gave a short version of it in over 700 years ago in his *Summa Theologica*. The reasoning of the cosmological argument was that the mere existence of the universe meant that there had to be a creator God. The design argument, on the other hand, notes that the universe has certain features, and infers that these features can only be explained by a designer God.

3.50 The nineteenth-century theologian William Paley gave the most famous version of the design argument. Paley presents the argument in the form of a very intriguing analogy. Suppose you are walking through the woods, and stub your toe on a rock. You might pick the rock up and ask, "What's this rock doing here?" Of course, it's the woods, and there are rocks. So a perfectly respectable answer is "well, it's just always been here." Fine. You move on. Now suppose that instead of a rock you stumble across a watch. Maybe you've never seen a watch before and have no idea what it is for. Nevertheless, you pick it up and ask the same question as before: hello, what's all this, then? Now it doesn't seem nearly as sensible to say that maybe the watch has always been there. Why not? Well, you can see from looking closely at the watch that it is assembled from an intricate mesh of **tiny gears**,[40] all interlocking, moving together, and turning tiny hands on the face at different speeds. Whatever the point of the watch it is clear that should even one of those little parts be disturbed, the entire mechanism would seize up. The watch is phenomenally complicated, and stands in sharp contrast to the plain, natural background of the woods. Paley says that you would naturally conclude that someone designed and made the watch, and they either dropped it by accident or left it in the forest on purpose. You can just see that the watch was designed, and that there was intelligence behind its manufacture.

Paley claims that the entire universe is analogous to the watch. When we 3.51
look around the universe, we see incredible complexity and orderliness. Consider the human eye, for example. The cornea focuses light rays on the retina, which contains three different sorts of cellular cones that respond to different light wavelengths and are the basis for color vision. There are other photoreceptor cells called rods that are sensitive to low light and responsible for night vision. The cells of the retina send information to the brain along the optical nerve, and the brain reconstructs this information into visual sensations about the world. The entire process is as intricate and precise as any watch. Or think about the march of the planets around the sun. Planetary orbits follow completely predictable ellipses around our star, and never fly off in all directions or radically change their paths. Everything, from the operations of the subatomic particles to the metabolisms of living creatures, to the interplay of celestial bodies, marches to the orders of the laws of nature. Paley's conclusion is that any explanation of such a complex world demands a designer every bit as much as the watch. Here's a schematic version of the design argument.

1. Everything in the universe is organized, detailed, complex, and precise.
2. Nothing explains this complexity and order except intelligent design.
3. If it is the result of design, then there must be a designer.
4. This designer is God.

3.52 *Objection 1: Weaknesses in the watch analogy* Paley's watch analogy is clever, but suffers from three weaknesses which undermine its claim to be a good enough reason to accept that the universe must be designed.

3.53 *Objection 1a.* The first problem with it is that the watch looks strikingly out of place against the plain background of the forest floor. There is no denying that in comparison the watch is astonishingly intricate and seems to cry out for an explanation in terms of design. However, the analogy is *watch is to forest as universe is to . . .* ? To what? The universe is everything, so against what background should we compare it to conclude that it is particularly orderly or complex?

3.54 The issue of what sort of things requires explanation is deep and subtle. On the one hand you could argue that since there is no background for the universe it is the natural state and exhibits exactly the level of complexity that we should naturally expect. In which case there's nothing to explain, much as Paley thinks that the complexity of the forest needs no explanation. On the other hand, there are various features of our universe, such as the laws of nature and the basic physical constants, which might have been quite different from what they are. In fact, if some of these parameters had been even slightly different, life could have never have arisen. For example, if the matter/energy in the very early universe had been smoothly and evenly distributed, then gravity would have never clumped it up into stars, planets, and such, and life could never have arisen. Likewise, if the matter/energy in the very early universe had been much clumpier than it in fact was, then gravity would have concentrated practically everything into giant black holes. The Oxford mathematician Roger Penrose has calculated that if the features of our universe were picked just by chance, then the probability is 1 in $10^{10^{123}}$ that the early universe would have just the moderately chunky structure it did. Hitting the sweet spot was stupendously unlikely, and a defender of the design argument might well argue that this shows that a designer fine-tuned the universe for life.

3.55 Of course, any specific structure of the early universe is fantastically unlikely, if we assume that all possible configurations of matter/energy were equally probable at the beginning. That alone does not cry out for an explanation. If you roll a die, each number that might come up is unlikely (1/6), but *some* number must come up. If the number you really want for whatever reason is 6, and you roll a 6, you needn't suppose that you have a magic touch, or God answered your prayers and nudged the rolling die. Some number or other had to come up and you merely got lucky. There may be no deeper explanation to why our universe turned out the way it did beyond "we just got lucky." Nevertheless, there is the feeling that given all the ways that the universe might have been configured, it seems sensible to ask *why did it turn out the way that it did*? It is beyond the scope of this book to work out exactly which events require an explanation and which are part of the assumed background. Here we note only this: Paley's views about which things need explanation and which do not are rather questionable.

Objection 1b. The next objection to the watch analogy is that, according to the design argument, the background conditions themselves are designed. That is, the forest, the trees, the rocks, are all designed by God. So there is no reason for the watch to have stood out at all. Paley might just as well have picked up a rock and said "Lo! Design!" But he didn't—in fact he explicitly claims that it would be perfectly reasonable to judge that the rock had always been there. But the intricacy of the watch *does* need explanation. Yet if everything's designed, then everything should stand out as needing an explanation, and the watch is nothing special or unusual. Paley needs the watch to be unusual, though, to get his appeal to design up and running. The upshot is that if everything is designed, then it undermines the force of the original analogy. 3.56

Objection 1c. The last problem is that surely it would be a mistake to pick up the watch, note its complexity, and promptly judge that God must have made it. That would be a hasty and mistaken inference, so why not think that the inference that God was the designer of the universe equally hasty and mistaken? A humorous example of this point is in the cult film ***The Gods Must Be Crazy***.[41] In the film, an empty **Coke bottle** is thrown out of a passing airplane over the Kalahari Desert in Africa. It is found by the Bushmen, a stone-age tribe indigenous to the Kalahari. The tribe naturally concludes that the bottle, which was spectacularly unlike anything they had ever seen, must have been given to them by the gods.[42] The Bushmen's reasoning is exactly like Paley's: an inexplicable object exhibiting an order and form unlike the environment is evidence of the divine. If you think that the Bushmen were wrong because of their ignorance about how the world really works, you ought to think that Paley's reasoning is equally faulty and based on ignorance. 3.57

Objection 2: Alternative scientific explanations Just as the cosmological argument faced the objection that modern science has an alternative, evidence-based account of the origin of the universe, so too the design argument faces the objection that modern science has an alternative, 3.58

evidence-based account of complexity and order. In fact, there are several such interlocking explanations. First, here is an easy example of how considerable order can be generated by a dumb, mechanical process.

3.59 Suppose that you want to get rich. In fact, you want to get rich by ripping people off as efficiently as you can. So here's what you do. Day one. Send a spam email to 10,000 people telling them that you would like them to invest their money in your stock-picking service. To prove to them what a great stock-picker you are, you will predict what tomorrow's stock market will do: 5000 people get an email saying that the Dow Jones Industrial Average will go up, and the other 5000 get an email saying it will go down. Now, either the market will go up or it will go down, right?

3.60 Day two. Suppose that the market went up. Forget about the 5000 people you told that the market would go down. They never hear from you again. Send out another email, with another prediction, this time about what the following day's stock market will do: 2500 people get an email saying it will go up, and the other 2500 get an email saying it will go down.

3.61 Day three. Suppose this time the market goes down. Forget about the 2500 people you told that the market would go up. They never hear from you again. Send out another email, with another prediction, this time about what the following day's stock market will do: 1250 people get an email saying it will go up, and the other 1250 get an email saying it will go down. You see how this goes. By the time you have winnowed it down to 10 people, those 10 have had 10 correct predictions in a row. Then you email them claiming that you have proven what a stock-picking genius you are, and get them to invest their money with you.

3.62 The incredibly simple selection procedure of "if and only if last prediction was correct, send email" did not require a great intelligence, and in fact could be easily programmed to run unsupervised on an iPhone. Yet it produced a very surprising order, namely 10 correct predictions of the stock market in a row, something that would be extremely unlikely to achieve by chance guessing alone. The string of correct predictions wasn't random, and it wasn't the work of a brilliant stock analyst. It was no more than a purely mechanical operation that winnowed out the losers (=recipients of an incorrect prediction) and promoted the winners (=recipients of a correct prediction).

3.63 The way in which order is produced in the stock-picking scam is the root idea in evolution by natural selection. Evolution explains the diversity of life, speciation, and extinction as the blind following of a relentless rule that winnows out the genetic losers and promotes the winners. The losers are those who fail to survive until they reproduce, and the winners are those who succeed in reproduction. That's it.

For example, finches with small, skinny beaks are able to eat small seeds 3.64
and insects, but if competition from other species for the seeds grows too fierce, or if a disease wipes out the little insects, then the **finches starve.**[43]

Only finches with somewhat larger than normal beaks can survive, as they are able to crack open large nuts and seeds for food. The finches with bigger and stronger beaks then pass on those traits to their young. In this way finches change over time. Physical attributes can develop more or less out of nothing, just as order arose in the stock scam. **Eyes,** for instance, started out as no more than the chance mutation of chemically-sensitive cells into molecularly similar light-sensitive cells.[44] Light sensitivity gave those organisms a mild survival advantage over the competition, and so the trait was preserved and refined. Modern eyes are amazingly sophisticated little devices, but they have been molded and developed by natural selection for at least 540 million years. After a couple of billion generations even a dumb mechanical process can produce something quite complex.

Evolution isn't the only scientific account of order and complexity. A 3.65
very recent theory develops the idea that there are self-organizing systems that spontaneously generate order. For example, a drop of oil in water is a sphere, and snowflakes have a **six-fold symmetry.**[45] Drops of oil and symmetrical snowflakes did not evolve, nor do we need to suppose that they were each designed by a micromanaging deity. With self-organizing systems, once they reach a critical level of complexity, order can arise as an emergent property. That sounds a bit complicated, but the idea of an emergent property isn't that alien. Consider a rubber band. The individual molecules that compose the rubber band are not themselves stretchy, or snap back when pulled. But if you string enough of them together, at some point the property of elasticity emerges and you get a little piece of stretchy material. In these examples, you get order for free—it arises like a phase transition between **states of matter** (like when liquid water freezes into solid ice).[46] Order can just happen.

In the end, design is not the only way to explain complexity, as premise 3.66
(2) of the design argument maintains. There are other well-developed, evidence-based scientific theories that show how order can arise without a designer. The challenge for a defender of the argument is to show how those other explanations are flawed and why design hypothesis is a superior alternative. Even if that challenge could be met, the move from there being a designer to the conclusion that the designer must be God is big step indeed.

3.67 *Objection 3: Problem of the attributes* Just as in the cosmological argument, the design argument faces the problem of the attributes. Let's grant for the sake of argument that the order and complexity of the universe is the result of design. The question is how to get from that point to the designer's being God. Remember, we're looking for an omnipotent, omniscient, omnibenevolent being. The design argument provides no reasons whatsoever to believe that the designer has even one of these attributes. Indeed, the argument provides no reasons to think that the designer, whomever or whatever it may be, is still alive.

3.68 You might be inclined to argue that God is omniscient—a great power to have if you're in the business of universe-designing. Therefore if there's something that designed the universe, it must be an omniscient being like God. Unfortunately, that's to reason exactly backwards. The design argument is attempting to use the complexity and order of our universe to infer the existence of God. You can't go the other way and assume that since there's an omniscient God, he could have designed this complex universe. That strategy assumes, and does not demonstrate or give evidence for, God's existence.

3.69 A related objection is the problem of uniqueness.

3.70 *Objection 4: Problem of uniqueness* The design argument concludes that there is a designer. That is, there must be at least one designer who drew the blueprints for the universe. Yet there are no reasons offered for thinking that there is *only* one designer. After all, designing the universe is quite a big job, and perhaps a team, or a committee, put together the plans, rather like in Douglas Adams's novel *The Hitchhiker's Guide to the Galaxy*. In the novel (and film version), the Earth is in fact designed—it was purpose built for hyperdimensional extraterrestrials who in our dimension look like mice. An enormous crew was behind the design, with one character, Slartibartfast, winning an award for his design of **Norwegian fjords**.[47] For all the design argument is able to show, perhaps this is what we should think. The argument offers no resources to conclude that a unique God is correct designer.

3.71 *Objection 5: Explaining the complexity of God* The final objection is that the design argument is supposed to explain all order and complexity as the handiwork of God. But what about God himself? Presumably God too is a complex thing. One would think that his thoughts are orderly, coherent, and intricate. His actions are not chaotic or random, but are the consequences of his desires. God has reasons for what he does, and those actions conform to the logic of his mind. God is, by definition, omniscient, which means not only that he possesses all facts, but also that his beliefs form an intricate, mutually supporting web appropriately tethered to reality. Surely God's mind is more complicated than human minds, indeed, infinitely more so.

The problem is that if God is complex, then he cannot explain all complexity. According to the design argument, the orderly structure of reality can be explained only by postulating a designer God. But surely God did not **design himself.**[48] Therefore we are left without an explanation of his complexity. Therefore the design argument is unable to give a fully general account of complexity. The present objection is similar to the Schopenhauer complaint about the cosmological argument. the cosmological argument wanted to insist that everything had a cause (except God), and the design argument attempts to explain all order and complexity (except God's). 3.72

There is a tradition, going back to Thomas Aquinas, in which God is considered "simple." A simple is an object that has no parts, for example, an electron. If God is partless, then his composition cannot be like that of an intricate watch. The watch has many tiny parts cleverly fitted together, but God has no parts at all, and so there is no need to explain the complexity of God—indeed there is nothing to explain. Thus God is suitable to the explain complexity of everything, being simple himself. 3.73

One problem with this attempt to escape Objection 5 is that, even if God has no parts, that does not show that he is simple in all relevant ways. For instance, God's mind, even if indivisible, is still rationally structured and complicated in all the ways just listed above. If one wants to argue that God's mind has no structure, that his thoughts are not even rationally or logically connected to one another, or deny that there are distinctions to be made among his thoughts, then there is no credible sense in which God does thinking or deciding. God is not a mind nor does he have one. Moreover, if God is without parts, and without discernible ideas or separable thoughts, then it is quite puzzling why we should think of God as any kind of being at all. That is a large price to pay to escape the complexity objection. 3.74

The ontological, cosmological, and design arguments are the three traditional philosophical attempts to prove the existence of God. There are other modern attempts, such as treating revelation as a legitimate method of gaining noninferential beliefs, that require more philosophical 3.75

background and sophistication than can be presented in an introductory book such as this one. The interested reader is encouraged to examine the annotated bibliography. However, the pro-God arguments are not yet over. There is one more argument to consider on God's behalf, one that takes a very different and intriguing approach.

Pascal's wager

3.76 In the seventeenth century, Blaise Pascal argued that it was in your rational self-interest to believe that **God exists.**[49] Pascal explicitly did *not* argue that God exists. Wait, you surely cry, how can it be possible for it to be rational to believe that God exists without having any sort of argument for God's existence? Therein lies the genius of Pascal's reasoning. As a young man, Pascal inherited a bit of money from his father, and devoted most of his twenties to partying, in particular, gambling. His wayward youth turned out to be a great thing for mathematics and philosophy. As the result of trying to solve gambling puzzles, Pascal made considerable contributions to probability theory and more or less invented decision theory. In his book *Pensées*, Pascal applied the logic of gambling to the problem of God. Believing in God, Pascal thought, is your best bet.

3.77 Pascal begins his famous wager argument by asserting that everyone has to make a choice about God's existence. We're all at the gaming table and have to lay our money down. So how will we bet? Well, before you decide, you'll probably want to know the odds. Pascal is well aware of that, and conveniently provides them. Either God exists or he does not, Pascal plausibly notes. The inference he makes is that the whole matter is just a coin toss—heads God exists, tails he doesn't. Since Pascal explicitly claims that the odds for God's existence are 50–50, it is clear that he does not think that evidence demonstrates God exists in any traditional sense. If we lack any reason to believe in God's existence, and the chance that he exists is no more than a coin toss, how does that motivate belief?

3.78 The answer, Pascal says, lies in the possible payoffs. There are four options:

1. You bet that there is a God, and he really does exist. You win.
2. You bet that there is a God, and he does not exist. You lose.
3. You bet against God's existence, there is no God. You win.
4. You bet against God's existence and there is a God after all. You lose your wager.

So what's at stake in God's casino? According to Pascal, if God really does exist, then you'd better believe in him. God will reward believers with eternal life, paradise, Heaven, harps, wings, and the whole shebang. Non-believers, on the other hand, not only miss out on the victory prize, but also lose huge. They face an afterlife of separation from God, Hell, torment, punishment, lakes of fire, and so on. Well, what if it comes up tails, and there is no God? Then, claims Pascal, it doesn't matter what you bet. In that scenario there's really nothing to win or to lose either way. Overall, wagering that God exists is the smart money. If you're right, you win big, but if you're wrong you lose nothing. If you bet against God, you have nothing to gain and everything to lose. Pascal's wager can be summarized in this way:

1. You must make a decision as to whether God exists.
2. The odds for his existence are 50–50.
3. If God exists and you believe, then you win big by believing.
4. If God exists and you do not believe, then you lose big by not believing.
5. If God does not exist and you believe, then you lose nothing by believing.
6. If God does not exist and you do not believe, then you gain nothing by not believing.
7. Therefore, it is in your rational self interest to wager that God exists.

The logic of the argument is compelling. The premises seem to make the conclusion very reasonable to believe. But what of the premises? Are there good reasons to accept them? Let's look at the premises one at a time.

Objection 1: Unforced wagering In the first premise, Pascal claims that we 3.79
are all forced to make a choice about God's existence, that we are all compelled to place our bets. However, it is hard to see why this is true. For one, there may be people who have no idea of God, or only vaguely have some notion of who or what he might be. Suppose you walk into a Vegas casino and someone invites you play a game of Pai Gow, a Chinese dominoes game that you've never heard of before. Are you compelled to play? Presumably not. Or even in the case of existence claims, it is very peculiar to insist that everyone has to decide whether the **Higgs boson particle** exists,[50] or whether there are still **ivory-billed woodpeckers**.[51] To be sure, physicists are very keen on finding Higgs bosons, and ornithologists are interested in

rare woodpeckers. But unless those are your interests, why should you care? Pascal might claim that lack of belief in God will send you to Hell just as quickly as disbelief in God does (assuming God exists). Of course, Pascal will have to give an argument for that claim; perhaps God has no stake in those who refuse to bet. Premise (1) may not be that essential to his argument, though. Pascal could easily reply that *if* you want to have a view about God, then, given the rest of his argument, you should bet that he exists. Let's look at some of the other premises.

3.80 *Objection 2: The odds of God* Pascal rightly observes that either God exists or he does not. Yet that fact does not mean that the odds of his existence are 50–50. Not every yes/no question is 50–50; in fact, very few are. Consider: suppose you were to fight martial arts expert **Jet Li**.[52] Either you would win or you would lose, right? Therefore your odds of winning are 50 percent! Probably not . . . Imagine that your high school junior varsity football team were going to play the Dallas Cowboys. Do you think the Vegas bookies are going to say that Cowboys are just as likely to lose, as they are to win? Obviously not. So why should we think that the chance God exists is 50 percent?

3.81 Pascal might rejoin that in the case of God that we have no credible evidence of his existence, and no decent evidence of his nonexistence. In modern probability theory there is something called the principle of indifference, which states that if you know nothing more than there are N mutually exclusive outcomes, then the chance of each outcome is 1/N. For example, suppose that you are rolling a six-sided die. You know nothing more about the dice rolling—for example, you don't know whether the die is unequally weighted, what its spin is, or anything else that would favor one outcome over another. In this case, as far as you are concerned, each face of the die is just as likely as any other to come up. There is a 1/6 chance of the dice roll coming up 1, a 1/6 chance it comes up 2, a 1/6 chance it comes up 3, and so on. If we have no evidence about God, and there are only two possible outcomes (he exists/he doesn't exist), then by the principle of indifference the chance of each outcome is ½.

3.82 For Pascal to rely on the principle of indifference as just sketched, he would have make out the case that we have no evidence about God's existence at all. Few people are likely to accept that. Believers in the proofs of God we have discussed so far will think that they make the chance of God's existence greater than 50 percent, and atheists convinced by the arguments against God (to be discussed later in this chapter) may think that the chance of God existing is zero. But perhaps fixing the odds of God's existence isn't that vital to Pascal's argument. If the rest of the argument goes through, the odds may not matter.

Objection 3: Assumes loads of Christian theology without argument One of 3.83
the most serious defects in Pascal's wager is that premises (3) and (4) assume all kinds of controversial and unsupported Christian theology. Remember, Pascal is hoping to persuade unbelievers—people who aren't already convinced that everything in the Bible is true. Like Anselm, Aquinas, and Paley, he thinks that reason alone will show the virtue of believing in God. What, then, is the reason for accepting the claim in premise (3) that if God exists and you believe, then you win big by believing? If someone asks you to bet your life savings on something, and promises you a possible payout of a billion dollars, at the very least you are going to tell them to **show you the money**.[53] Has Pascal shown you the money? No. All he has done is *claim* that there is this wonderful payout for believing in God. He hasn't given any evidence of such a prize. Nor has he shown that God cares a whit if you believe he exists. Premises (3) and (4) are true only if these presuppositions are true:

- God cares whether you believe he exists.
- God cares so much that he will reward you for belief and punish you for nonbelief.
- God will judge you.
- There is an afterlife.
- There is a good afterlife and a bad one.
- The good afterlife is colossally, perhaps infinitely, preferable to the bad afterlife.

Now imagine that Pascal is trying to persuade you to believe in God with his wager argument. That is, suppose you don't already believe in God, and you're not already religious in any way. Then all those bulleted points look rather ridiculous, just myths about living after death and some kind of judgmental superbeing. Without reasons to believe all those things, reasons that Pascal fails to provide, premises (3) and (4) are unacceptable. It's worth noting that Pascal can't offer up the Bible to support his presuppositions—that's to give up the game entirely. He might as well just tell people to believe that God exists because the Bible says so and not bother with the wager argument.

3.84 *Objection 4: The value of your life* Premises (5) and (6) assume that there is no God, and then follow out the consequences of belief and disbelief in God. According to Pascal, if there is no God, then it doesn't matter what you believe—you gain nothing by being right and lose nothing by being wrong. What makes this hard to believe is that genuine belief affects your actions; belief isn't just some harmless, abstract add-on to your life. For example, suppose that the way you really want to live your life is to pursue mindless hedonism. If it were entirely up to you, you'd pass your days smoking dope, having casual sex, and playing video games. But instead you've decided to believe in God. You take this belief seriously, and have come to the conclusion that God doesn't approve of hedonism. Instead you become a monk, wear a coarse woolen cloak, and spend your days in **ascetic devotion**.[54] If there is no God, isn't there a clear sense in which you wasted your entire life? You spent it denying and rejecting what you truly wanted to do, so you could devote yourself to the nonexistent. Maybe you'll never find out that you were wrong. Yet objectively you squandered everything you had—your whole life—for nothing. Nevertheless, Pascal thinks that you didn't lose anything at all by making a losing bet on God.

3.85 Premise (6) states that if there is no God, then you gain nothing by not believing. Again, it is hard to see the force of this claim. At a minimum you gain the truth, something that most think has intrinsic value (see Chapter 7 on knowledge). Even more, there is a sense in which you gain control over your own life; you gain the liberty to decide how you want to live, without being in thrall to some nonexistent God. By possessing the truth that there is no God, you can shake off the chains of religious superstition and live free. That seems like a great deal more to gain than the "nothing" Pascal thinks the nonbeliever stands to win.

3.86 *Objection 5: An alternate ending* Imagine the following scenario. Suppose that, sometime in the future, you die. Well, so far this story will definitely happen. Now imagine that after your death you find yourself dressed in a flowing white robe and standing in a very long line behind similarly dressed people. You seem to be standing on a cloud. Your spirits brighten immediately. Up ahead you can see towering pearly gates, and the line of people is going through it. You pass through the gates and now ahead you can see that there is an enormous golden throne ahead, with a white-bearded, berobed giant sitting on it. Light seems to be radiating from the giant, and people in the line are pausing to speak with him before moving on.

You are exultant! It is obviously God on his throne, passing judgment, 3.87
and you can't wait to get to the front of the line. Eventually you do, and finally you are standing before God.

"Lord," you begin, "I just want you to know that I've always believed in you, so I'm ready to head on into Heaven."

"Ah, well," rumbles God, "why have you believed in me?"

"Pascal's wager, my Lord. I read his argument as a youth and knew right away that believing in you was the best bet. And now I'm here to cash in my chips and get the payoff."

"So let me get this straight. You believed in me out of *greed*? That's the reason?"

"Yep, greed. Now, where's my wings?"

Let's just pause here for a moment. You might be a bit doubtful that God 3.88
thinks **greed is good**,[55] and can't wait to reward it, or that clever gambling is the right way into his good graces. Yet that's the very essence of Pascal's wager. Let's modify the exchange a little and spin the tale in a different direction.

"Ah, well," rumbles God, "why have you believed in me?"

"Faith, my Lord. Always believed in you on faith."

"So what you mean is that you didn't have a good argument or credible evidence of my existence, but you believed in me anyway?"

"Of course! Blessed are those who have not seen and yet believe."

God chuckles. "Let me fill you in on a little secret. The greatest gift I gave 3.89
human beings was the gift of reason, which you have obviously failed to use. I made sure that there was no good evidence of my existence when I set up the universe. If you had used your reason, you would have come to the conclusion that I do not exist. Now I'm rewarding only those who used my greatest gift, and not those who squandered it. It is only the atheists who get into Heaven. Everyone else is sentenced to Hell."

How do you know that this isn't how things will go? Pascal certainly gives 3.90
no reasons to think otherwise. Maybe you don't believe it because it's not what the Bible says. Appealing to the Bible isn't available to Pascal, however, since he is attempting to give a rational argument for belief to people who don't already accept the Bible. If you believe the Bible on faith, well, you'd better hope you never hear God's little speech above!

Objection 6: The problem of other gods Pascal is trying to motivate belief 3.91
in the Christian God. However, there is nothing in his argument that singles out any particular god as the one deserving of your bet. His wager will work

just as well with any god anyone has ever believed in. You must make a decision as to whether Odin exists. The odds for Odin's existence are 50–50. If Odin exists and you believe he does, then you will be rewarded with eternal combat and endless mead in the golden halls of Valhalla. Just plug in any god. You must make a decision about Allah, the odds of whose existence are 50–50. If Allah exists and you believe that he does, then you will be rewarded with 72 virgins in paradise. And so on. If Pascal's wager works for the Christian God, then it works for any deity. In short, if it works it proves way too much—can you really believe in the thousands of gods that have been worshiped throughout the **ages**?[56] What paradise will you expect? Which punishments will you fear? And if you decide to just believe in one God on the basis of the wager, what if you choose the wrong one? You'd hate to pick the Christian God and then find a disappointed Krishna judging you in the afterlife.

3.92 *Objection 7: The involuntarism of belief and self-deception* The final objection to Pascal's wager has to do with the involuntary nature of belief. The wager argument recommends that you up and start believing in God because it is your best interest to do so. But can you really do that so easily? Suppose that your philosophy professor walked into the room pulling a large suitcase. She plops it on the desk and tells you that there's $2 million inside the suitcase, and it's all yours if you start believing that she is Wonder Woman, and that she has bracelets that can stop bullets and a magic golden lasso. Unlike Pascal, your professor shows you the money. She pops the top on the suitcase and shows you that it's packed with bundles of $100 bills. Do you think you could do it? You could believe that she's Wonder Woman? Not whether you can *act* as if she's Wonder Woman, or pretend to believe it for the money. The question is whether you can really start *believing* something so silly just because it is manifestly in your self-interest to do so. It's not easy to accomplish.

3.93 The point is that wagering God exists is not the same as believing that he exists. Even if the wager convinces you, you may be psychologically unable to up and believe in God. To his credit, Pascal is quite aware of the fact that our beliefs are in some way involuntary and that we do not have complete command over what we believe. Pascal offers an astonishing solution to the problem: he says that you should just hang around with the Christians, go to mass, take the sacraments, and eventually you'll come around. No one starts off believing in God, Pascal says, they just go to church and act like they do, and then one day find that they really do believe. You should just fake it until you make it. Is that a logical, rational solution to the problem of the involuntariness of belief, or a sort of self-deception and brainwashing? You decide.

So far in this chapter we have been examining arguments that try to show 3.94
that God exists (the argument from scripture, the ontological argument, the cosmological argument, the design argument) or that it is rational to believe that God exists (Pascal's wager). The remainder of the chapter will review arguments that God does not exist. It is worth noting that nothing said so far offers a reason to deny that God exists. Even if you think that the pro-God arguments all fall to the objections we've considered, that will not be enough to reject the existence of God. At most it will motivate agnosticism.

- Theism: judging that there is a God
- Agnosticism: withholding judgment about the existence of God
- Atheism: judging that there is no God

An agnostic may not have enough information about the existence of God to have an informed judgment and so refuse to believe there is a God and also refuse to believe that there isn't one. Analogously, someone who doesn't follow baseball may refuse to have an opinion on whether the Phillies will win the World Series this year. Or an agnostic may think that the matter of God's existence is unprovable either way and so refuse to have an opinion about whether God exists. Analogously, you may decline to believe that the number of stars in the universe is odd and also reject the claim that the number is even, on the grounds that it is impossible to prove one way or another. Atheists go further—they actively deny that there is a God. Let's proceed to examine the reasons to accept atheism.

Why There Is No God

Atheists are widely disliked and distrusted. There is essentially no chance 3.95
that an atheist could be elected to the presidency of the United States, no matter what their qualifications. Irrespective of their ethnicity or gender, Americans would prefer to vote for Jews, African Americans, women, senior citizens, and even homosexuals before they would vote for an **atheist**.[57]

Atheists are more frightening than Muslims for most Americans. They would rather that their children marry not only Muslims, but also Jews,

African Americans, Hispanics, and every other group studied before they marry an **atheist.**[58] Recent research even indicates that atheists are distrusted as much as **rapists.**[59] On the totem pole of marginalized groups, atheists are at the very bottom. Against these powerful social forces it is striking that nearly three quarters of professional philosophers are **atheists,**[60] and 93 percent of the members of the ultra exclusive National Academy of Sciences are either atheists or **agnostics.**[61] So what puts them at odds with popular belief? What arguments are there for concluding that God does not exist?

Proving a negative

3.96 There is a surprisingly widespread belief that it is impossible to prove that something does not exist, often phrased as "you can't prove a negative." The idea is that you may be able to prove that something does exist, but cannot prove that it does not. If that's right, then it is impossible to prove that God does not exist, and the atheist is stopped in his tracks. Even **Richard Dawkins**[62]—a famous atheist—apparently concedes, writing that "you cannot prove God's non-existence is accepted and trivial, if only in the sense that we can never absolutely prove the non-existence of anything" (Dawkins, 2006, p. 54). According to Dawkins and many others, it is impossible to prove that God, Santa Claus, unicorns, the **Loch Ness Monster,**[63] aliens in Roswell, pink elephants, ghosts, and Bigfoot don't exist.

3.97 Logicians universally reject the notion that you can't prove a negative. There are many ways to demonstrate that a negative claim is true. Here are a few examples. Can you prove that your wallet contains no money? Sure; just open it and look. Now you've proven that something does not exist (namely, money in your wallet). Too easy. How about a more general claim? Can we prove that there are no gases that fail to decrease in volume when they increase in pressure without changing the temperature? Again, the answer is yes. **Boyle's Law** states that the pressure and volume of a gas are inversely proportional (when one goes down, the other goes up).[64] All gases in a closed system at a fixed temperature decrease in volume when the pressure goes up = there are no gases that fail to decrease in volume when they increase in pressure without changing the temperature. This is a basic law of nature that holds everywhere in the universe, and can be formulated as a negative claim about what does not exist.

3.98 Another way of putting the point is that all the evidence we have for the positive claim that gases in a closed system at a fixed temperature decrease in volume when the pressure goes up also counts as evidence in favor of the negative claim that there are no gases that fail to decrease in volume when they increase in pressure without changing the temperature. There could not possibly be a gas that expands when its pressure increases (without changing the temperature). That is a negative existence claim we know to be true because it is not physically possible for it to be true.

Other things can be shown not to exist because their existence is logically 3.99
impossible. Here's an example. Suppose there is a village barber who shaves customers who don't shave themselves. He lathers their faces and gives them a nice hot shave. If someone shaves at home, then they don't need to go to the barber, so the barber shaves only those who don't shave themselves. Does he also shave *everyone* who doesn't shave himself? The answer is no. Think about the barber—does he shave himself? If he does, then he doesn't need to go to the barber for a shave. Therefore he is not shaved by the barber, and must be unshaved since he himself is the barber. But if he doesn't shave himself, then the barber has to do it for him, in which case he does shave himself! Therefore it is logically impossible that a barber exists who shaves all and only those who do not shave themselves.

The upshot is that we can have evidence that a thing does not exist in 3.100
the same way that we can have evidence that something does exist. We could be mistaken in our conclusions about what the world contains, of course, but all we can do is reason our way to what there is and what there is not. Evidence against God's existence can be provided—in principle—no less than evidence in favor of God's existence.

The argument from religious pluralism

One sort of argument that motivates skepticism about God is the observa- 3.101
tion that there have been thousands of gods believed in by human societies all over the world. If you believe in a Judeo-Christian style God, that's no more than an accident of your birth. If you had been born in Indochina, you'd be Buddhist. If you were born in Saudi Arabia, you'd be Muslim, bow to Mecca and praise Allah. If you had been born in Israel, then you would be Jewish, read the Torah in Hebrew, and **worship** יהוה.[65] If in India, then you would most likely be Hindu, if you had been born in the sixteenth-century Aztec Empire, you would worship Huitzilopochtli (among the other 100 Aztec gods), and so on. Yet you think all of those other gods are just mythological. Jupiter and Hera are part of Roman mythology, right? They aren't out there in reality. Baal, Zeus, Horus, Loki, Bacchus, and Isis

are all phony, false gods. In other words, you are *already* 99 percent an atheist—you think that nearly all of the gods ever believed in are myths, superstitions, and nonexistent. So just go one step further and realize that *all* gods are just fantasies that people in different societies are raised to believe in. Let's formulate the argument as follows.

3.102 If you had been born and raised in a different culture, then you would have different religious beliefs from what you presently have. If you had been born in ancient Rome you would be completely convinced that Sol Invictus, Minerva, and the other state gods are absolutely real and that upstart Jesus cult is ridiculous heresy. You have no more reason to accept your god than those others; ancient Romans relied on faith, or their sacred scriptures, or the priests and church authority, or the cosmological argument, no less than you. It is inconsistent to believe that all these thousands of gods are fake and your god alone is real, when the evidence for any of these gods is the same. Since you have no reason to believe that any particular god is real (and the others aren't), the best way to make your beliefs consistent is to reject them all as myths.

3.103 *Objection* This time it is the theist who can respond with a scientific analogy. If you had been born in thirteenth-century China, you would have believed that Earth is flat. If you had been a Greek citizen during the time of Hippocrates, you would have believed that diseases were the result of an imbalance among the four bodily humors of blood, black bile, yellow bile, and phlegm. There is no end of now-discredited scientific theories that you would have believed if you had been born in a different culture or at a different time—Newton's mechanics, a luminiferous ether, the phlogiston theory of combustion, the caloric theory of heat, the geocentric model of

the **universe**, etcetera.[66] All of those theories were once the best that science had to offer, and all have since been pitched into the dustbin of history.

3.104 Yet if we were to apply the same reasoning here as in the religious pluralism case, then it is inconsistent to believe that current science is right and all those other scientific views are wrong. We have the same reasons to accept what scientists tell us now that our ancestors had to believe the scientists of their time. Therefore we need to reject all scientific claims as myths. Obviously that is a big mistake; we *should* believe that contemporary science has hold of the truth and that those old discredited theories really are false. So something went wrong somewhere with the argument from religious pluralism, and it does not provide a good reason to be an atheist. There's no inconsistency involved in accepting one god and rejecting the others, any more than there is a problem with accepting one scientific theory and rejecting its predecessors.

Response The problem with the theist's objection is that there is a crucial 3.105
disanalogy between the plurality of scientific theories and the variety of religious belief. The disanalogy is this: there is publicly available, widely accepted evidence that a replacement scientific theory really is superior to its predecessor. When physicists chucked out the idea that the universe was suffused with a luminiferous ether through which light moved in favor of Einstein's Theory of Relativity, they had convincing reasons to prefer relativity. When physicians accepted germ theory and gave up on the notion that sickness was the result of miasma,[67] or "**bad air**," they had powerful evidence in favor of germs. So what compelling evidence is there that your preferred god is the only real one and all those other gods are just mistakes?

At this point the theist will have to go back to the pro-God arguments 3.106
that were discussed earlier in this chapter and try to fix them up in response to the objections that were raised then. The atheist can only say: good luck with all that. In science there is a real sense of advancement, as flawed or incomplete theories are discarded and better theories of the world take their place. If we all still thought Newton's understanding of the laws of nature was as good as Einstein's, much of the modern world would be impossible (cell phone technology relies on understanding **general relativity**,[68] for example). In the case of religion there is no evidence-driven progress, just a great buffet of thousands of incompatible gods and theologies. You may put one on your plate and head to the cashier, but so long as your selection was based on faith, then it really is just arbitrary.

Let's move on to examine another argument for atheism. 3.107

The problem of evil

The most famous argument against the existence of God attempts to show 3.108
that the nature of God is incompatible with how the world actually is, and so it is impossible for there to be a God. To get things started, let's review some facts about the world we live in. First off, your life is sweet. Merely by reading this book you are more educated than the vast majority of people who have ever lived. You will probably live longer than the vast majority of people in the world. You are also richer than nearly everyone who has ever lived. You'll probably balk at that, since we're all accustomed

to wealth-porn TV and therefore lament that we don't live in a mega-mansion like those rap stars. But you *are* **rich**—about two billion people live on less than $1.25 per day.[69] It is extremely likely that you are a citizen of a wealthy first-world nation and enjoy a stable government, reliable prices, public education, and at least some social safety net. In comparison with most of your fellow human beings, your life is gravy. Now reflect on the amount of suffering that you personally have experienced. Have you been close to someone who died, or had cancer or Alzheimer's? Have you been affected by mental illness? Broken bones? Been terribly sick? Addicted? Suffered anguish, loss, fear, loneliness, grief, shame, terror, or regret? Been burned, cut, or bruised? Ever had a **hangover**?[70] Your life is about as easy as it gets, and even you have endured physical and emotional pain.

3.109 It is extremely difficult to appreciate the vast extent of the suffering and misery the world contains. An untold number of people are **tortured**, even to death, every year.[71] Tens of millions have **died** in wars, genocides, and massacres,[72] hundreds of millions have died in **plagues and pandemics**,[73] and millions more have died in **floods, earthquakes, tsunamis, famines, volcanoes, tornadoes, and hurricanes**.[74] This brief review doesn't even touch on the rivers of blood spilled by nonhuman animals every year, 54 billion of whom we annually kill for food. To make a very long and gruesome story short, people's lives are marked by pain, from headaches to AIDS, and the world is soaked in gore and torment.

3.110 What's all this have to do with God? The problem of evil is that the manifest existence of all the world's suffering shows that there cannot be an omnibenevolent, omniscient, and omnipotent God. If there's suffering (and there is!) then there cannot be a God. Here's the argument.

1. Suppose that there is a God who is omnibenevolent, omniscient, and omnipotent.
2. The world is filled with suffering and misery.
3. Since God is omniscient, he knows about human and animal suffering and misery.
4. Since God is omnipotent, he could effortlessly prevent such suffering if he wanted to.
5. Anyone who knows about suffering and could effortlessly prevent it, but doesn't do so, is not perfectly good.
6. Therefore God is not perfectly good.
7. This contradicts (1)—therefore there is no God.

Premise (1) is no more than the assumption that God exists, which the argument makes in order to derive a contradiction, in classic *reductio ad absurdum* form. A theist would be hard pressed to deny premises (3) and (4), as they are really just elaborations on what it is to know everything and be all powerful. Premise (5) is more of a lynchpin in the argument, and it is worth a brief pause to defend it.

In April 2010, Queens resident **Hugo Alfredo** Tale-Yax attempted to help 3.111
a woman who was being attacked.[75] In return he was stabbed to death by her assailant. While he bled to death on the sidewalk, two dozen people walked by and did nothing to help him. Even though video surveillance footage showed that one person snapped a cell phone picture of the dying man, and another shook him, no one could be bothered to call 911 or render first aid. Would you say that those bystanders are *perfectly* good? The absolute paragon of virtue and righteousness? No way. They're not even willing to push three numbers on their phones to save a man's life. Yet God's even worse than they are—he doesn't even have to dial 911. God's all powerful; it isn't heavy lifting for him to end suffering, indeed it literally is no effort at all. Yet, like pedestrians in Queens, he can't be bothered. That doesn't sound like the actions of a morally perfect, worshipful hero. Unless you think those passersby deserve a medal for ignoring Hugo Tale-Yax, the obvious inference is that God is not perfectly good either.

Objection 1: Just give up an attribute One response to the problem of 3.112
evil is to just give up one of God's attributes. For example, suppose that God is all knowing and perfectly good, so that he knows about all the suffering in the world, and he wants to do something about it, but he just doesn't have enough power to stop it. God's kind of a wimp. Or we could give up omniscience. God is both perfectly good and all powerful, and he would eliminate suffering if he only knew about it. But he's kind of a dope and just doesn't have a clue. Or we abandon the attribute of omnibenevolence: God's all powerful and all knowing, but he's a malicious bastard, or a bloodthirsty tyrant. He knows about the world's suffering, all right, but like a Roman emperor at the **Colosseum**,[76] he enjoys the screaming and the blood. One wag has suggested that given the way the world is, the best inference is that God is 100 percent malicious but only 80 percent effective.

It is certainly true that God can keep any two out of the three traditional 3.113
attributes and escape the problem of evil. The problem with this approach is that it is really just a way of conceding to the atheist. The atheist is

arguing that there is no God, where God is understood as a being that is omnipotent, omniscient, and omnibenevolent. Giving up one of the attributes is admitting defeat—it's conceding that there is no God with all three of the classical attributes. The atheist will say "Mission accomplished!" and have a cup of tea. You may want to argue that your conception of God is of a being that has only two of the three traditional attributes, and you believe *that* God is real. Unfortunately, such a reply is really to throw in the towel. The atheist will simply scratch one god off the list and move on to the next.

3.114 *Objection 2: It's all part of God's greater plan* The fundamental idea behind the God's greater plan objection is that our suffering is all part of God's grand plan for our happiness and flourishing. God's wisdom is beyond the wisdom of the world; his designs are subtle and mysterious. There is no denying that we suffer in this world and do not know why, but that does not mean that there is no God; it only shows that we fail to fathom the reason that we need to suffer. Perhaps our suffering in this world is a test, a way to prove our faith in God and demonstrate our worthiness for the afterlife. Or maybe without enduring pain in this life we will never be able to appreciate or comprehend the glories of the next. Whatever God's plan may be, we can rest assured that he has one, and that our earthly, temporal sufferings are but a drop in the bucket of eternity.

3.115 The "God's greater plan" proposal is often taken to refute what is called the logical problem of evil, namely the idea that the existence of suffering shows that it is logically impossible for there to be a God. God *might* have some good reasons as to why suffering is necessary, and instrumental to our greater happiness. Since he might, it is not downright impossible for God and evil to coexist. Of course, the possibility of God's existence isn't nearly as desirable as his actual existence. Will the "God's greater plan" idea show that it is really is reasonable to continue to believe in God, given the vast suffering in the world?

3.116 One response to the greater plan idea, as skillfully presented by **David Hume**,[77] is to object that it is nothing but pure, unprovable conjecture to suppose that there really is such a plan. At best it is a *possible* way out, not a genuine way out. Suffering is evident and manifest, and the plan is nothing but unfounded speculation. Even if the problem of evil is not conclusive, doesn't it show a superb reason to deny that there is a God? The idea of a greater plan is a *possible* solution, but not an *actual* one until we have reason to believe (1) that there really is such a "greater plan," (2) this plan could not be accomplished without suffering, or at least, (3) this plan could not be accomplished without as much suffering as there actually is.

Compare: suppose that your philosophy professor walked out into class 3.117
and just started **slapping** you.[78] Would you turn the other cheek, or would you at least say, "Whoa, what's up with the face-slapping?" Imagine he tells you, "it's all part of my greater plan for your education." What would your response be then? "Oh, well, in that case, slap away!" Or would you say, "Hold on, at least tell me what the plan is." Probably you'll want some serious details on the plan before you submit to another round of beatings. Would you be satisfied with "Oh, don't worry, I have your best interests at heart and know what I'm doing."? Rather doubtful. But this is exactly what the theist is telling you to do: let God slap you around and just trust that he's doing it because he really loves you. Why do you think that he has some glorious plan? It can't be because you assume that God is perfectly good—that's the very attribute that is under criticism here. The "greater plan" idea sounds more like an excuse for domestic violence. You deserve God's beatings, which he's only doing because he truly loves you. Just trust in his love! We could imagine that God has some unknown and mysterious plan, but, as Hume writes, these are "arbitrary suppositions" built "entirely in the air; and the utmost we ever attain by these conjectures and fictions is to show that [God's having a greater plan that explains away evil] is *possible;* we can never in this way establish that it is *true*" (**Hume**, 1779, pt 10).[79]

Whatever the greater plan is supposed to be, it is rather hard to imagine 3.118
that it must include the murder and torture of innocents, babies, and those who have never heard of God. Such a plan is seriously the best one that an all-knowing God could think up? It's reminiscent of the **Vietnam War-era idea** of destroying a village in order to save it.[80] An often-floated hypothesis is that the sufferings of the world are a test for the faithful to demonstrate their worthiness. Apart from the complete lack of evidence for this conjecture, it is extremely puzzling as to why an all-knowing God would need to administer any sort of a test. He would already know in advance who will pass and who will fail; he could peer directly into a person's mind (or metaphorical heart) without any need for some pointless test. It is irrational for God to test on the face of it.

In fact, rejoins the atheist, if God really does have some sort of greater 3.119
plan, then why isn't he really a sort of terrorist? God intentionally created everything, including diseases, floods, famines, earthquakes, tornadoes, hurricanes. It's not just the wicked who suffer from these things; **God** sends the rain on the just and the unjust alike.[81] Suppose God does have a plan

for all this indiscriminate killing—it's to teach us a lesson, to punish us, revenge, get us to change our ways, test our faith, or something like that. How is that any different from what Osama bin Laden did? Osama, too, was out to teach the West a lesson, punish us for our various sins, get us to change our ways, and so on. In fact, God is a much, much worse terrorist than Osama—God's death toll is in the billions. Whether God really loves you is frankly irrelevant to the conclusion that he is a terrorist. Perhaps you sympathize with Osama's view that Western nations are filled with materialistic infidels, just as one may agree with God that we are all wicked sinners. They are terrorists either way. The atheist concludes that not only do we have no reason at all to suppose that there really is some greater plan that justifies our massive suffering, but even if there is one, all that really shows is that God is a terrorist.

3.120 *Objection 3: Free will* The most famous and popular response to the problem of evil is known as the free will defense, which goes like this. The atheist rightly observes all the suffering, pain, and misery in the world, but then makes the mistake of blaming God for it. Suffering is not God's fault, it is *our* fault. *We* are the ones who have freely chosen to disobey God and ignore his rules and commandments. When we sin, yes, it leads to suffering; that should be no surprise. Yet God is not to blame for the stupid and wicked deeds that we perform, any more than a father who has done his best to instruct his children is at fault when those children go astray. To be sure, there is suffering in the world, but God is not on the hook for it—we are. God made us free to choose how to live our lives, but the consequence of his gift is that he allowed us to create a world with substantial evil in it.

Response 1: Moral vs. natural evil

3.121 There are two kinds of evils in the world, moral evil and natural evil.

- Moral evils: murder, war, rape, torture, theft, deception, assault, etc.
- Natural evils: diseases, floods, famines, earthquakes, tornadoes, hurricanes, volcanoes, etc.

Even if the free will defense absolves God of the suffering caused by moral evil, that doesn't touch the suffering caused by natural evil. Far more people have been killed by cancer, smallpox, and bubonic plague than by war. Humans do terrible things to each other, granted. But they cannot compare to the suffering imposed by famines and floods. Those things are all on God—an omnipotent, omniscient being could surely have designed the world so that it didn't have the flu (which killed over 40 million people in

just two years: **1918–1919**).[82] The physician Sir William Osler wrote, "Humanity has but three great enemies: fever, famine, and war; of these by far the greatest, by far the most terrible, is fever." Osler died of pneumonia in 1919.

It would take extremely tortuous reasoning to try to blame natural evils 3.122
on human beings; a clear case of blaming the victim. God's the one dishing out cancer, he's the one we should blame. Wars and murder may be our fault, but smallpox and earthquakes are God's fault.

Response 2: What's the value of free will?

At the heart of the free will defense is the idea that having free will is incred- 3.123
ibly valuable; indeed it is so valuable that possessing it is worth all the suffering in the world. But what makes it so wonderful? That notion needs some defense. Since the reason we suffer is supposedly our free will, God might have made the world so that no one had any free will but we were all perpetually happy. What makes free will + massive suffering better than having no free will + universal happiness? It sounds rather implausible. Even now we limit people's behavior (through laws) precisely to prevent them from freely performing evil. So we do think it is better to limit people's freedom than to allow them to do whatever they want. Why not take that reasoning to the logical limit: God, in his infinite knowledge and compassion, should create a world in which no one is able to perform evil acts and all live in bliss and harmony. Or he might have made the world so that everyone *could* perform evil acts if they wanted to, but no one ever had the desire to do so. There's a name for such a world: Heaven. Sounds better than this place, right? Wouldn't you rather be there? Maybe having free will is not all it's cracked up to be.

Response 3: The irresponsible owner

Imagine a dog owner who trains his pit bull to be a ferocious killing 3.124
machine. The dog has a bad attitude, strong teeth, and jaw muscles that can tear the tires off a Honda. Imagine the dog owner takes **Cujo**[83] down to the town park and lets him off the leash. After the dog savagely mauls some innocent bystanders at the park, the owner is arrested. His defense to the judge is this: "Your honor, I didn't tell Cujo to attack anyone. The dog has his own free will and freely chose to chomp those people. I yelled at him and told him to stop, but Cujo's not such a good listener. It's not my fault and I can't be held accountable for what Cujo does."

Do you figure that the dog owner is complete absolved of responsibility? 3.125
The owner knowingly trained Cujo to be a killer and intentionally set him

loose in the park. Surely the owner had a good idea of what the likely consequences were going to be, and at the very least is criminally negligent, regardless of Cujo's free will. God is in exactly the same situation as the dog owner. Presumably God intentionally created people with their own drives and motivations, each with their own character and nature. Some people are pacifists, some are violent—we're not all stamped from the same cookie cutter. Yet God knew perfectly well which people were the wolves and which the sheep and went ahead and set the wolves loose. God may have yelled at the wolves and told them to stop, but they're not such good listeners. Just like the dog owner, God is still at fault for moral evil, free will notwithstanding.

Response 4: Why doesn't God intervene?

3.126 Here's one last criticism of the free will defense. One kind of morally good action is to prevent suffering, or to intervene in the wicked actions of others. In January, 2007, Wesley Autrey was waiting for a subway train in New York City. A nearby man, Cameron Hollopeter, suffered a seizure, which caused him to stumble off the subway platform and into the path of an incoming train. Without hesitation, Mr Autrey leapt onto the tracks and pulled Hollopeter into a foot-deep drainage trench between the tracks, covering Hollopeter's body with his own. The train roared overhead, passing inches from their heads, but both men survived with only minor scrapes. There can be little doubt about **Autrey**'s heroic and admirable behavior; few people would have risked their own lives so spectacularly to save the life of a stranger.[84] Afterwards, Autrey was awarded the **Bronze Medallion**, New York City's highest award for exceptional citizenship and outstanding achievement.[85]

3.127 Or consider the anonymous bystanders who foiled a robbery in New Hampshire. In October, 2010, Sean Cullen entered a Manchester, NH convenience store, handed the clerk a threatening note, and told her, "Give me your money, or you're going to die." One store patron saw what was happening and tackled Cullen, while another bashed him over the head with a large squash. Surely these bystanders were the proverbial Good Samaritans, helping others in time of need. Sean Cullen was acting out of his own free will, but nevertheless the morally right thing to do was to stop him from **causing harm**.[86]

3.128 If Wesley Autrey had stood by and let Cameron Hollopeter be killed, or had the New Hampshire bystanders done nothing and let Sean Cullen rob the store, they would have been less morally praiseworthy. The morally best thing to do in both cases was to intervene and prevent harm, even when it meant interfering with someone's free action. Having free will does not mean getting a free pass. Thus if God does not intervene when he can—stop the bullet, cure Grandma's cancer, prevent the Holocaust—he is morally inferior to mere mortals wielding squash. God can't hide behind an excuse of free will, pretending that justifies his hands-off policy.

It is true that if God steps up Superman-style and flies to the rescue every 3.129
time then that will prevent human beings from developing or exercising such virtues as self-sacrifice, helping, and bravery. A theist might argue that allowing moral evil is justified because the world is better off if we have genocide and war, but we also have courage and selflessness. In essence, God allows suffering because it builds character. Still, replies the atheist, it is difficult to see that such a view will be convincing to the parents of the children murdered in Rwanda, who would much prefer their children to live than enjoy whatever character-building they supposedly received because their children were slaughtered.

Finally, you may wish to consider how convincing the free will defense 3.130
really is after you read the chapter in this book on free will. There are reasons to believe that we don't even have free will in the sense of being able to make undetermined choices. If you are skeptical about the existence of free will at all, it won't serve as a legitimate way to escape the problem of evil.

Conclusion

While the pros and cons of the most prominent arguments concerning the 3.131
existence of God have been discussed in the present chapter, there are still many theistic and atheistic arguments out there. Unexamined are pro-God arguments based upon reports of miracles or on personal religious experience. One of the most sophisticated contemporary theistic strategies is to treat divine revelations as basic sources of knowledge, akin to perception. That too is beyond the reach of the present chapter. Likewise unaddressed are anti-God arguments based on **Ockham's razor**,[87] which argue that positing a God has no explanatory value and should be avoided. Beyond the issue of God's existence are defenses of religion that find value in rituals and community building, even while not believing in a God. Buddhism and Unitarianism are examples of such religions. Whether God exists is a vital issue to decide in order to have a comprehensive view of the

contents of reality. All major philosophers have staked out a position on this topic, and now that you have an introduction to their arguments, it is up to you to decide which ones you find the most compelling.

Annotated Bibliography

Anselm of Canterbury (1078) *Proslogion*, full text available at www.ccel.org/ccel/anselm/basic_works.iii.iii.html, accessed May 15, 2012. In Chapter 2 Anselm gives his ingenious ontological argument.

Aquinas, Thomas (c. 1270) "The Five Ways," full text available at www.ccel.org/ccel/aquinas/summa.FP_Q2_A3.html, accessed May 15, 2012, in *Summa Theologica*. Aquinas is the preeminent Catholic theologian, known as The Angelic Doctor. *Summa Theologica* is Aquinas's masterwork, and in it he presents five arguments to prove God's existence, including versions of the cosmological argument and the design argument.

Bostrom, Nick (2009) "Pascal's Mugging," *Analysis* 69:3, 443–445. A short and wickedly funny take-down of Pascal's wager.

Dawkins, Richard (2006) *The God Delusion* (New York: Houghton Mifflin). A muscular defense of atheism written for a popular audience. The book is a bit uneven, but Dawkins is at his strongest when discussing the design argument, as his area of expertise is evolutionary explanations of complexity.

Dawkins, Richard (2009) *The Greatest Show on Earth: The Evidence for Evolution* (New York: Free Press). Dawkins, a well-known evolutionary biologist at Oxford, reviews the empirical evidence for evolution by natural selection in a comprehensive but accessible volume.

Dennett, Daniel C. (2007) *Breaking the Spell: Religion as a Natural Phenomenon* (New York: Penguin). Dennett investigates the nature and persistence of religious belief, drawing on anthropology, psychology, and evolutionary biology. He treats the study of religion with the same sort of skeptical approach typically brought to other areas of inquiry.

Descartes, René (1641) *Meditations on First Philosophy*, full text available at www.earlymoderntexts.com/pdfbits/dm3.pdf, accessed May 15, 2012. In his Fifth Meditation, Descartes defends a version of the ontological argument. Descartes's presentation is heavily dependent on other aspects of his philosophy, such as clear and distinct perception and innate ideas, and is thus more theory laden than Anselm's original version.

Gaunilo of Marmoutier (c. 1079) *In Behalf of the Fool*, full text available at www.ccel.org/ccel/anselm/basic_works.v.i.html, accessed May 15, 2012. Gaunilo, a contemporary of St Anselm, gives his "lost island" objection to the ontological argument.

Hume, David (1779) *Dialogues Concerning Natural Religion*, full text available at www.gutenberg.org/ebooks/4583, accessed May 15, 2012. The preeminent work of natural theology in English. The arguments for God's existence are pursued and critiqued by characters in a dialogue format. Hume thought this book so radical that he forbade its publication during his lifetime.

Kant, Immanuel (1787) *The Critique of Pure Reason*, full text available at www.earlymoderntexts.com/pdfbits/kc24.pdf, accessed May 15, 2012. Kant's criticism of the ontological argument begins at section 620, and his complaint that existence is not a property is at section 626.

Kauffman, Stuart (1995) *At Home in the Universe: The Search for the Laws of Self-Organization and Complexity* (Oxford: Oxford University Press). A polymath and iconoclast, Kauffman here presents his theory of how order can spontaneously arise in complex systems. He argues that his ideas complement the evolutionary explanation of life.

Leibniz, Gottfried (1710) "Making the Case for God in terms of his Justice which is Reconciled with the rest of his Perfections and with all his Actions," full text available at www.earlymoderntexts.com/pdf/leibmaki.pdf, accessed May 24, 2012. Starting at section 41, Leibniz attempts to solve the problem of evil by arguing that ours is the best of all possible worlds.

Manson, Neil (forthcoming) *This Is Philosophy of Religion: An Introduction* (Oxford: Wiley-Blackwell). A comprehensive introduction to the philosophy of religion that discusses religious language, the nature of God, life after death, the role of faith, religious diversity, and delves more deeply into the arguments for and against God's existence. Manson also addresses some conundrums of the divine, such as the Paradox of the Stone.

Mlodinow, Leonard (2008) *The Drunkard's Walk: How Randomness Rules Our Lives* (New York: Pantheon Books). A fascinating and readable discussion of randomness and probability, with applications to sports, gambling, stock markets, and more. There is a nice discussion of Pascal in Chapter 4.

Paley, William (1802) *Natural Theology*, full text available at http://ocw.nd.edu/philosophy/introduction-to-philosophy-1/readings/paley-natural-theology-selections, accessed May 15, 2012. Paley's presentation of the design argument is one of the most influential and most carefully developed. Darwin specifically discusses Paley's reasoning in *The Origin of Species.*

Pascal, Blaise (1660) "The Wager," full text available at www.ccel.org/ccel/pascal/pensees.iv.html, accessed May 15, 2012, in *Pensées*. Pascal gives his wager argument starting at section 233. It is a surprisingly short discussion, which has generated a tremendous literature.

Plantinga, Alvin (2000) *Warranted Christian Belief* (Oxford: Oxford University Press). A sophisticated book meant for professionals, this book represents the state-of-the-art in Christian apologetics. Plantinga's hefty tome is devoted to defending the claim that if God exists, then Christian beliefs have warrant.

Price, Huw (1996) *Time's Arrow and Archimedes' Point: New Directions for the Physics of Time* (Oxford: Oxford University Press). A technical book for philosophers, included here because it is the source for Roger Penrose's calculation of the improbability of the conditions in the early universe (it is on p. 83).

Smoot, George and Keay Davidson (2007) *Wrinkles in Time* (New York: Harper-Perennial). A beautifully written account of the standard model in cosmology. Smoot tells a thrilling story of his work on the experimental evidence for the Cosmic Microwave Background, for which he won the Nobel Prize in physics. Accessible to the educated lay audience.

Voltaire (the pen name of François-Marie Arouet) (1759) *Candide*, full text available at www.gutenberg.org/ebooks/19942, accessed May 15, 2012. An hilarious satire on Leibniz's view that this is the best of all possible worlds.

Online Resources

1 The Gallup Poll's claim that "83% say there is a God who answers prayers, while 9% believe there is a God who does not answer prayers": www.gallup.com/poll/127721/Few-Americans-Oppose-National-Day-Prayer.aspx

2 The Gallup Poll's evidence that 79 percent of Americans believe that the Earth revolves around the Sun: www.gallup.com/poll/3742/New-Poll-Gauges-Americans-General-Knowledge-Levels.aspx

3 The Gallup Poll's evidence that 4 percent of Americans believed that Elvis was still alive almost a quarter century after his death: www.gallup.com/poll/2638/August-23rd-Anniversary-Elvis-Death-Americans-Still-Conside.aspx

4 The history of the temple of Athena known as the Parthenon: www.ancient-greece.org/architecture/parthenon.html

5 Facts about the exquisite Blue Mosque in Istanbul, Turkey: www.sacred-destinations.com/turkey/istanbul-blue-mosque

6 The history of Angkor Wat, the largest Hindu temple complex in the world: http://en.wikipedia.org/wiki/Angkor_Wat

7 Information on Michelangelo Buonarroti's 1499 sculpture of the Virgin Mary holding the body of her son Jesus Christ after his death: http://saintpetersbasilica.org/Altars/Pieta/Pieta.htm

8 A discussion of Michelangelo's famous painting on the ceiling and walls of the Sistine Chapel in the Vatican: www.sacred-destinations.com/italy/rome-sistine-chapel

9 An excerpt from Johann Sebastian Bach's *Mass in B Minor*: www.youtube.com/watch?v=tdLCcQixNvg

10 The first part of John Coltrane's *A Love Supreme*: www.youtube.com/watch?v=558bTG0D-xg

11 George Harrison performs "My Sweet Lord": www.youtube.com/watch?v=wynYMJwEPH8

12 The iconic beginning of Strauss's *Also Sprach Zarathustra*: www.youtube.com/watch?v=lyJwbwWg8uc
13 A dicussion of Raphael's fresco *The School of Athens*, another treasure of the Vatican: http://en.wikipedia.org/wiki/The_School_of_Athens
14 The Metropolitan Museum of Art's entry on Jacques Louis-David's painting *The Death of Socrates*: www.metmuseum.org/Collections/search-the-collections/110000543
15 The definition and history of the view that faith and reason are in conflict with each other, a position traditionally attributed to Tertullian: http://plato.stanford.edu/entries/fideism/
16 A biography of Martin Luther, along with a discussion of his theological views: www.iep.utm.edu/luther/
17 Luther's 1540 treatise *Disputation on the Divinity and Humanity of Christ*: www.iclnet.org/pub/resources/text/wittenberg/luther/luther-divinity.txt
18 A brief discussion of natural theology: www.giffordlectures.org/theology.asp
19 An entertaining list of fool's errands and practical jokes: http://en.wikipedia.org/wiki/Snipe_hunt
20 A few of God's killings, as attested in the Bible: http://drunkwithblood.com/index.html
21 The sacred Hindu text *The Rig-Veda*: www.sacred-texts.com/hin/rigveda/index.htm
22 The sacred Hindu text *The Bhagavad Gita*: www.sacred-texts.com/hin/gita/agsgita.htm
23 The Buddhist holy scripture *Pali Canon*: www.palicanon.org/
24 The Islamic holy scripture *The Qur'an*: http://quran.com/
25 *The Book of Mormon*, sacred to members of The Church of Jesus Christ of Latter-Day Saints: www.lds.org/scriptures/bofm?lang=eng
26 The most comprehensive online source for the sacred texts of religions from all over the world: www.sacred-texts.com/
27 A discussion of the logical fallacy of begging the question: www.fallacyfiles.org/begquest.html
28 A journalist's summary of recent critical scholarship concerning the historical claims of the Torah: www.worldagesarchive.com/Reference_Links/False_Testament_(Harpers).htm
29 The full text of Homer's *Iliad*: http://classics.mit.edu/Homer/iliad.html
30 The full text of Homer's *Odyssey*: http://classics.mit.edu/Homer/odyssey.html
31 An in-depth discussion of various versions of the ontological argument: http://plato.stanford.edu/entries/ontological-arguments/
32 Psalms 14:1, "The fool has said in his heart, "There is no God.": http://bible.cc/psalms/14-1.htm
33 The website for professional tennis player Rafa Nadal: www.rafaelnadal.com/

34 The cosmological argument in classical Islam: www.muslimphilosophy.com/ip/pg1.htm
35 The life, philosophy, and theology of Thomas Aquinas, the greatest of Catholic theologians: http://plato.stanford.edu/entries/aquinas/
36 An introduction to cosmology from NASA: http://map.gsfc.nasa.gov/universe/
37 A fine, detailed primer on cosmology from NASA: http://map.gsfc.nasa.gov/universe/WMAP_Universe.pdf
38 The full text of Schopenhauer's book *On the Fourfold Root of the Principle of Sufficient Reason*, the source of his line that the cosmological argument uses the principle of universal causation like a "hired cab": http://openlibrary.org/books/OL7040205M/On_the_fourfold_root_of_the_principle_of_sufficient_reason
39 "Pay no attention to that man behind the curtain" scene from *The Wizard of Oz*: www.youtube.com/watch?v=YWyCCJ6B2WE
40 The Calibre 89 by Patek Philippe, the most complex pocketwatch ever made: http://stylefrizz.com/200803/the-worlds-most-complicated-pocket-watch-patek-philippe/
41 Allmovie's synopsis of *The Gods Must Be Crazy*: www.allmovie.com/movie/the-gods-must-be-crazy-v20084
42 The opening scenes of *The Gods Must Be Crazy* when the Bushmen of the Kalahari encounter a Coke bottle that fell from the sky: www.youtube.com/watch?v=gCQIGiXf0JA
43 The finches of the Galapagos Islands, and their role in helping Darwin formulate the theory of evolution by natural selection: http://en.wikipedia.org/wiki/Darwin's_finches
44 Details on how eyes evolved: http://en.wikipedia.org/wiki/Evolution_of_the_eye
45 A discussion of snowflakes, crystals, and six-fold symmetry by a Caltech scientist: www.its.caltech.edu/~atomic/snowcrystals/faqs/faqs.htm
46 A fun kitchen experiment that instantaneously changes beer from liquid to solid: www.youtube.com/watch?v=n_H5ZIoZSBo
47 The creation of the Earth scene from *The Hitchhiker's Guide to the Galaxy*: www.youtube.com/watch?v=MbNtlS69HhU
48 M. C. Escher's drawing of self-creating hands: http://en.wikipedia.org/wiki/Drawing_Hands
49 An in-depth discussion of Pascal's wager: http://plato.stanford.edu/entries/pascal-wager/
50 The nature of the Higgs Boson particle and why it matters to physics: http://en.wikipedia.org/wiki/Higgs_boson
51 Facts about the rare ivory-billed woodpecker: http://web4.audubon.org/bird/ivory/ivory.php
52 The fighting talents of Jet Li: www.youtube.com/watch?v=2SK9kFyQxNw

53 The "show me the money" sequence from the film *Jerry Maguire*: www.youtube.com/watch?v=Lnrb8HnQvfU&feature=related
54 Ascetic monks in *Monty Python and the Holy Grail* chant "Pie Jesu Domine, dona eis requiem": www.youtube.com/watch?v=YgYEuJ5u1K0
55 Gordon Gekko's speech that greed is good, from the film *Wall Street*: www.youtube.com/watch?v=Muz1OcEzJOs&feature=related
56 A guide to over 3000 deities, demons, and spirits from around the world: www.godchecker.com/
57 A Gallup Poll showing that Americans would rather vote for someone Jewish, Catholic, Mormon, a woman, black, Hispanic, homosexual, 72 years of age, or someone married for the third time before they voted for an atheist: www.gallup.com/poll/26611/Some-Americans-Reluctant-Vote-Mormon-72YearOld-Presidential-Candidates.aspx
58 Sociological research that shows Americans would rather their children marry someone from every other marginalized group studied before marrying an atheist: https://www.soc.umn.edu/~hartmann/files/atheist%20as%20the%20other.pdf
59 A report on research showing that atheists are distrusted as much as rapists: http://digitaljournal.com/article/315425
60 Survey evidence about the beliefs of professional philosophers over a wide variety of topics, including God: http://philpapers.org/surveys/results.pl
61 A survey of what the members of the National Academy of Sciences believe about God and personal immortality: www.stephenjaygould.org/ctrl/news/file002.html
62 A discussion of the life and work of biologist Richard Dawkins: http://en.wikipedia.org/wiki/Richard_Dawkins
63 The self-described "ultimate and official Loch Ness Monster site": www.nessie.co.uk/
64 The history and definition of Boyle's gas law: http://en.wikipedia.org/wiki/Boyle's_law
65 The history of the god Yahweh: http://en.wikipedia.org/wiki/Yahweh
66 A list of superseded, obsolete scientific theories: http://en.wikipedia.org/wiki/Obsolete_scientific_theory
67 A discussion of the discarded view that disease is caused by "bad air" instead of contagion: http://en.wikipedia.org/wiki/Miasma_theory_of_disease
68 An article that explains why the global positioning system (GPS) depends upon the truth of general relativity: www.metaresearch.org/cosmology/gps-relativity.asp
69 The World Bank's poverty statistics and indicators: http://web.worldbank.org/WBSITE/EXTERNAL/TOPICS/EXTPOVERTY/0,,contentMDK:22569498~pagePK:148956~piPK:216618~theSitePK:336992,00.html

70 Allmovie's synopsis of *The Hangover*: www.allmovie.com/movie/the-hangover-v420157
71 Information on torture from Amnesty International: www.amnestyusa.org/our-work/campaigns/security-with-human-rights?id=1031032
72 A sobering death toll of wars, genocides, and other anthropogenic causes: http://en.wikipedia.org/wiki/List_of_wars_and_disasters_by_death_toll
73 The death toll of diseases and natural disasters: http://en.wikipedia.org/wiki/List_of_natural_disasters_by_death_toll#Contractible_diseases
74 A list of natural disasters by death toll: http://en.wikipedia.org/wiki/List_of_natural_disasters_by_death_toll
75 A news report on the murder of Hugo Alfredo Tale-Yax and the indifferent passers-by:http://gawker.com/5523739/more-than-20-people-passed-as-homeless-new-york-man-bled-to-death
76 The history and description of the Flavian Amphitheater, better known as the Colosseum of Rome: http://en.wikipedia.org/wiki/Colosseum
77 A detailed discussion of David Hume's writings on the philosophy of religion: http://plato.stanford.edu/entries/hume-religion/
78 A faceslap in super slow motion: www.youtube.com/watch?v=3BRw_ihZRJI
79 The complete text of David Hume's *Dialogues Concerning Natural Religion*: www.earlymoderntexts.com/pdfbits/hd3.pdf
80 The money quote: "Writing about the provincial capital, Bến Tre, on 7 February 1968, [AP correspondent Peter] Arnett cited an unidentified US military official as follows: 'It became necessary to destroy the town to save it', a United States major said today. He was talking about the decision by allied commanders to bomb and shell the town regardless of civilian casualties, to rout the Vietcong.": http://en.wikipedia.org/wiki/B%E1%BA%BFn_Tre
81 Matthew 5:45: God sends the rain on the just and the unjust alike: http://bible.cc/matthew/5-45.htm
82 The history of the 1918–1919 flu pandemic: www.flu.gov/pandemic/history/1918/index.html
83 A synopsis of Stephen King's novel about a killer dog, *Cujo*: www.stephenking.com/library/novel/cujo.html
84 The heroism of Wesley Autrey, who saved a stranger from being killed by a subway train: www.nytimes.com/2007/01/03/nyregion/03life.html?_r=3
85 A photo of New York City mayor Bloomburg presenting Wesley Autrey with the Bronze Medallion, the City's highest award for exceptional citizenship and outstanding achievement: www.nyc.gov/portal/site/nycgov/menuitem.1cac08e0805942f4f7393cd401c789a0/index.jsp?eid=11708&pc=1095
86 The story of a would-be robber foiled by squash: www.wmur.com/r/25578010/detail.html
87 A detailed discussion of theoretical parsimony, simplicity, and Ockham's razor: http://plato.stanford.edu/entries/simplicity/

4

FREEDOM

There are loads of ways in which you are said to be free. Here's a small sample: 4.1

- You are free to speak your mind.
- You are free to bear arms.
- You are free to worship how you please.
- You are free from hunger.
- You are free from poverty.
- You are disease-free.

The first three kinds of freedom are largely political. That is, according to certain laws you are free from governmental interference or constraint. No one's stopping you from criticizing the leaders, packing heat, or practicing Scientology—feel free! The other forms of freedom above are also a kind of absence of outside barriers, such as disease, poverty, and hunger that impede you from living your life as you choose. These senses of freedom are important in discussions of **political philosophy**,[1] and how the existence of political authority might reduce some freedoms (you are less free to spend your money as you wish because of taxation) while at the same time increasing other freedoms (you are free from ignorance because of taxpayer-funded education). As interesting as these freedoms are, they aren't the main sort of freedom that has troubled philosophers for two millennia. The big worry has been over free will.

So what is free will exactly? Well, that's part of what the brouhaha is all 4.2
about, but here's a fair first attempt:

This Is Philosophy: An Introduction, First Edition. Steven D. Hales.

Free will: Your will is free just in case you can choose to perform one action instead of another.

The idea here is that free will means being able to direct your own actions, to pick one thing over an alternative. The past is fixed and immutable, and you are not free to change it. But the future is open to you, and you are at liberty to direct its course. Imagine standing at a fork in the road with a dozen branches ahead of you, each representing a future path that you could follow. All it takes is for you to decide, to pick one over the others. There aren't any barriers, and no one is pushing you from behind: the choice is yours. To be free at a time is to be standing at that fork, facing the open future. You can choose vanilla ice cream or chocolate, you can choose to listen to Bach or Lady Gaga, you can choose to study or go to the party. Furthermore, "choice" means effective choice—your choosing to study brings about the event of your studying. True choice is not idle, like "I choose to be invisible." There is nothing you can directly or indirectly do to make yourself invisible. Your free will is the power you possess to set foot on one path into the future over another. The future is not set; there is no fate but what you make for **yourself**.[2]

4.3 There is little doubt that you believe that your will is free and that you can choose your own future. The problem is, as the eighteenth-century British wit Samuel Johnson once remarked, "**all theory is against the freedom of the will; all experience is for it**."[3] Let's proceed to what these theories might be that are against the freedom of the will.

Why There Is No Free Will, Part 1: Divine Foreknowledge

4.4 Philosophers and theologians have been troubled since the Middle Ages that if there is an omniscient God, then free will seems impossible. Think about how well you are able to predict the behavior of your friends. With your close friends, you can guess quite well how they will act in certain circumstances. You know that if you go with your best friend for coffee, he takes it black, and when the coffee comes he will not add milk or sugar. You know that another friend is paranoid about running out of gas and that she always gets fuel when the tank is down to a quarter full. On a road trip with her, you can easily predict when she will pull over for gas. Admittedly, you can't predict each and every action by even your best friend. But that only shows that your knowledge of others is imperfect; you can't know every last thought or impulse in their heads, or every possible circumstance they might find themselves in. You can't, but God can. God is omniscient—he knows *everything*, every sparrow in the sky, the number of hairs on your head, how many grains of sand are at the beach. You might be able to predict your friends' behavior fairly accurately, but God is 100 percent infallibly certain of what they will do. Yet if God knows what they will do, how is it possible for them to have done anything else?

Presentation of the argument

Here's a concise version of the problem of divine foreknowledge. 4.5

1.	Assume there is an omniscient God.	(premise)
2.	If God is omniscient, then he infallibly knows every fact about the past, present, and future.	(premise)
3.	Therefore, God infallibly knows every fact about the past, present, and future.	(from 1, 2)
4.	Therefore, God infallibly knows everything that you will do, every action you will perform, and everything that will happen to you.	(from 3)
5.	If God infallibly knows everything that you will do, then it is impossible for you to do anything other than what God knows you will do; you have no choice.	(premise)
6.	Therefore, you have no choice in what you will do.	(from 4, 5)
7.	If you have no choice in what you will do, then you are not free.	(from the definition of free will)
8.	Therefore, you have no free will.	(from 6, 7)

Objection 1: Atheism and agnosticism

Theists are generally keen on salvaging free will. If God knew since the 4.6
beginning of the world that Lucifer would defy him, that Judas Iscariot would betray Jesus, and that Pharaoh would refuse to liberate God's chosen people, why would God punish those folks? It's not like they had any choice in the matter. It seems unreasonable to hold them responsible for actions they were doomed to perform. The problem of free will and

moral responsibility will be discussed in more general terms later in this chapter. In addition, appeal to human free will is one of the classic responses to the problem of evil (discussed in the chapter on God). If divine foreknowledge really means that no one is free, then the existence of suffering cannot be blamed on people making the wrong choices; there is no such thing as choice. So eluding the divine foreknowledge problem is important.

4.7 There is a really easy way to solve the problem: reject premise 1. Either deny that there is an omniscient God (atheist style) or refuse to have an opinion either way (agnostic style). God's existence is addressed in some detail in the chapter on God. If you aren't convinced that God really does exist, then of course you have no reason to be troubled about whether his knowledge of the future precludes your freedom. This may seem terribly obvious, but it is worth pointing out that the problem of divine foreknowledge isn't a wholly general threat to the possibility of free will. It is only a puzzle for theists. Now, if you do think that there is an omniscient God, then you have to look for some other way to get out of the argument. Here's another escape route.

Objection 2: Aristotle's answer

4.8 In ***On Interpretation*** (section 9),[4] which is part of his treatise on logic, the Greek philosopher **Aristotle**[5] insisted that there are no facts about the future. Suppose that the Persian fleet is sailing towards Athens. Aristotle argued that there most definitely either will or will not be a sea battle tomorrow. But that's not a fact about the future. *Any* claim of the form "either p is true or p is false" is true; that's no more than a general logical law. However, it is not true that "the Persians and Athenians will have a sea battle tomorrow" nor is it true that "the Persians and Athenians will *not* have a sea battle tomorrow." In other words, no statement about the future is either true or false. There are concrete facts about the present and the past, but the future is no more than a formless void. Here's how things stand according to Aristotle:

a. Either there will be a sea battle tomorrow or there won't be. (true)
b. There will be a sea battle tomorrow. (no truth value; neither true nor false)
c. There will be no sea battle tomorrow. (no truth value; neither true nor false)

God knows (a) but doesn't know (b) or (c). Until tomorrow comes, there is nothing to know.

If Aristotle is right that there are no future facts, then premise (2) of the 4.9
divine foreknowledge argument is false. God's omniscience does not extend to the future because there is nothing to know. God does indeed know everything knowable—every truth of the past and present. But since there are no truths about the future for him to know, it is no limitation on his omniscience to say that God does not know what the future will bring. When the future arrives and becomes the present, then God knows whether the Persian and Athenian navies do battle. But not a moment before.

There are various logical objections to the idea of some propositions 4.10
having no truth values at all, even if they are only statements about the future. The **worries** of logicians are beyond what can be addressed here.[6]

However, if Aristotle is right and there are no facts about future, then what explains the fact that we can often accurately predict the future? It is mysterious as to why our present speculations about such a nebulous future should have any legitimacy at all. You might insist that there are present facts about what is probable in the future, for example, "it is probable now that there will be a sea battle tomorrow." That's a perfectly legitimate sentence for Aristotle, because it refers only to what is true now in the present moment. However, this sentence: "tomorrow it is probable that there will be a sea battle" remains neither true nor false, since it refers to some future fact. That result seems strange and arbitrary.

Let's set the divine foreknowledge argument aside and look at another 4.11
argument against free will, one that is applicable no matter what you think about God.

Why There Is No Free Will, Part 2: A Regress of Reasons for Acting

Did you decide to read this chapter? There are only two possible answers, 4.12
namely "yes" and "no." Suppose the answer is "no." That doesn't mean you aren't reading it; we all do plenty of things that we don't particularly decide to do, things that we do out of habit, as a matter of routine, or perhaps even randomly. Ever drive a familiar route and then realize that you can't remember any part of the drive for the last ten minutes? The drive is just part of a routine that you don't really think about; you do it subconsciously. Or when you brush your teeth—do you really make a decision about every

stroke? "Up," you think, "now down . . . all the way, OK, now up again, don't press so hard . . . down once more." Of course not. You probably daydream, or worry, or plan your day like everyone else when you brush your teeth. You don't think about the brushing. You just do it. So maybe reading this chapter is like that—without really deciding to, you found yourself sitting in your chair with this book in your hand. You started reading this chapter without thought, zombie-like.

4.13 No, you say? You actually decided to read it? Good for you. How did you decide? Of your own free will? Let's think about that for a bit. There are lots of other things you might have done instead; you could have slept in, consumed a refreshing adult beverage, studied for another class, played some tennis, kissed your lover. How did you decide to read about free will instead of those other things? Presumably you thought it over, you weighed out the reasons pro and con for reading the chapter, and the pros won out. There are many good reasons for reading it after all—nothing is more exciting and stimulating than philosophy, the writing style is breathtaking in its excellence, free will is a great topic, and let's not forget the weight contributed by the fact that it will be on the test and you desperately need to pass this class to graduate. There were reasons on the other side to blow it off, true, but it turns out that they just weren't as weighty. The image of deliberation here is that of pair of scales, a mental balance if you will. In one pan are the reasons for performing the action and in the other are the reasons against performing the action. The balance tips in one direction or other, and that's the action you perform. What explains your decision to read this chapter? You weighed out the options, and reading the chapter won.

Previous decisions vs. outside forces

4.14 There is still a mystery to be solved, though. Why should the things that counted as a reason to read the chapter (or not read it) be reasons at all? And why do they have the relative weight that they do? If your **GPA (grade point average)** is 0.0,[7] maybe you don't especially care about the upcoming test or passing the class. So the fact that reading this chapter is instrumental to passing the test just has no value, no weight for you. It doesn't even count as a reason to read it. Likewise, if you've had plenty of sleep, the option of sleeping in doesn't have much pull either. We can put it on the scale on the "con" side, but it doesn't weigh very much. It is clear, then, that which things count as reasons to keep on reading this chapter and which things count

as reasons not to read it are going to vary from person to person, perhaps even from moment to moment. What explains which things are reasons for you, and how much they weigh? There seem to be only two possible answers, namely that the explanation is rooted ultimately in you and your decision-making, or that the explanation is rooted outside of you in other forces and factors. Here are our alternatives.

Previous decisions: Your reasons for acting are the result of some previous decisions you made.

Outside forces: Your reasons for acting somehow came from forces and influences outside of your mind (for example: authority, family, society, environment, or innate biological instincts).

With the previous decisions option, you made choices in the past, and these choices determine your preferences and desires now. For example, in the past you decided to come to college and be successful, and this prior decision is what gives weight to the value of studying and reading assigned texts. Likewise for the other reasons pro and con: their relative weight, and that they amount to reasons for acting at all, is the result of earlier decision-making.

The problem with this answer is that it apparently leads to an infinite regress. Your decision to read this chapter is explained by your earlier decision to study in college, which is the result of your prior decision to do some action A which is explained by your even earlier decision to do B, and on back. If we think about decision-making as the tipping of scales, then it looks like Figure 4.1. 4.15

We can just keep adding little balances back in time. You didn't make an infinity of decisions before deciding to read this chapter. You haven't had enough time. As a baby did you make some first decision that determined everything else in your life? How did you make *that* decision? It couldn't be the result of any prior decision-making, being the very first one. Therefore it can't be the case that *all* of your decisions are the causal consequences of earlier decisions. Suddenly decision-making seems inexplicable. 4.16

Maybe the outside forces option is the right answer. The reason that you care about education (and therefore passing the class and reading this chapter) is because of the values instilled in you while you were growing up. The reason that you like philosophy is because of your fortunate genetic heritage along with the inquisitive nature that your parents, friends, and teachers always encouraged. Your values, your reasons for acting, are 4.17

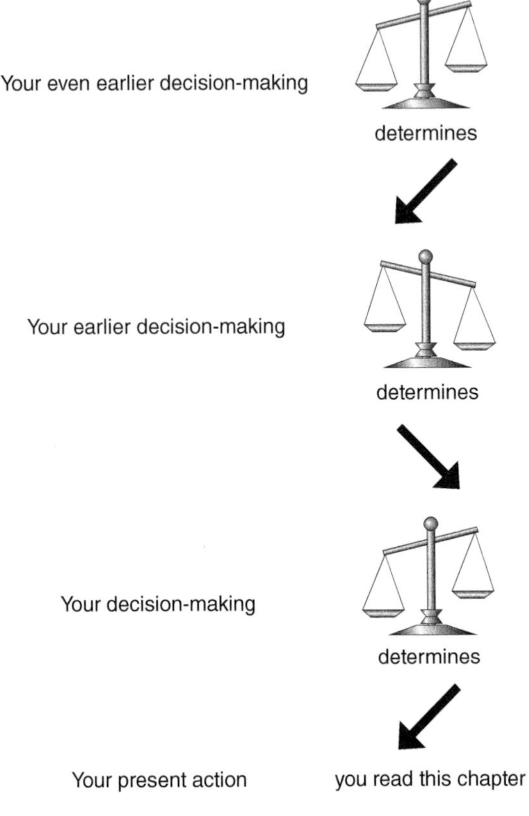

Figure 4.1 Decision-making regress

thereby the result of these outside influences that have molded and shaped you into the person you are. When we ask the question "How did you decide to read this chapter?," the answer is that you weighed out the pros and the cons. When we press on to ask what determines a reason to be a pro or a con, and what fixes how much each reason weighs, the answer is that your biology, experiences, upbringing, and environment determine these things. The important thing to notice here is that all of these forces are outside of your control and not the result of your choosing. No one chooses their families, or what society they were born into, or what teachers they have, or any of those other things. Your present decision to read this chapter isn't the result of some earlier decision that you made, but the outcome of forces completely outside of you. The argument against free will is just around the corner.

The regress of reasons argument against free will

1.	You always act according to your greatest desire.	(premise)
2.	Your desires and their relative strengths are outside of your control.	(premise)
3.	Therefore your actions are outside of your control.	(from 1, 2)
4.	If your actions are outside of your control, then they are not the result of your choices.	(premise)
5.	Therefore your actions are not the result of your choices.	(from 3, 4)
6.	If your actions are not the result of your choices, then you have no free will.	(from the definition of free will)
7.	Therefore, you have no free will.	(from 5, 6)

The defense of the first premise is implicit in our discussion so far. The image of a mental balance represents the weighing of your desires, and when it tips, it tips in the direction of the greatest weight, that is, the overall greatest desire, upon which you then act. "Your greatest desire" in this context doesn't mean your greatest wish or fondest hope. The statement of premise (1) that you always act on your greatest desire does not mean that you can fly like Superman, buy a Ferrari, travel in time, or whatever else you may fantasize about. It's not physically possible for you to fly, it's economically impossible to get the Ferrari, and (probably) not metaphysically possible to travel in time. But of all the actions you can possibly perform, you always perform the one you want to do the most. If premise (1) were false, then your intentional actions would be inexplicable; why didn't you do the thing you wanted to do the most? The answer is that you actually wanted to do something else even more. Accidental acts or those that stem from the subconscious might not be your greatest desire, but such actions aren't good candidates for free actions either. 4.18

You might object that you don't always act on your greatest desire. You might suppose that if you're on a diet, you may want to scarf a pint of Ben 4.19

and Jerry's Chunky Monkey more than anything else, but nevertheless manage to resist. If you're sleepy and hungover, you may want to stay in bed more than get up for work, yet still drag your carcass to the shower and out the door. There is no doubt that we frequently have many conflicting interests—desire for Chunky Monkey vs. desire to stay on the diet, desire for sleep vs. desire for continued gainful employment, desire to go to the party vs. desire to study for the test. In these situations you can't do both. If you wind up pigging out on Chunky Monkey, then your greatest desire was to have the ice cream, something proven by the fact you are eating it. The desire for rich, creamy banana ice cream stuffed with nuts and chocolate chunks was a stronger desire than staying on the diet. Conversely, if you stayed on the diet, *that* action really was the result of your greatest desire. So you do act on your greatest desire, even if there is a powerful conflicting desire that pulls you in the opposite direction. In the tug-of-war among your wants, the victory goes to the strongest.

4.20 The second premise was just defended—it is factors outside of you, independent influences that you can't control, that determine the existence and strength of your desires. (3) seems to be a straightforward consequence, your actions themselves are, in some fundamental and ultimate way, outside of your control. Yet if you aren't in control of your actions, then it seems that you are not free, that you are a mere puppet of external forces, and that your own sense of freedom, your feeling of making a choice out of nowhere is an illusion. Keep in mind that the argument at this point isn't that you can't act against your greatest desire, but that your greatest desire at any given moment has, in some deep sense, little to do with you.

4.21 Wait, you say, perhaps our desires are *influenced* by outside events, our upbringing, our church, family, etcetera, but *I'm* the one who decides how I'll react to those influences. Well, it sure feels that way, doesn't it? Unfortunately, this response just sends us right back to the question we began with: "How do you decide? How do you make your decisions?" It was in trying to answer this question that we were driven to the idea that your desires are outside of your control, that you have no choice over them. So claiming that you decide how to react to outside influences is no help at all; it assumes that we've already made sense of the very thing we're puzzled about, thus committing the error in reasoning that logicians call "begging the question." The very issue before us is trying to figure out how it is possible to make a free decision; the answer cannot simply appeal to having made one.

The digger wasp

The argument we've been examining so far suggests that our desires and actions are in some sense mechanical, the mere outcomes of prior forces. In fact, consider the case of the digger wasp, ***Sphex ichneumoneus***:[8] 4.22

> When the time comes for egg laying, the wasp *Sphex* builds a burrow for the purpose and seeks out a cricket which she stings in such a way as to paralyze but not kill it. She drags the cricket into the burrow, lays her eggs alongside, closes the burrow, then flies away, never to return. In due course the eggs hatch and the wasp grubs feed off the paralyzed cricket, which has not decayed, having been kept in the wasp equivalent of deep freeze. To the human mind, such an elaborately organized and seemingly purposeful routine conveys a convincing flavor of logic and thoughtfulness—until more details are examined. For example, the wasp's routine is to bring the paralyzed cricket to the burrow, leave it on the threshold, go inside to see that all is well, emerge, and drag the cricket in. If the cricket is moved a few inches away while the wasp is inside making her preliminary inspection, the wasp, on emerging from the burrow, will bring the cricket back to the threshold, but not inside, and will then repeat the preparatory procedure of entering the burrow to see if everything is all right. If again the cricket is moved a few inches while the wasp is inside, once again she will move the cricket up to the threshold and re-enter the burrow for a final check. The wasp never thinks of moving the cricket straight in. On one occasion the procedure was repeated forty times, always with the same result. (Dennett, 1984, p. 11)

What makes you any different from the digger wasp? Aren't you the least bit sphexish? You might argue (and probably will!) that we're far more complex than poor *Sphex*, and don't engage in the same repetitive actions that she does. Furthermore, all the wasps behave in the same way with the cricket—it's not just a case of one wasp with obsessive-compulsive disorder. Yet human beings are infinitely variable in their behavior, we don't all do the same thing in the same circumstances. Maybe it is hard to say exactly *why* we're not sphexish, but surely we're not.

Regrettably, this rejection of sphexishness is not that great an argument. 4.23
In the first place, one *can* see common behaviors among humans on large scales. Numerous psychological studies show us that in the same situation, there is a great deal of predictable, similar behavior. In the second place, even if no two individuals behave in precisely the same way in the same

circumstance, this is no proof at all that our actions are free or not determined by natural forces. Consider two **leaves falling** from a tree: no two fall in exactly the same way.[9] However, this hardly means that leaves freely *decide* how to fall—obviously their falling patterns are the result of differences in the wind, subtle variations in the shape of the leaves, and so on, all physical facts that have nothing to do with willing.

4.24 Maybe you can't see yourself falling into sphexish behavior. But perhaps that's because you're just not smart enough. Consider the wasp: she's not smart enough to see the repetition in her behavior and may well have (for all we know) a feeling of freedom, of deliberation and freely choosing to move that cricket. Still not convinced? Imagine a race of extraterrestrials whose ratio of intellect to our own is the same as the ratio of our intellect to that of *Sphex*. They're not just a little bit brighter than we are. Humans are titanically smarter than wasps (most of us, anyway). Imagine the ETs are just that much more intelligent than we are. It is perfectly conceivable that these big-brained ETs could perform little experiments on us, just like we do to *Sphex*. "**Hey Kodos**,[10] come here and check out these humans. Every time I do X, they do Y. Isn't that hilarious? They kill me." In the end we may just be larger, more complicated versions of the digger wasp, big lumbering robots programmed by natural selection for the reproduction of our genes, not smart enough to examine our own source code. Our psychological feelings of freedom are nothing more than a transparent, gauzy overlay on top of the coldly impersonal biological mechanism of ourselves. Perhaps we differ from *Sphex* in degree, but not in kind.

Why There Is No Free Will, Part 3: The Dilemma Argument

4.25 The divine foreknowledge and regress of reasons arguments are in some ways warm-up acts. In contemporary philosophy the main objection to free will is put in terms of a dilemma, one that centers around determinism. With divine foreknowledge, God knows the facts at every point in time, past, present, and future. But the argument does not insist that God creates those facts, or that he has some sort of predestined plan for everyone and we are all marching towards our destinies. Those things could be true, but the foreknowledge problem simply relies on the idea that God surveys—that he can see—what happens at every moment. With the regress of reasons problem we get the sense that our actions are pushed from behind. What we do is the inexorable result of those tilting balances that represent our decision-making. Just like the digger wasp, prior forces ultimately beyond our control determine what we do. It is this idea of earlier events fixing what happens in the future that is the heart of determinism. Let's examine the idea of determinism more directly, as we lead up to the dilemma argument.

The threat of determinism

In 1814, the French mathematician **Pierre-Simon Laplace**[11] published a book entitled ***A Philosophical Essay on Probabilities.***[12] A couple of pages in, Laplace writes: 4.26

> We ought to regard the present state of the universe as the effect of its anterior state and as the cause of the one which is to follow. Given for one instant an intelligence which could comprehend all the forces by which nature is animated and the respective situation of the beings who compose it an intelligence sufficiently vast to submit these data to analysis it would embrace in the same formula the movements of the greatest bodies of the universe and those of the lightest atom; for it, nothing would be uncertain and the future, as the past, would be present to its eyes.

All we need is a snapshot of the universe, one so finely detailed that we could tell the position and momentum of every particle, and we could in principle figure out the entire future history of the universe and everything in it. Well, maybe we couldn't figure it out, but a vast intelligence could—perhaps a future supercomputer with full knowledge of all the forces and laws of nature. What Laplace is defending is the idea of **determinism.**[13] Here's a more precise definition:

> *Determinism*: Given the laws of nature and a set of initial conditions, there is exactly one physically possible future.

This sounds kind of technical, so let's try to break it down with an analogy. Think about shooting a game of pool. When you **break,**[14] what determines where the balls go isn't random, and the balls don't decide for themselves. The 11 ball doesn't think, "Hey, I think I'll bounce off the 2 ball, hit a side rail, rattle around the corner pocket and then bounce out again." So what makes them go where they do? Well, we can list lots of factors:

- where the balls are in the rack
- the velocity of the cue ball
- the spin of the cue ball
- the angle the cue ball hits the racked balls
- the tightness of the rack
- the condition of the table felt

No doubt we could expand this list further. But you get the idea. These factors are the *initial conditions* of the break. When these vary, the balls wind up going in different directions after the break. Good pool players can replicate and control the initial conditions—they hit the cue ball with the same speed, spin, and at the same angle time and again. There's one other key factor that isn't on the list, one that is essential to shooting decent pool: the laws of nature. For example, laws concerning momentum, force, ball and rail elasticity, rolling friction, angle of incidence equaling the angle of reflection, all affect where those balls go. These don't change. However, if you have no clue about how any of these physical laws will affect the motion of pool balls, you aren't going to be a very good player. Thus there are two things that determine where the balls go after the break: the initial conditions of the break, and the laws of nature.

4.27 Determinism is basically the far-reaching global thesis that the entire universe is like a gigantic game of pool. The initial conditions of the universe are the physical facts at the moment of the Big Bang. Those facts, coupled with the laws of physics, determine everything that has happened since. The universe is simply in the process of unfolding, and it is all just forces and little pool balls bouncing off of each other. We ourselves are no more than physical creatures, made up of physical parts, subject to the same laws as anything else in the universe. Our brains too are electrochemical mechanisms and their operation is simply the result of prior states of the universe and the laws of nature.

4.28 The threat that determinism poses to free will is this: determinism states that there is exactly one physically possible future. If you have free will, then you have a choice, you could do either action x or action y. In other words, if you are free, then you somehow decide what the future is going to be like, whether it contains the performance of x or the performance of y instead. If you are free, then the future is open. If determinism is true, then the future is closed; there is only one way things could go. If you perform action x, then that was the only thing that you could have done, no matter how much it felt like you could have done something else. The feeling that you could have done otherwise was no more than an illusion, self-deception of some kind. The view that free will and determinism are in conflict is called "incompatibilism."

Incompatibilism: Either we have no free will or determinism is false.

"C'mon," you say. "What kind of a dope do you think I am? I've heard that modern physics has disproved determinism, that some things just flat-out happen for no reason at all, that they are uncaused and undetermined by what happened before." Good point. It is true that the mainstream interpretation of the equations of quantum physics is that some things happen randomly. This is a truly difficult view to wrap one's mind around, but the idea is *not* that we can't explain or discover what caused certain events, but literally that they have no cause at all. The future could contain event *x*, or it could contain event *y*; either is physically possible. A good example of such an event is radioactive decay. There's even a website at a Swiss physics lab that uses the randomness of the atomic decay of Krypton-85 to generate authentically **random numbers**.[15] Here's a nice passage on randomness from that website:

> Even though we're absolutely certain that if we start out with, say, 100 million atoms of Krypton-85, 10.73 years later we'll have about 50 million, 10.73 years after that 25 million, and so on, there is no way *even in principle* to predict when a given atom of Krypton-85 will decay into Rubidium. We can say that it has a fifty/fifty chance of doing so in the next 10.73 years, but that's *all we can say*. Ever since physicists realised how weird some of the implications of quantum mechanics were, appeals have been made to "hidden variables" to restore some of the sense of order on which classical physics was based. For example, suppose there's a little alarm clock inside the Krypton-85 nucleus which, when it rings, causes the electron to shoot out. Even if we had no way to look at the dial of the clock, it's reassuring to believe it's there—it would mean that even though our measurements show the universe to be, at the most fundamental level, random, that's merely because we can't probe the ultimate innards of the clockwork to expose its hidden deterministic destiny.
>
> But hidden variables aren't the way our universe works—it really *is* random, right down to its gnarly, subatomic roots. In 1964, the physicist John Bell proved a **theorem**[16] which showed hidden variable (little clock in the nucleus) theories inconsistent with the foundations of quantum mechanics. In 1982, Alain Aspect and his colleagues performed an experiment to test

Bell's theoretical result and discovered, to nobody's surprise, that the predictions of quantum theory were correct: the randomness is inherent—not due to limitations in our ability to make measurements.[17] So, given a Krypton-85 nucleus, there is no way whatsoever to predict when it will decay. If we have a large number of them, we can be confident half will decay in 10.73 years; but if we have a single atom, pinned in a laser ion trap, all we can say is that is there's even odds it will decay sometime in the next 10.73 years, but as to precisely when we're fundamentally quantum clueless.

While these facts are enough to undermine the global thesis of determinism stated earlier, they do not imply that every event is random, just that some are. Determinism is the global thesis that *everything* is determined; to reject it we need only show that *some* events are not determined. Nevertheless, even atomic physicists agree that there are still plenty of events whose occurrence is the inexorable outcome of prior forces. Quantum randomness tends to wash out at the macro level. The rolling of those pool balls is still determined by the initial conditions of the break and the laws of nature. In fact, one way to understand ordinary physical and chemical laws is that they just are certain kinds of generalized descriptions of causal regularities; that is, if everything were random there would be no physical laws. So it looks like events are going to fall into one of two groups: those that are random, like the radioactive decay of Krypton-85, and those that are determined. Is any of this enough to save free will? Can quantum randomness somehow provide for our freedom?

Will randomness make us free?

4.29 It's awfully hard to see how it can. If an action is undetermined, if it occurs randomly, then its happening is a matter of chance or luck, and not a free action. The whole idea behind free will, as we have defined it, is that we have a choice in what we do, that we have a sort of volitional control over our thoughts and actions. But random actions aren't under the control of anything. If our actions are the amplified result of some random quantum event, then our actions would be surprising and spontaneous, like **Tourettic outbursts**[18] or **epileptic seizures.**[19] This sense of chance, random action is more indicative of diminishing control, a loss of freedom, than a sign that we are free. We might be unaware of the real causes of our actions in a deterministic world, and thereby still feel free, but how could we even *feel* that our choices were free ones if they are as random as atomic decay?

Perhaps even worse is this apparent consequence: if an event is truly 4.30
random, then it might not have occurred given precisely the same initial conditions and laws of nature. For example, if your reading this chapter is the result of randomness, then when you decided to read it (assuming you still are!) all of your deliberative decision-making and weighing of the pros and cons could have been exactly what they in fact were right up to the moment of choice and yet you did not read it. Such a consequence is truly weird—if decision-making is infected with randomness, it suddenly becomes irrational, arbitrary, and capricious. It no longer looks free. In a nutshell, random action is not the result of anything, and so not the result of free will.

We have now assembled the pieces—determinism, randomness, 4.31
incompatibilism—needed to build what may be the most powerful argument against free will.

The dilemma argument against free will

1.	Either determinism is true, or it is false.	(trivial)
2.	If determinism is true, then you can never choose to perform one action instead of another.	(incompatibilism thesis)
3.	If you can never choose to perform one action instead of another, then you do not have free will.	(from the definition of free will)
4.	Therefore, if determinism is true, no one has free will.	(from 2, 3)
5.	If determinism is false, then some events are random (those not random are determined).	(premise)
6.	If you do something randomly, then it is not the result of choice.	(premise)
7.	Therefore, an action that is random is not the result of free will.	(from 6 and the definition of free will)
8.	Therefore, if determinism is false, there is no free will.	(from 5, 7)
9.	Therefore, there is no free will.	(from 1, 2–4, 5–8)

Either determinism is true, or it is false. If it is true, we have no free will. 4.32
If determinism is false, we have no free will. In short, any way you slice it,

no matter what you think about determinism, we're not free. At this point you might well be thinking, "Oh well. So I don't have free will. It's a bummer, but what am I going to do? Nothing. Just another illusion shattered by reading philosophy." Whoops, maybe that's going too far. But you might be thinking that it's not that big a deal to have no free will. We're not free, but so what?

Free will and moral responsibility

4.33 One big reason that people have cared about free will is its connection to moral responsibility. Suppose you and the supervillain The Pusher are in a 10-story apartment building. It is a beautiful day, and you have opened the window to get some fresh air. You're standing at the window, enjoying the view, when The Pusher comes up behind you and suddenly pushes you out. You plummet to the sidewalk below, and land squarely on a hapless pedestrian, plowing into him at about 27 mph. Fortunately for you, especially considering the day you've had so far, the pedestrian was hugely fat, and cushioned your fall. You get up and walk away unharmed. Unfortunately for the pedestrian, you killed him. Should you be arrested for murder? No? How about manslaughter? Negligent homicide? Something? No doubt you'll complain to the arresting officers that you didn't have any choice in the matter, that you were pushed out of the window, and once gravity had you in its tenacious grip, there was not a thing you could do. True, all true. Oh? You're going to blame The Pusher? Go on, send the cops upstairs. He'll tell them just what you did: he had no choice in the matter, his pushing you was either determined or random, and either way there was not a darn thing he could do about it. The Pusher refers the officers to the dilemma argument above. Really, he's not any more responsible for that poor pedestrian than you are. If you're not responsible because you had no choice in the matter, then neither is The Pusher—and for exactly the same reason.

4.34 See, if you're not free, then there was *never* anything else you could do, no matter *what* you do. Either forces outside of your control determine every action you perform, in which case you never had a choice, or your actions are the result of randomness, in which case you never had a choice. Either way, you were never free to do anything differently; there was nothing you could have done to produce a different outcome. In other words, every single thing you do is exactly like getting shoved out of the window. You're not free to do otherwise than you did. So if you think that prosecuting you for killing that pedestrian is unjust, then prosecuting you for *any* action is unjust. The preceding bit of reasoning presupposes the following principle:

> *The principle of alternate possibilities*: you are morally responsible for an action *x* only if at the time you did *x*, there was alternate possible action *y* that you could have done instead.

This extremely appealing principle was widely accepted until Harry Frankfurt proposed some **counterexamples** to it in 1969.[20] Frankfurt argued that there were cases in which one was intuitively still responsible for an action, even when one's action was completely unavoidable. The basic idea behind his counterexamples is that that of a manipulator waiting in the wings who will guarantee that you do *x*, should you not choose to do *x* on your own.

Here's an example. Suppose that Kathy is deciding whether to poison her 4.35
boss. The mad scientist Dr Zorg can't stand the SOB either, and is fervently hoping that she will. Dr Zorg isn't taking any chances; he's going to make sure that Kathy does the deed. Yet he's subtle in his manipulations, and Kathy has no idea that Dr Zorg even exists. Zorg's plan is to use his newly invented Mind Control Machine. The MCM is a masterpiece of cognitive engineering by which he can not only inspect Kathy's beliefs, thoughts, emotions, and desires, but change the strength of those desires. Dr Zorg can turn the dials on the machine and increase Kathy's desires or lessen them. As she deliberates about whether to poison the boss, Dr Zorg keeps a close eye on the proceedings; he watches her reasoning process and assesses the strength of her desires. While Dr Zorg would prefer that Kathy choose to poison the detested boss on her own, should he detect that her desires to poison just aren't sufficiently strong to overcome her moral compunctions and fear of the law, he will turn the knobs on his Mind Control Machine until the desire to kill overwhelms everything else and Kathy whacks her boss.

There are only two possible futures in this scenario. Future (1): Kathy 4.36
decides to poison the boss, Dr Zorg does nothing, and Kathy poisons the boss. Future (2): Kathy decides *not* to poison the boss, Dr Zorg uses the MCM to give Kathy an overwhelming desire to kill the boss, and Kathy poisons the boss. Let's just assume that Kathy is morally responsible in future (1), where she decided to poison and did so. In ordinary cases of supposedly free action someone decides to do *x*, is not coerced by others,

does *x*, and is responsible for it. That's just what we have in future (1). However, surely Kathy is not responsible in future (2), where she decided against poisoning but was forced to by Dr Zorg. Here is Frankfurt's important discovery: in neither case could Kathy have done otherwise than she actually did. Kathy was going to poison the boss no matter what; there was no possible alternative action that she could have performed instead. Nevertheless, when Kathy decided to poison, and was uncoerced by Dr Zorg, she is, by hypothesis, morally responsible. Therefore the Zorg scenario is a case in which someone is morally responsible for an action, despite the fact that at the time the action was performed there was no alternate possible action that she could have done instead. Thus the principle of alternate possibilities is false. The existence of a possible alternative action to what one actually did is not a requirement for moral responsibility.

4.37 If the principle of alternate possibilities is false, then perhaps the lack of free will does *not* mean that no one is morally responsible for her actions. Of course, even if that principle is false, we still need to explain what's happening in the pushing out of the window case discussed previously. Why should The Pusher be on the hook for pushing you, yet you're not responsible for killing the pedestrian? If the principle of alternate possibilities were true, then neither of you is responsible. Since that principle is apparently false, we are back to square one. Plenty of philosophers have tried to plug this gap, with a variety of different proposed moral principles. (This is how it goes in philosophy: ever more precise and careful principles and definitions are needed to avoid counterexamples.)

4.38 Frankfurt himself suggested that *one is not morally responsible for what one does if one does it only because one could not have done otherwise*. Here's how Frankfurt's revised principle is supposed to work. When Kathy decides not to poison her boss, and Dr Zorg forces her to do so with his Mind Control Machine, she is not morally responsible for her action because she poisoned the boss only because she could not have done otherwise. Dr Zorg made sure that she could not have done otherwise. But when Kathy decides to poison her boss and follows through with the plan, she is morally responsible—Frankfurt's revised principle gets her off the hook only if she poisoned *only because* she could not have done otherwise. The assumption of the Kathy/Dr Zorg case is that if Kathy chooses to poison, then it was a free choice. When she chooses on her own to poison, it wasn't because Dr Zorg coerced her; it was because she hated her boss. It looks like Frankfurt's revised principle gives the right answer in the Kathy/Dr Zorg case.

What about our original case of The Pusher pushing you out of the window? You're not responsible for killing the pedestrian after he pushed you out of the window; the only reason you killed the pedestrian is because you could not have done otherwise than crush the poor sap with your speeding body. But wait—it looks like he's still not responsible for pushing you out of the window. Remember, his act of pushing you was either determined (an inexorable consequence of the pool-balls of the universe that The Pusher could have done nothing to prevent) or random (a spontaneous quantum belch that he could have done nothing to prevent). There's a powerful argument to be made that the only reason The Pusher pushed you was because he could not have done anything else, despite his delusions of free choice. We might add that he also wanted to push you, but The Pusher's wants are also either determined or random and so he only has the wants he does because he could not have done otherwise. Thus it looks like a lack of free will still kills moral responsibility. 4.39

What's more, there are complications with omissions instead of acts. Often we are held morally responsible for failing to take action, not just for taking the wrong actions. For instance, suppose you are a mechanic. You inspect a car and do not fix or even notify the owner that his brakes are about to fail. It seems like you did something morally wrong. On the other hand, suppose you attempt to fix the brakes, and reasonably believe that you have successfully repaired them. However, unknown to you or the Guild of Auto Mechanics the brakes are inherently maldesigned and irreparable. In this case you did the best you could with the brakes, and it is not your fault when they fail. Frankfurt's revised principle only addresses when one is not morally responsible for acts, and says nothing about omissions. Thus some supplementary principle will be needed to address moral responsibility and omissions. Of course, if you have no free will, then when you fail to perform an action, your failure is—like everything else—either determined or random, and your lack of action is unavoidable. 4.40

Subsequent philosophers have proposed all sorts of moral principles with various amendments, codicils, revisions, supplements, and riders designed to escape the problems we have been discussing, but these matters get very complicated very fast, and here we're just sketching the landscape, not hacking through every jungle. Nevertheless everyone agrees that if the dilemma argument against free will is right, there is at least a prima facie case that you are never morally responsible for anything you do. You may feel liberated by this result or frightened by it, but either way you should at least be surprised and a bit disturbed. So now what do we do? 4.41

Agent causation

4.42 One way out of the dilemma argument is to deny premise (5), the assumption that if determinism is false, then some events are random (those not random are determined). People who reject premise (5) defend *agent causation*. The idea of agent causation is that the alternative to determinism isn't randomness at all, but our own free will. How does this proposal escape the evil clutches of the determinist without just assuming the very thing we're trying to prove? That's a good question. The answer is that human beings, in fact any willful agent, can just spontaneously begin a new chain of causation is the world, one that has no causal history prior to the act of willing. As Aristotle wrote, "thus, a staff moves a stone, and is moved by a hand, which is moved by a man" (***Physics***, VIII, 5, 256a, 6–8).[21] Your decision to read this chapter was literally caused by nothing outside of yourself. You decided, chose, as a sort of unmoved mover, and then the reading began. Through our freedom we are in a way outside of the causal order of the world; our choices are undetermined, but not precisely random either. Our choices are free, picked by ourselves as free agents, neither determined by the outside world nor arbitrary happenings.

4.43 Prominent philosophers have defended agent causation, including **George Berkeley**[22] and **Thomas Reid**[23] in the eighteenth century, and **Roderick Chisholm**[24] in the twentieth century. It remains a minority view, however, because it is so difficult to give a really convincing and detailed explanation of how this sort of causation is supposed to work.

4.44 *Objection 1: Mystery* The first problem for agent causation is the mystery objection. You do things for a reason. If you raise your arm, you do so because you wanted to wave hello to a friend, or signal to the waiter, or salute the captain, or lift the comb to your hair, or put on your hat. If someone asked you why you raised your arm and the honest and literal answer was "no reason," one might wonder if you really were in control of your bodily movements. Perhaps you have neurological problems. When we explain the behavior of others, we do so in terms of the reasons they have for acting. Why did the **Grinch steal Christmas**?[25] Answer: he hated the Whos. The fact that the Grinch hated the Whos was the reason he stole Christmas, and moreover that reason is the causal explanation of his stealing Christmas. That is, the reasons you have for acting are generally the causes of action. You wanted to wave hello to a friend, and that was the cause of you raising your arm the way that you did. There is a cause (in terms of a reason) for you raising your hand. Is there a reason you had that reason?

You act for reasons. Either (a) those reasons for acting are due to causes outside of you, or (b) you choose which reasons are important to you and to what degree. If (a), and your reasons for acting are the result of outside causes, then agent causation is obviously wrong. Agent causation supposes that you are the first cause, the originator of causal chains, insulated from the larger world. If we pick (b), and you choose your reasons for acting, then presumably you had reasons for that choice as well, and reasons for *that* choice, and we are off to an infinite regress of reasons for acting, as we saw earlier. You have to have an infinite number of reasons to perform any action, a terribly challenging demand. Yet if you spontaneously create your reasons for acting out of thin air, then it smells suspiciously capricious and arbitrary. Randomness, of course, is not freedom. We're back to the problems we looked at earlier in this chapter—either your reasons for acting are due to causal forces outside of you, you have an infinite chain of reasons for acting to do anything, or your reasons are random and not the exercise of free will. The mystery is how agent causation can escape the earlier arguments against freedom at all. 4.45

Objection 2: Magic Agent causation insists upon a sort of causation that is connected to the rest of the physical world in a most peculiar way. Humans aside, the universe is filled with events that cause other events, which cause other events, in a complex kaleidoscope of interaction. Natural science is tasked with discovering the laws of nature that govern these interactions and so allow us to predict future events. Knowing what we know about electromagnetism we can predict that passing a current through a copper wire wound around a magnet will increase its magnetism. Agent causation insists that human beings stand apart from the web of causation that holds everything else; our actions are free and uncaused. We are only partly outside the causal order of the physical world, however. While our actions are uncaused, we can cause things, we can begin whole new chains of causation with lasting effects outside of ourselves. The universe does not leave its mark upon us, but we can leave our mark upon it. Surely for agent causation our choosing is beyond the reach of science to treat; there can be no psycho-physical laws or rigorous predictions of our behavior. We are magicians, casting spells, with causal powers outside the domain of science. 4.46

If agent causation is committed to the view that human beings have magical abilities, it faces a whole host of hard questions. Does every 4.47

decision-making animal have agent-causal powers? Or are humans special? Is agent causation driven to the controversial view that persons are not completely physical (since we have scientifically indescribable magic powers)? What's the relationship between ordinary event causation and agent causation? If our agent-caused decisions are themselves uncaused, then what's the difference between agent causation and plain old random action? Such troubling questions have made most philosophers leery of agent causation.

Compatibilism

4.48 Without doubt the most prominent response to the dilemma argument is to reject premise (3), namely, if you can never choose to perform one action instead of another, then you do not have free will. "Wait," you say, "Premise three comes straight from the definition of 'free will;' how can anyone deny *that*?" The answer is by rejecting the definition itself. This is the strategy of *compatibilism*. Compatibilists concede that the dilemma argument against free will is sound—the knockout blow against free will. We just don't have any of that sort of freedom. Yet, they say, there is a kind of freedom we *do* have, and this freedom is compatible with determinism. All we need to do, compatibilists argue, is redefine "free will." The kind of free will under attack so far in this essay has traditionally been called libertarian free will. Just to remind you:

> *Libertarian free will*: Your will is free just in case you can choose to perform one action instead of another.

Here's the compatibilist's new and improved definition of "free will":

> *Compatibilist free will*: Your performance of an action is free just in case it is the result of your beliefs, desires, and intentions.

The central idea is behind libertarianism is that you have a choice in what you do. Compatibilists agree with the dilemma argument that you never have a choice in what you do, you're never libertarian free. Nevertheless, they think, there is a plausible and powerful sense in which you're free: you're free as long as you're doing what you want. That's the compatibilist idea. What exactly is doing what you want compatible with? Why, determinism. Suppose all of your desires are the result of forces outside of you, going back to the initial conditions of the universe itself. Given those initial conditions and the laws of nature, you were bound to have the desires and beliefs that you do. However, as long as you are acting on your desires, doing what you want, in accordance with your beliefs, then you are free. When your actions are random or the result of randomness, you are still unfree. If you do something randomly, then your action isn't the result of your beliefs and desires. It is literally the result of nothing. Therefore it's not a free action according to compatibilism.

The compatibilist is quick to note that this idea of freedom fits well with 4.49
our everyday concerns about being free. Why do you want to avoid prison? It's not because you don't have choices, or that at any time you never have a choice between doing an action *x* and an action *y*. Ignoring the dilemma argument for a moment, it seems that you have lots of choices in prison, at every moment: to open your eyes or close them; what to think about; whether to shift your weight to your right foot or your left. No, the reason you don't want to go to prison is because *you can't do what you want* in prison. That's the way in which prison robs you of your freedom. Freedom is acting on your desires, beliefs, and intentions, and prison prevents you from acting in that way.

Objection 1: Too little freedom One objection to compatibilism is that it 4.50
means that the plain ordinary facts about the world imply that we're still not free. Suppose what you want to do right now is lie on a Caribbean beach, deciding whether to have the lobster or the cracked crab for lunch. But you can't act on those desires; you're not in the Caribbean and can't afford either lobster or cracked crab. The unfortunate state of your finances prevents you from acting on your tropical desires and intentions. Since compatibilist freedom is doing what you want, you're still not free. In fact, freedom may be just as impossible under compatibilism as it was under libertarianism. If you desire immortality (or to breathe under water, to fly by flapping your arms, or to have zero mass), then you want the impossible, and you could never be free to act on your desires. Compatibilism was supposed to save free will from the dilemma argument; we gave up on the unobtainable libertarian free will in favor of humble compatibilist freedom. But it looks like compatibilism is no better in securing our freedom than libertarianism was. We're still not free. The challenge for the compatibilist is to explain how a lack of omnipotence does not entail a lack of freedom.

4.51 *Objection 2: Too much freedom* Another objection to compatibilism is that cases where we are intuitively unfree come out as free action under compatibilism. For example, suppose a mugger points a gun at you and demands your money or your life. After due consideration, you hand over your wallet. By giving the mugger your wallet, you acted on your greatest desire, didn't you? Wasn't your desire to give him your money greater than your desire to get killed? Of course it was! Therefore you did what you wanted, you acted on your desires and beliefs, and so according to the compatibilist giving your money to a mugger is a free action. The problem is that compatibilism then looks absurdly inclusive—everything you do is free, no matter what. You're every bit as free in prison as you are on the outside. A nice slogan for a police state, but not too convincing otherwise. A paragraph ago it seemed that we were never compatibilist free, but now it looks like we are inevitably compatibilist free. That doesn't seem to get things right either. The challenge for the compatibilist is to explain coercion in such a way that coerced acts aren't free ones, even though apparently you're always acting on your desires, even at gunpoint.

4.52 Intuitively, sometimes our actions are free ones, and sometimes they are not. If compatibilism is to be an adequate theory of free will, it must be capable of sorting these things out. One way a compatibilist could respond to the *too little freedom* objection is to argue that freedom comes in degrees. It's a mistake to think that we're either free or not free, end of story. We can be partly free and partly unfree, more free and less free. So sure, you're not free to kick back on that Caribbean beach right now. But you might still be free to act on plenty of your other desires—you can get yourself a cup of coffee, keep reading this chapter, take a nap, or whatever other actions are within your power. Notions of political and economic freedom tie nicely into compatibilist free will here: the fewer governmental or fiscal constraints on your behavior, the more free you are to do what you want, which is, of course, the essence of compatibilism.

4.53 What about the *too much freedom* objection? One avenue for the compatibilist is to draw a distinction between those desires that are a part of one's own intrinsic character and those that are the result of manipulation or coercion. If you give your money to a beggar because you are an inherently sympathetic and generous person, then it was a free action. You acted on beliefs, desires, and intentions that were a part of the sort of person that you are, and in that sense they were *your* desires. By acting on your desires, you acted freely. If you give your money to a mugger because he is holding a pistol to your head, then it was not a free action. While you desired to give your money to the mugger (given the unpleasant alternative posed by the gun), that desire did not arise out of the character traits that make you who you are. Instead, the mugger forced the desire on you. It is not a matter of determinism, since compatibilists are happy to admit that your desires may be determined by outside forces no matter what. Your character traits are determined too. However: somebody else does not coerce them, and that's the key difference.

Compatibilists will have to do more fancy footwork than the quick 4.54
sketch of the preceding paragraph, though. Suppose that right now you do not desire a doughnut. Here are two different ways someone could get you to want one: (1) she points a gun at your head and demand that you eat the damn doughnut or else; (2) she waves a box of warm, freshly baked Krispy Kremes under your nose. Obviously, compatibilists will write off the first option as intentionally coerced, forced, and unfree. What about the second? Surely the fiend is amping up your desires for a doughnut when she wafts those sugary delights in front of you. Moreover, she is intending to change your desires; perhaps she hates eating doughnuts alone and she's trying to get you to join her. It doesn't seem right, however, to conclude that in case two your doughnut-eating was unfree and coerced. In case one she is intentionally modifying your desires via gun and in case two she is intentionally modifying your desires via doughnut. In both cases you wind up wanting a doughnut and eating one. Compatibilists have to find a plausible way to distinguish between the two cases if they hope to escape the *too much freedom* objection.

The Feeling of Freedom

If we don't have free will or, at least, if we don't make free choices in the 4.55
libertarian sense, then why are we so convinced that we *are* free? In 1888, Friedrich Nietzsche argued that our belief in free will is the residue of our religious heritage, writing, "men were thought of as 'free' so that they could become *guilty*: consequently every action *had* to be thought of as willed, the origin of every action lying in the **consciousness**."[26] In his view, a religious insistence on moral responsibility led to the invention of free will.

Recent scholarship in neuroscience and experimental psychology sug- 4.56
gests a different answer, namely that our feelings of freedom are more neurological than moral in origin. Our brains organize and interpret our

experience to make a whole, unified human life. They are not mere passive receptors for the data of the senses. The creative work of brains is exposed when there are failures of one kind or another; reading through neurological case studies gives a cornucopia of examples. For example stroke victims who suffer from left side neglect lose the entire left side of the world, for them the very idea of "**leftness**" has lost its meaning.[27] They will shave only one side of their face, not recognizing that there is an entire side unshorn on the left. Such persons won't pick up an object on their left, and draw clocks like half-circles, all while failing to recognize or even sincerely denying that anything is amiss.

4.57 Benjamin Libet and subsequent researchers have explored the **neuroscience of free will.**[28] It turns out there is a difference in the brain between a freely voluntary act, such as you consciously lifting your arm, and involuntary motions, such as your arm jerking up as a result of cerebral palsy, Parkinsonism, Huntington's chorea, Tourette's, etcetera. Voluntary—but not involuntary—actions are preceded by a specific electrical change in the brain called the readiness potential. **Libet** asked test subjects to move their wrist at a time of their own choosing and to note the precise time when they decided to do so.[29] What he discovered is that the reported intention to move one's wrist occurred, on average, 200 milliseconds before the wrist-moving act itself. However, the electroencephalographic measurements of the motor cortex show that the readiness potential ramps up 350 milliseconds before the time of the reported intention. That is, Libet's experiments showed that the readiness potential in the brain increases prior to the subject's awareness of a conscious will to move.

4.58 Libet argued that since the mental beginnings of an act happen before the feeling of willing the act, this proves that voluntary actions are initiated unconsciously, and the conscious mind comes on board after the fact. If Libet is right, his results give potent ammunition to critics of free will. If conscious decision-making is no more than the brain's window-dressing on the foregone conclusion of the unconscious mind, then our "decisions" play no causal role at all. It would be a mistake to even refer to our actions as the result of conscious, free choice.

4.59 In a similar vein, the psychologist **Daniel Wegner** has recently argued that the internal sensation or perception of conscious control over our actions is an illusion.[30] Wegner claims that people experience conscious will when they interpret their own thought as the cause of their action. But, he argues, the feeling of conscious will has a rather loose and tenuous connection to the actual physical mechanisms that cause action. For example, there are cases in which people experience a lack of will over actions they cause. In the nineteenth century fad of séances, people sincerely believed that the tables around which they sat were raised off the floor and moved about by spirits from beyond the grave. In one famous experiment, the scientist Michael Faraday placed force measurement devices between the séance participants' hands and the table. He showed that it was the hands that moved the table, and not the other way round. Of course, such scientific proof failed to convince the participants, who felt most sincerely that they had not moved the table. Science has an uphill fight against sincere feelings. Ouija boards and spirit channeling provide similar examples of people performing actions that their conscious minds do not recognize as their own, as do schizophrenics, who do not interpret their own thoughts as coming from themselves. There are also cases in which people believe themselves to be author of actions and events that they have absolutely nothing to do with, as in the case of certain mental illnesses in which sufferers believe they are the ones who caused events in the remote past, or that their thoughts have faraway effects.

Wegner concludes that such results ought to lessen our confidence that 4.60
our feelings of conscious will or sensations of freedom have very much to do with our actions. Sometimes we do things that we do not think we did, and sometimes we think we did things that we could not have done. Our internal feelings about our abilities aren't very accurate; feeling free proves nothing at all. The mistake we make, according to Wegner, is that we confuse correlation with causation. We're aware of a conscious thought or intention to perform an action, then we observe the action happening, and so we conclude that our conscious thought caused the action to occur. Really, though, it was unconscious mental processes that did all the work—they caused both the conscious intentions and the action. The inferred connection between consciousness and action is the superfluous step.

Conclusion

When amputees have **phantom limbs** they continue to feel sensations in 4.61

their missing limbs, feeling pain in a hand that plainly doesn't exist, or a cramp in a missing foot.[31] The feelings are certainly real, and in some cases phantom pain has driven amputees nearly to suicide. Nevertheless, a missing hand just *can't* hurt; there's nothing there *to* hurt. Even though there is no longer a limb, the sufferer's brain continues to map an intact body, stubbornly refusing to update some important data. It may be that free will is, like an itch in a nonexistent hand, a persistent and troubling illusion that our brains have built for us. Like the amputee who feels the phantom limb long after knowing that there is no limb there at all, we may well continue to feel free despite the most persuasive arguments to the contrary.

Annotated Bibliography

Dennett, Daniel (1984) *Elbow Room: The Varieties of Free Will Worth Wanting* (Cambridge, MA: MIT Press). The first of Dennett's fine books on free will, in which he defends compatibilism and discusses the digger wasp.

d'Holbach, Paul Heinrich Dietrich (1770) *System of Nature*, full text available at www.gutenberg.org/ebooks/8909, accessed May 15, 2012. Baron d'Holbach's materialist treatise. In Chapter 9 of Book 1, he defends determinism and argues that there is no free will as a result.

Edwards, Jonathan (1754) *A careful and strict enquiry into the modern prevailing notions of that freedom of will which is supposed to be essential to moral agency, vertue and vice, reward and punishment, praise and blame*, full text available at www.earlymoderntexts.com/pdf/edwafree.pdf. Edwards argues against libertarianism by providing the decision-making problem and regress argument.

Hobbes, Thomas (1656) *The questions concerning liberty, necessity, and chance: clearly stated and debated between Dr. Bramhall, Bishop of Derry, and Thomas Hobbes of Malmesbury*, full text available at http://archive.org/details/englishworkstho00hobbgoog, accessed May 15, 2012. Hobbes's famous debate with Bramhall over free will, with Hobbes providing an early statement of compatibilism. Perhaps the opening salvos in the modern debate over free will.

Hume, David (1748) *An Enquiry Concerning Human Understanding*, full text available at www.earlymoderntexts.com/pdfbits/he2.pdf, accessed May 15, 2012. In Chapter 8, Hume gives his best-known, and most accessible, account of free will. His defense of compatibilism was the gold standard for two centuries.

Kane, Robert (ed.) (2002) *Free Will* (Oxford: Wiley-Blackwell). A fine collection of influential essays on free will, primarily from the twentieth century.

Libet, Benjamin (2004) *Mind Time: The Temporal Factor in Consciousness* (Cambridge, MA: Harvard University Press). Libet's summary of his experiments concerning the subconscious causes of supposedly volitional actions.

Manson, Neil (forthcoming) *This is Philosophy of Religion: An Introduction* (Oxford: Wiley-Blackwell). Contains a more in-depth discussion of the divine foreknowledge problem.

Ramachandran, V. S. and Sandra Blakeslee (1998) *Phantoms in the Brain* (New York: William Morrow). A book on popular neuroscience, with fascinating case studies, including a fine discussion of the neurology of phantom limbs.

Reid, Thomas (1788) *Essays on the Active Powers of Man*, full text available at www.earlymoderntexts.com/reac.html. In Chapter 4, Reid rejects compatibilism and presents his classic defense of agent causation.

Wegner, Daniel M. (2002) *The Illusion of Conscious Will.* Cambridge, MA: MIT Press. Skepticism about free will on the basis of contemporary cognitive science.

Online Resources

1 A discussion of positive and negative liberty in the context of political philosophy: http://plato.stanford.edu/entries/liberty-positive-negative/
2 A discussion of the film *Terminator 2*, which explores issues of free will, and is the source for the line "the future is not set; there is no fate but what you make for yourself": http://en.wikipedia.org/wiki/Terminator_2
3 The passage in Boswell's *Life of Johnson* in which Johnson is quoted as saying "all theory is against the freedom of the will; all experience is for it": http://books.google.co.uk/books?id=TmShu9cK3IUC&pg=RA1-PA169&dq=All+theory+is+against+freedom+of+the+will+all+experience+is+for+it+boswell&hl=en&ei=DTTVTdTrBIzqgQfTusj_Cw&sa=X&oi=book_result&ct=result&redir_esc=y#v=onepage&q=All%20theory%20is%20against%20freedom%20of%20the%20will%20all%20experience%20is%20for%20it%20boswell&f=false
4 Aristotle's book *On Interpretation*. In part 9 he discusses statements about the future and gives his sea-battle example: http://classics.mit.edu/Aristotle/interpretation.1.1.html
5 A discussion of the life and works of Aristotle, arguably the greatest thinker in human history: http://plato.stanford.edu/entries/aristotle/
6 A sophisticated overview of nonclassical logics, including those that allow propositions with no truth values: http://plato.stanford.edu/entries/logic-manyvalued/
7 Quotations from *Animal House*, including Dean Wormer's observation that Bluto Blutarsky's grade point average was 0.0: www.imdb.com/title/tt0077975/quotes?qt=qt0479924
8 Video of a great golden digger wasp burying a paralyzed cricket: www.youtube.com/watch?v=5t2p4ukzL74

9 Some thoughts on the freedom of falling leaves, from the writer Ambrose Bierce: http://thinkexist.com/quotation/decide-v-i-to_succumb_to_the_preponderance_of_one/288637.html

10 Kang and Kodos, the irrepressible space aliens from *The Simpsons*: http://en.wikipedia.org/wiki/Kang_and_Kodos

11 A biography of Pierre Simon Laplace, a great and inventive mathematician. As a human being, though, "That Laplace was vain and selfish is not denied by his warmest admirers; his conduct to the benefactors of his youth and his political friends was ungrateful and contemptible; while his appropriation of the results of those who were comparatively unknown seems to be well established and is absolutely indefensible.": www.maths.tcd.ie/pub/HistMath/People/Laplace/RouseBall/RB_Laplace.html

12 The full text of Laplace's *A philosophical essay on probabilities*: http://archive.org/details/philosophicaless00lapliala

13 A detailed discussion of determinism, especially as it is understood in the philosophy of science: http://plato.stanford.edu/entries/determinism-causal/

14 A pool break: www.youtube.com/watch?v=_S8FhWNBkHM

15 A Swiss physics lab that provides genuinely random numbers, generated by atomic decay: www.fourmilab.ch/hotbits/how.html

16 A sophisticated discussion of John Bell's theorem regarding hidden variables in quantum mechanics: http://plato.stanford.edu/entries/bell-theorem/

17 A biography of Alain Aspect, a physicist who provided an experimental confirmation of Bell's Theorem: http://en.wikipedia.org/wiki/Alain_Aspect

18 Surprisingly funny montage of a man with Tourette's Syndrome: www.youtube.com/watch?v=rqtr_RvR3sY

19 Video of a grand mal epileptic seizure: www.youtube.com/watch?v=MRZY2a2jnuw

20 Harry Frankfurt's article "Alternate Possibilities and Moral Responsibility": http://hamishpat.com/Courses/99631/631-article-frankfurt-alternate-possibilities.pdf

21 Book 8 of Aristotle's *Physics*, where he discusses motion, causes, and agent causation: http://classics.mit.edu/Aristotle/physics.8.viii.html

22 The life and works of George Berkeley, Bishop of Cloyne, one of the great philosophers of the early modern period: http://plato.stanford.edu/entries/berkeley/

23 A discussion of the thought of Thomas Reid, one of the seminal figures in the Scottish Enlightenment: http://plato.stanford.edu/entries/reid/

24 The life and works of the greatest epistemologist of the twentieth century, Roderick Chisholm: http://plato.stanford.edu/entries/chisholm/

25 The Internet Movie Database entry on *How the Grinch Stole Christmas*, along with some clips: www.imdb.com/title/tt0060345/

26 *Twilight of the Idols*, "Four Great Errors," §7. The full text of Friedrich Nietzsche's book *Twilight of the Idols, or, How to Philosophize with a Hammer*: www.lexido.com/EBOOK_TEXTS/TWILIGHT_OF_THE_IDOLS_.aspx?S=7

27 A video study of a patient suffering from left side neglect: www.youtube.com/watch?v=ymKvS0XsM4w

28 A discussion of Benjamin Libet, a pioneer on the neuroscience of free will: http://en.wikipedia.org/wiki/Benjamin_Libet

29 Video of Libet's free will experiments: www.youtube.com/watch?v=IQ4nwTTmcgs

30 A discussion of psychologist Daniel Wegner, who argues that free will is a cognitive illusion: http://en.wikipedia.org/wiki/Daniel_Wegner

31 An explanation of phantom limbs, and how some neuroscientists address the problem of phantom limb pain: www.youramazingbrain.org/brainchanges/phantomlimbs.htm

5

SELF

In this chapter we'll look at the philosophical issue of what makes you *you*, what philosophers call the problem of personal identity. Who are you exactly? *What* are you? Imagine your own corpse, lying on a slab in the (hopefully) distant future. Your body is lying there, but you are gone. What's missing, and what happened to it? One way to begin to get a handle on these questions is to consider the problem of difference. 5.1

The Problem of Difference and the Problem of Sameness

The problem of difference

You have a lot in common with your friends and other people of your own age and cultural background. You're about the same size as your peers. You speak the same language, have similar musical tastes, fashion sense, food preferences, religious views, and have the same general background knowledge of the world—knowledge of sports, politics, history, and pop culture. If you're reading this sentence in English you probably don't wear a loincloth, eat grubworms, **play buzkashi**,[1] or listen to **Indonesian gamelan**.[2] But you do speak English, own a pair of blue jeans, know who Shania Twain is, can ride a bicycle, and have eaten a hamburger. You're probably religious and, if you are, you're a monotheist. Nevertheless you're a different person than your friends. There are things about you that make you different. 5.2

So what makes you different? You might quickly come up with a laundry list—you listen to Sufjan Stevens, not Metallica. You play soccer, not field 5.3

This Is Philosophy: An Introduction, First Edition. Steven D. Hales.

hockey. You watch Celebrity Apprentice, not House. You grew up in one part of town and not another. You're good at math and your best friend isn't. No one else has exactly your physical appearance—height, weight, hair, and distribution of freckles. It's those qualities, skills, preferences, and beliefs that make you the person that you are. Different people have different traits. The problem of difference is easy to answer, right? Yes it is. The real challenge is how to give a plausible answer while also solving the following conundrum, the problem of sameness. What makes this pair of puzzles especially tricky is that any solution to the first problem seems to preclude a solution to the second problem and vice versa.

The problem of sameness

5.4 One of the things you believe is that you were once a baby. Your parents showed you pictures of a baby and said it was you, which you accepted without question, despite the fact that you look nothing like a baby. And all your biology teachers taught you that every organism grows from some smaller form, be it egg, seed, or spore. So the person you are today grew out of that baby of however long ago. Of course, you are not a baby *now*, but supposedly you were once a baby. The question is *what makes you the same person as that baby of 20 (or whatever) years ago?* To say that you are the same person is to claim that:

> you right now = some particular baby 20 years ago.

The claim is not that you resemble such a baby, but in fact that you are *identical* to the baby of two decades ago. That baby is *you*. But why on earth should we think that you are identical to a baby of long ago? You have virtually nothing in common with such a baby: you don't look alike (except vaguely), aren't the same height or weight, don't have the same abilities, interests or thoughts, don't have the same tastes, friends, or knowledge. In fact, you have almost nothing in common; you have much more in common with your friends. The things you have in common with that baby tend to be very general characteristics, such as vague similarities of personality or appearance. More generally, the problem of sameness is how we can account for remaining the same person despite change.

5.5 The solution to the problem of difference was to list the fine-grained distinctions between you and your friends. A lot of small dissimilarities served to set you apart from others who are more or less like you. In the seventeenth century, the German philosopher **Gottfried Leibniz** argued that two objects that had all the same properties in common were identical; they were really just one object.[3] He called this principle the identity of **indiscernibles.**[4] A corollary of Leibniz's idea is the principle of the non-identity of discernibles. When two objects have different properties (they are discernible), then they really are two different things. For our purposes, let's put the principle like this:

> *Principle of the non-identity of discernibles*: Small differences between person A and person B prove that A and B are not identical.

Hold on, though. There are enormous differences between you and the baby of long ago that is also supposed to be you. Suppose person A is you right now, and person B is some particular baby 20 years ago. You are so vastly unlike that baby that according to the principle of the non-identity of discernibles it couldn't be the same person as you. The overall problem can be put as a dilemma. First horn of the dilemma: Let's assume that small differences prove non-identity. A great solution to the problem of difference, but a terrible solution to the problem of sameness. Second horn of the dilemma: Let's assume that minor similarities prove identity. A fine answer to the problem of sameness, but a horrible answer to the problem of difference.

The mystery of personal identity is figuring out how we can solve both 5.6
the problem of difference and the problem of sameness at once.

Preliminary Positions

A natural thought is to look for some property that (1) doesn't change, (2) 5.7
only you have, and (3) you have from birth until death. *That's* the thing that makes you who you are. Such a trait would solve the problem of difference (because you uniquely have this quality) and the problem of sameness (because you've always had this quality) in one fell swoop.

The luz bone

In the Jewish **Midrash** (*Kohelet* folio 114, 3)[5] there is the legend of the **luz** 5.8
bone.[6] According to this legend, the Roman emperor Hadrian once asked Rabbi Joshua ben Chanania,

> "From what shall the human frame be reconstructed when it rises again?"
>
> "From Luz in the backbone," was the answer.
>
> "Prove this to me," said Hadrian. Then the Rabbi took Luz, a small bone of the spine, and immersed it in water, but it was not softened; he put it into the fire, but it was not consumed; he put it into a mill, but it could not be pounded; he placed it upon an anvil and struck it with a hammer, but the anvil split and the hammer was broken.

The luz bone was supposed to be an unchanging, immutable thing that made each person who they were. It was the kernel ("luz" is also Aramaic for "almond") for the resurrection of the body; the rest of a person could be built out of and around the luz bone.

Fingerprints

5.9 Would anything count as the modern equivalent of the luz bone? Here's a thought: fingerprints. Fingerprints are apparently unique to each person; even identical twins don't have the same fingerprints. Moreover, they are widely reported to be unchanging over time. You're different from others because no one else has your fingerprints, and you're the same since birth since, despite massive change in other ways, your fingerprints are the same. Problem solved!

5.10 Well, not so fast. Let's grant for the sake of argument that fingerprints are unique to each person. While it is frequently asserted that fingerprints never change, that claim is false. They do change. For one thing, an infant's finger is a fraction of the size of an adult's. Your present fingerprints have a much larger area than those of any baby, and therefore can't be the same as the fingerprints you had as a child. Moreover, fingers may become scarred or even amputated. The loss of your fingerprints does not mean the loss of you; if you were to lose your fingers in battle, that is not your death sentence. *You* could survive the loss. Yet if we were to insist that your personal identity is bound up with your fingerprints, then without a fingerprint whomever is left just wouldn't be you.

5.11 The deeper point is that something as arbitrary and meaningless as fingerprints has nothing to do with the person that you are. It is a bit silly to say "I know who I am and what it is to be me. I'm the person with these little ridges and patterns in my skin!" Whatever is the right explanation of personal identity, it needs to have a real connection with being a unique, living, thinking being, and not just some random property that's along for the ride.

DNA

One idea that might naturally occur to you is DNA. DNA is the large molecule that encodes the blueprints for building every living organism. What makes you different from your friends and neighbors? Each of you has a distinct genetic blueprint. What makes you the same over time despite change? The information in your DNA—the recipe of you—stays the same. The DNA proposal is looking pretty good. Furthermore, unlike fingerprints, DNA really does have something to do with you. It is one of the essential keys to understanding life, explains individual differentiation, and is the source of heritable traits. If your DNA were different your personality, abilities, and appearance would not be the same as they are now. 5.12

Unfortunately, DNA won't work as an account of personal identity because it does not ensure uniqueness. Identical twins have the same DNA, as do clones (cloning is essentially delayed twinning). Identical twins have the very same DNA but are not the very same person, since, of course, there are two of them. Therefore there must be some further fact that explains what makes them different people. Identity of DNA is not sufficient for personal identity; while better than the fingerprint idea, DNA does not solve the problem of difference. 5.13

The Soul Criterion

One very common way that people attempt to say what makes them who they are is to refer to a soul, *their* soul. Before we can begin to evaluate the idea of a soul as a serious proposal for solving the problems of personal identity, we must first try to get some sense of what a soul is. Often "soul" is used metaphorically, or as an adjective. So James Brown is the Godfather of Soul, someone uncommonly mature may be said to have an "old soul," collard greens are soul food, and ideal lovers are soulmates. None of these uses are the slightest help when it comes to personal identity. However, there are four distinct senses of "soul" with legitimate historical lineage that may be of help. 5.14

Conceptions of the soul

Soul$_1$: soul = mind There is a long-standing tradition, stemming from **Plato**,[7] in which "soul" simply means "mind." Plato himself, it must be 5.15

noted, conflated different uses of "soul." For him it was on the one hand the rational part of the mind, but also the body's animating force, and still further something immortal, three distinct ideas of the nature of souls. Nowadays people sometimes equate their soul with their personality, or use "soul" to refer to the ethical faculty of the mind. Thus a conscienceless psychopath might be called "soulless." But if "soul" is just an old-fashioned or confusing name for "mind," then the soul criterion is really just the proposal that your identity through time is to be explained by your psychology—your thoughts, beliefs, emotions, and perceptions. The view that psychology is the key to personal identity is an important and venerable approach to the problem and will be discussed later. Thus the view that soul = mind doesn't provide an *alternative* theory of personal identity; it just is a cumbersome way to state the psychological criterion of the self.

5.16 *Soul$_2$: soul = ghost* Perhaps when you think of souls you think of the Hollywood portrayal of **ghosts**.[8] The most striking feature of movie ghosts is that they are physical entities. They have location, are visible, have shapes, move objects, make noises, and even wear ghost clothes (a truly puzzling feature if you think about it), all physical properties. Movie ghosts are just a physical part of nature, and if they exist they'll get a scientific explanation like the rest of the natural world. In other words, if a soul is a movie-style ghost, and souls are the thing that explains personal identity, then you are a physical, material object. There is a respectable physicalist answer to the problem of personal identity that will be discussed later in this chapter. But if we are going to go physicalist, there is no good reason to drag in bizarre hypothetical entities like movie ghosts. Like the previous sense of soul, the view that souls = ghosts doesn't provide a different theory of personal identity; it just is a confusing way to state the physicalist criterion of the self.

5.17 *Soul$_3$: soul = vitalist force* Somewhat more promising is the notion of a soul as the *élan vital*, the animating spark of life. According to the traditional view of **vitalism**,[9] the mechanistic principles that describe the motion and forces of nonliving objects cannot explain the behavior and actions of living organisms. Living things are supposed to possess some vital force that nonliving things do not, analogous to idea that some metals are magnetic and others are not. In death the vital force dissipates or leaves the body, which then returns to the status of a mere inanimate object.

Vitalism was an active theory of scientific investigation into the nineteenth century. The vitalist view was that there is a fundamental difference between organic matter and inorganic matter. Because of this essential difference, vitalists hypothesized that chemists would never be able to synthesize organic materials from inorganic ones. In a landmark scientific experiment in 1828, **Friedrich Wöhler** successfully created urea, a compound in organic urine, from inorganic components.[10] He famously wrote that his experiment had demonstrated "the great tragedy of science, the slaying of a beautiful hypothesis [in this case vitalist chemistry] by an ugly fact." While the nomenclature of inorganic vs. organic chemistry persists into the present day, Wöhler showed that there is no scientific difference between the two. Wöhler's experiment, along with cell theory and evolutionary theory, largely killed off vitalism by showing how living functions can be explained mechanistically. By the early twentieth century vitalism was in full retreat, and since the discovery of DNA it has been regulated to the dustbin of discredited ideas. 5.18

Soul$_4$: soul = supernatural stuff Probably when you think of souls, you think of a religious conception of souls. The ***Catechism of the Catholic Church***, for example, states that persons are composed of a body and a soul, and that the soul is a supernatural immortal entity (pt I, sec. 2, ch. 1, art. 1, para. 6, II).[11] In traditional **Hinduism**, the soul is *atman*—the breath of life—an incorporeal, eternal, unchanging inner self.[12] Suppose, then, that a soul is like what the Hindus or Catholics think it is—something non-physical, incorporeal, immortal, and unchanging. Such a view is a genuine alternative to psychological and physical solutions to personal identity; supernatural souls aren't minds, or movie ghosts, or vitalist forces. The proposal that the nature of you is best explained by a supernatural soul does face problems, though. Here are some objections to the supernatural soul criterion. 5.19

Objections to the supernatural soul criterion

Objection 1: Definition According to the view just outlined, souls are supposed to have all sorts of wonderful qualities. They are supposed to be immortal, incorruptible, and make you who you are. Well, that sounds nice, but what exactly is this thing with all those great features? It's not your body; in fact it's not physical at all. It's not your mind, your personality, or 5.20

your conscience. It's not what makes you alive. So what the heck is it? And what does it do for you? Without some story about what souls are, it sounds like "soul" is just a word for a bunch of fanciful properties collected together.

5.21 One might address the identification objection by simply claiming that a soul is whatever has those characteristics. All we need to do is find some entity that is unchanging, eternal, immaterial, and somehow uniquely related to you. Then we'll declare that we've located your soul. That's not an unreasonable approach, but it does give rise to the next objection to the soul criterion, namely the problem of providing any evidence to believe in this marvelous thing.

5.22 *Objection 2: Evidence* Suppose your friend Keesha tells you that she's got something with the body of a lion and the head and wings of a eagle. Sounds pretty cool, you might reply. What is it? She tells you it's a **gryphon**.[13] You ask if you can come see it. Well, no, she's forced to answer. No one's ever actually seen one, there is no presence of them in the fossil record, there are no transitional forms that would predict gryphons, and eagles and lions are not just different unmateable species, but are in widely separated taxonomic phyla.

5.23 You figure that Keesha must mean that she has a mental image of a gryphon. That is, she has a gryphon all right, but it's in her head, like an idea or a concept. No, not at all, Keesha replies. There are real gryphons, and not just in her mind. You might well scratch your head at this point and ask her why she believes that there are gryphons in extra-mental reality.

5.24 Easy! she tells you. Look at the rich history of people who have talked about gryphons, written about them, and painted them. There are frescos of gryphons in the Bronze Age Palace of Knossos in Crete, they appear throughout classical Greek art, they show up in the art of fifth-century BCE central Asia, were written about by medieval Irish scholars, and appear in medieval heraldry. Even Dante referred to them in *The Divine Comedy*. Sure, gryphons are elusive and shy. No doubt if we were to capture and study a gryphon we would be forced to rewrite zoology and maybe even evolutionary biology. But the alternative is to declare that all those thousands of people who wrote about, drew, and believed in the existence of gryphons were just plain wrong.

5.25 Yet surely that's just what we do and should say. Gryphons are fabulous, mythological beasts from legends in the deeps of time. But they're not paid-up members of reality. There is no evidence of their existence, evidence we would expect to find were they real; their existence does not fit in with the best scientific understanding of the world; and there are no reasons apart from a misguided appeal to tradition to posit their existence.

The question before us is this one: why should we think souls are any more real than gryphons? We needn't insist that evidence for souls has to be physical or scientific evidence. By hypothesis we're supposing that souls are some kind of supernatural entity, and as such are beyond the reach of science. However, we're going to need *something*. It's true that many people feel horror at the thought that there is nothing after their deaths, just non-existence and the peace of the grave. So they may choose to believe that they have an eternal soul that will survive the death of the body. Yet that's just wishful thinking, not an argument. 5.26

Put another way, what phenomenon will positing souls explain? Most psychologists believe that there is a genetic basis for primary schizophrenia, even though they don't know what those genes might be. They think that schizophrenia is a heritable characteristic because of **twin studies**.[14] If one identical twin has schizophrenia, then their twin is very likely to have it too, even if the twins are raised in different families. That's not true for fraternal twins, though, which indicates that it's genes, not environment, that's behind schizophrenia. So positing a yet undiscovered genetic basis for schizophrenia explains the twin studies results. What does positing an undiscovered soul explain? It does no good to insist that it explains personal identity (tempting though it is), since, going back to Objection 1, we have no account of what souls are. Q: What is the answer to the problem of personal identity? A: Souls! Q: What are souls? A: They are whatever solves the problem of personal identity. Such reasoning is circular and unhelpful. 5.27

Objection 3: Identification Are you your soul? That is, are you identical to your soul, so that you = some particular soul? There are only two answers: yes and no. 5.28

If no: If your soul is not you, then what is its relationship to you? Two possibilities come immediately to mind. One is that your soul is solely part of you (no pun intended). This seems to be the Catholic view, according to which persons are made of two parts: body and soul. Another idea is that your soul is a possession of yours, the sort of thing that you might sell, trade, lease, or lend. The concept of soul-as-possession is a common one in popular culture; for example, **Homer Simpson** once sold his soul to the Devil for a doughnut.[15] However, if your soul is a part of you or a 5.29

possession or yours, its reputed immortality doesn't provide for *your* survival. If you are an organ donor, then many of your parts might survive your death. Your eyes, heart, and liver may go on—but your body won't. Your body is dead and dismembered. Likewise your possessions might survive your death. That's not really something you can personally look forward to, though, since you'll be dead. If you are not your soul, it's rather hard to see why you would care what happens to it after you die. Analogously, maybe you care about what happens to your corneas or stereo after your death, but you probably don't care all that much.

5.30 Thus if you're not identical to a soul, and your soul is just a part or possession or yours, then we still don't have a solution to the personal identity problem. We want to know what *you* are, not what one of your parts is, or about the things you own.

5.31 *If yes*: How do you recognize people that you know? How do you recognize your friends, parents, professors? The answer seems obvious: you identify them by how they look, how they act, what they say and do. You can recognize someone by their voice over the phone, or at a distance by the way they walk or the clothes they wear. In sum, you recognize others by observing (seeing, hearing, etc.) their physical properties (appearance, behavior, etc.). Now, we are presently supposing that persons are souls. You are a soul, your friends are souls. Souls aren't physical, though, they are supernatural, incorporeal sorts of things. So how can you recognize your own friends? Here's an argument.

1. Suppose that your friend Juan is identical to his soul. Juan is a soul.
2. Souls have no physical properties.
3. The only way to recognize someone is by observing his or her physical properties.

It looks like the next step is to swiftly conclude that you can't possibly recognize Juan or anyone else. But maybe we can hold that off for a moment. We might suppose that there is some kind of correlation between physical properties and souls. Maybe souls are attached to bodies in some kind of way, or they have something to do with how you act and what you say. Let's assume:

4. If someone has the same physical properties as the last time you saw them, then the same soul is present as well. Let's abbreviate this as *same body, same soul.*
5. Therefore you can recognize Juan.

The problem with this argument is there is no reason at all to believe (4). It's just guesswork. Here's an analogy. Suppose that a friend gives you a box of chocolates. They are the kind of chocolates with different fillings—raspberry, caramel, nuts, cherry, coconut, etcetera. There's no kind of key on the box as to what is what. But caramel is your favorite. Without piggishly eating the entire box, how can you pick out the candy with the caramel filling? Well, you might respond that you've eaten a lot of chocolates in the past, and you've come to realize that the outside of each chocolate indicates with what's inside. The round dark chocolate ones have a cherry inside, the rectangular wrinkly ones have nuts, and the square ones with a swirl on top have caramel. So you pick out one of those to eat.

Notice that your principle for identifying caramel chocolates was this: 5.32
same outside, same inside. You had evidence for this principle, namely your vast chocolate-eating experience. You've bitten into a lot of chocolates in the past, and square ones with a swirl always had caramel inside. To be sure, there's no guarantee that the same outside, same inside principle will always work, but you do have genuine evidence for it, inductive reasons based on past experience.

Here's the point. In the case of souls, the assumption in premise (4) 5.33
above is just the same outside, same inside principle again. You see someone's physical properties (the outside) and infer the presence of the same soul (the inside). The problem is that, unlike the chocolate case, there is no way to give evidence for thinking that this correlation holds. With the chocolates you've bitten into loads of them in the past and have had direct experience of what's inside. But there's no way to bite into someone and sample his or her soul. Basically you have no way to recognize or identify your own friends (assuming they are souls). You can tell yourself that the same body, same soul principle is true, but there is no reason to believe it. Even more, it doesn't look like we could even *get* a reason to believe it. Yet surely we do recognize our own friends and family. The implication is that therefore they cannot be souls.

To sum up the identification problem, if persons are not identical to 5.34
souls (souls are a part or possession), then souls are no help in solving the problem of personal identity and explaining what it is to be a person over time. If persons are identical to souls, then we have no way to show that their physical characteristics are related to their souls in any way. As a result, it is not possible to recognize or reidentify other people, since we do so on the basis of physical characteristics. But since we *do* recognize other people, it follows that they are not identical to souls.

5.35 Are there souls? The question has no straightforward answer because it is ambiguous. Are there souls in the sense of minds? The answer is clearly yes: there are souls, since there are minds. However, if souls are just minds, then the soul criterion is no more than a disguised version of a psychological view, which will be discussed later. It is not an independent solution to the personal identity problem. Are there movie ghost-type souls? Probably not. But since movie ghosts are physical, it is an empirical question to be answered by science. Yet if there really are movie-style ghosts, then the soul criterion is just a roundabout way of giving a physicalist solution to personal identity, a solution that will be discussed two paragraphs from now. Are there souls in the sense of vitalist forces? Definitely not: vitalism is firmly discredited and recognized as no more than a blind alley in the history of ideas. Are there supernatural souls? A satisfactory answer to that question is well beyond the present book, although it is worth noting that the hypothesis of supernatural souls does face the challenges of explaining what they are and coming up with evidence to believe in them. Even if there are supernatural souls, though, their existence does not seem to help with the puzzle of personal identity because of the identification problem discussed above.

5.36 Let's see if changing tactics completely leaves us any better off. Instead of you being some supernatural soul, maybe you're no more than a physical, material object.

The Physicalist Criterion

5.37 An initially attractive feature of the physicalist view is that we don't have to suppose that in addition to the physical world we see around us every day that there is also a hidden and secret realm of supernatural substances. We're just like everything else in the universe: concrete physical objects, made up of smaller parts, and held together by natural forces. We're each members of *Homo sapiens*, a primate species noted for large brains and unusual intelligence. We're animals—human animals—made out of flesh and blood and bone. The facts about us are like the facts about any other creature and are to be figured out by the scientific method. Human beings may be special, but we're not so unique that we're not even members of the natural world.

5.38 There may be philosophical mysteries about our identity, but problems of identity aren't restricted to persons. Ordinary material things change over time, just as we do—they gain parts, lose parts, change shape and size.

What makes them the very same object despite all these changes? A famous puzzle from antiquity concerns the ship of the Greek hero **Theseus.**[16] After Theseus slew the Minotaur and performed other feats of derring-do, the Athenians preserved his ship, as a memorial to Theseus and also as a general tourist attraction. Over time, various repairs had to be made to the ship; boards were replaced and freshly pitched, new pegs hammered in, new ropes and sails rigged, and so on. After a while, there were so many replacement parts and renovations that people started asking whether it was really Theseus's ship. That is, they wondered whether it really was the *same* ship that carried Theseus on his adventures.

Like the ship of Theseus, you lose parts; you lose your hair, pare your 5.39
fingernails, lose baby teeth, and may suffer more serious losses too. You also gain parts; you may gain weight, grow adult teeth, let your hair grow long, and so on. Sometimes the gains and losses can be seen as replacements. Your cells die off and are replaced with new ones, you may get a new heart or kidney in an organ transplant. The physicalist answer to the problem of difference is straightforward: you are a material object that at any moment in time occupies some portion of space. No one else is the same material thing and is in the same location as you at the same time. We need an answer to the problem of sameness, to be sure, but whatever that answer is, it will be in terms of you being a live human organism.

Abigail—the case of ordinary aging

Let's imagine Abigail, a person, who, like all of us, changes dramatically 5.40
over time. According to the physicalist criterion, Abigail is a living material entity, a particular human animal. Figure 5.1 is a graphic depicting her physical changes over time.

The question at hand is the problem of difference: what makes Grandma 5.41
Abigail the very same person as Toddler Abby? The key to the physicalist answer is to realize that Grandma Abigail, Mother Abigail, College Abby, and Little Abby are all related to each other in a very important way. In fact, they are connected to each other in a way unlike how they are related to anyone or anything else in the world. Each successive Abigail is the *closest physical continuer* to the previous one.

Closest physical continuer relation

Let's unpack the idea of being a closest physical continuer. There are two 5.42
components to this idea:

Figure 5.1 Abigail through time

1. *Causation.* The later editions of Abigail were caused by the earlier versions. College Abby is in some sense the causal result of Little Abby; the biological processes of Little Abby produced College Abby.

There's more to the idea of being a closest physical continuer than just the notion of being a causal successor, though. There's a clear sense in which Abby is her parents' causal successor. Baby Abby was the causal result of too many margaritas and the capacious backseat of an Oldsmobile. Moreover, Abby is her parents' successor in that she is their legal heir and perpetuates her parents' genes. However, Abigail is obviously not the same person as her parents. So we also need:

2. *Similarity.* Not only did the physical processes and mechanisms of Little Abby produce, create, and cause College Abby to come into existence (not in the same way that various physical processes of Abby's parents caused Baby Abby to come into being, of course!), but College Abby is physically more similar to Little Abby than she is to anyone else and this similarity is the result of the causal connection to Little Abby.

You might object that hey, what if Abigail has an identical twin? Call her Schmabigail. The physicalist criterion here is using the idea of physical similarity to establish identity. But College Abby is definitely more similar to College Schmabby than she is to Little Abby. So why isn't the physicalist committed to the mistaken idea that identical twins are the same person?

Figure 5.2 Closest physical continuers

The answer is that physical similarity isn't the whole story. Schmabby is not causally connected to Abby, but College Abby *is* causally related to Little Abby. We need both parts to being a closest causal continuer: causation and similarity. Baby Abby is in a sense a causal successor of her mother, but she is not physically more similar to her mom than anyone else. Her mother is more similar to herself than to Baby Abby. Therefore Abigail is not the closest physical continuer of her mother. College Abby is more physically similar to College Schmabby than she is to Little Abby, but Abigail and Schmabigail are not causally connected. Therefore neither is the closest physical continuer of the other. 5.43

Figure 5.2 is a diagram of the physicalist criterion of personal identity. Each person in the diagram is Abigail at a particular moment in time, and the entire picture represents Abigail's lifespan over time. The arrows are the closest physical continuer relation. Toddler Abby causes her closest physical continuer, Little Abby. Little Abby causes her closest physical continuer, College Abby, College Abby causes her closest physical continuer, and so on up to Grandma Abigail. The "glue" of the closest physical continuer relation holds all of the successive Abigails together. While it is true that Grandma Abigail is the not the closest physical continuer of Toddler Abby, she is connected back through time via the closer physical continuer relation to Toddler Abby. They are each links in the same chain, each of them Abigail at a moment in time. 5.44

5.45 Grandma Abigail almost certainly does not have a single physical part in common with Toddler Abby. The parts of our bodies naturally replace through ordinary metabolic processes. It is sometimes claimed that some of our cells—neurons in the brain, for example—are unchanging throughout our lives and do not replace themselves. That's not quite right. While brain cells do not replace or regenerate in the same way that skin cells or hair cells do, every cell in the body replaces its molecular components over time through cellular metabolism. Biologists regard something as the "same" cell if it performs the same functional role in the body as a predecessor cell it is causally connected to. In other words, biologists rely on something like the closest physical continuer relation to identify cells over time despite them changing their parts, just as we have been using it to identify someone as being the same person over time despite change. Viewed in terms of the molecules involved, however, the heap of molecules that Grandma Abigail is built out of is a completely different heap from the one that composes Toddler Abby. The closest physical continuer relation lets us identify the two as the same person at different moments in time.

Kenny—the case of loss

5.46 The physicalist criterion is looking good so far. It seems to handle Abigail—the ordinary case of maturing and aging—just fine, and it doesn't have the problems that confronted supernatural souls. But how does it fare with unusual cases of persistence? Consider the case of Kenny. Now, Kenny is a very unlucky chap. He is incredibly accident prone, which is quite unfortunate, considering that he juggles flaming chainsaws in the circus. Kenny is constantly losing parts at work. Figure 5.3 is a graphic of Kenny over time.

5.47 Poor Kenny. First he loses one leg, then the other, then an arm. Then he is a basket case, a term that was originally World War I British slang for a quadruple amputee. So far, everything that's happened to Kenny is physically possible, and compatible with his survival. While increasingly diminished, each is Kenny at a moment in time, connected by the closest physical continuer relation. Then Kenny loses the remainder of his body, and is nothing but a head. Given the current state of medical technology no one can survive as just a head; not for very long, anyway. But there's nothing philosophically profound about that fact, and it's just a matter of time before medicine advances to the point that it can keep a human head alive on machines. We have just as much reason to think that Just-a-Head is still

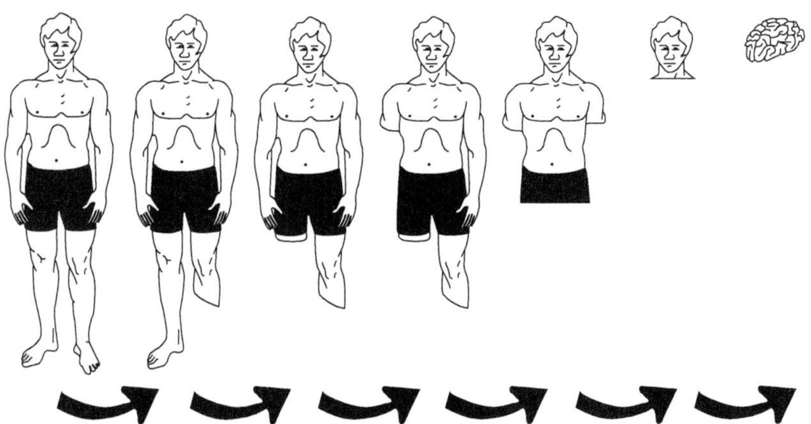

Figure 5.3 Kenny over time

really Kenny as we do to think that Basket Case is Kenny. Just-a-Head is the closest physical continuer of what came before, of what Kenny just was.

To extend things even further, why couldn't Kenny lose his nose and still 5.48
remain in existence? Or lose his ears and still survive? These things happen to people and they go on. Or perhaps Kenny could lose his entire face and survive, as have victims of animal maulings. Some folks have had titanium plates replace sections of damaged craniums, and continued to live. So even Kenny's face and skull might be gone and yet he could continue in existence, perhaps solely as a brain. As with Just-a-Head, medical science does not yet allow disembodied brains to be kept alive. Yet we can keep hearts pumping outside of a body, and other organs alive for transplantation, so again, surely it's just a matter of time before science catches up with science fiction. By the end of Figure 5.3, Kenny is no more than a living, thinking, brain. Brain Kenny is the closest physical continuer of what came before, ultimately connected to the fully intact Kenny at the beginning of his circus career. They are, by the physicalist criterion, the same person.

Perhaps you think that's going a bit too far. Maybe by the end we've killed 5.49
Kenny. If you're not sure what to think at this point, here's a thought experiment to support the idea that Kenny really is just the brain. Imagine brain transplantation—some mad scientist takes your brain, transplants it into the skull of another person, and takes that person's brain and puts it into your (now empty) skull. Scientists have already done whole **head transplants** on chimpanzees, dogs, and rats.[17] Human brain transplants can't be far behind.

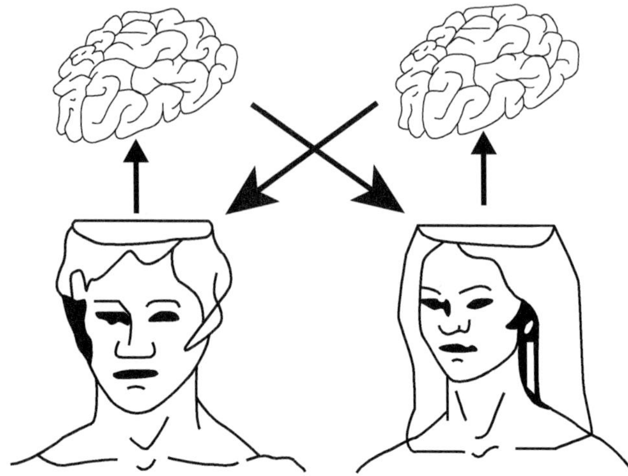

Figure 5.4 Trading brains

Brain transplants

5.50 Here, then, is the question to consider: after your brain transplant, *did you get a new brain or did you get a new body*? One way to think about the brain-switching scenario is this. Suppose that one person is going to be tortured tomorrow in a really horrible, gruesome, full-on medieval way. You get to decide right now who it will be. After your decision there will be a brain transplantation; your brain is going to be swapped just as Figure 5.4 illustrates. Who do you pick to be tortured? Here are your two choices:

1. Your brain + new body
2. Your body + new brain

Think about who is going to feel the suffering. Remember, the body may get the thumb screws, but its the brain that's going to register the pain. Which option do you pick so that you're not the one getting tortured? Or think about a case of pleasure. Who would you rather win the lottery tomorrow? Your brain + new body, or your body + new brain? While it will be the body that's driving the new Ferrari, it will be the brain that has the experience of it and feels the pleasure of newfound wealth. Most likely in the torture you're going to decide that your body + new brain is going to the rack and in the lottery case you want your brain + new body to win. If those are your decisions, then presumably you think that where your brain goes, you go. Which suggests that you believe that you are your brain, after all.

Your consciousness, personality, beliefs, and values all travel along with your brain. You may be in for some new experiences, and maybe a few surprises, with your new body, but it's a new body. Your old body may have received a new brain, but *you* didn't. In fact, this is just a case of total replacement of body parts, something that happens gradually anyway, as we saw with the case of Abigail above. Through normal metabolic processes all of your molecular components are slowly replaced over time. Brain transplant accomplishes the same thing, just more quickly. "Brain transplant" might best be called "whole body transplant." Instead of getting a new heart, lungs, or liver through transplantation, you get a whole new body. These reflections suggest that Kenny did in fact survive as no more than a brain. 5.51

But wait—why not think that all along Kenny was really no more than a brain? Apparently he didn't need the remainder of his body to survive. Why not think that *you* are a brain? The rest of your body is terribly handy to have, and no doubt you have grown quite attached to it, but the body switching example suggests that it's just along for the ride. Or, put another way, your brain drives your body around like a car, but you, the brain, are the driver and the car is replaceable. If you could survive mild brain damage, then you might even be a part of your brain. All of these reflections are physicalist ones. Brains are 3.5 pounds of squishy grey matter, which is physical, material stuff. If you are a brain, then you are a physical object. 5.52

In the brain transplantation thought experiment, your brain is divided from your body. Unlike the case of Kenny, both your brain and your body continue in existence, they are just no longer connected to each other. We've considered some reasons to think that after division you go along with your brain (and perhaps *are* your brain); you don't go along with your body. Let's dig into that a little deeper. The motivations for thinking that you go where your brain goes is that it is the repository of your memories, your personality, your thoughts, intellect, desires, hopes, dreams, wishes, fears, and intentions. In short, your brain is the seat of your psychology. Why didn't you think that you go where your liver goes? It's the source of bile! The obvious answer is that who you are has a lot to do with your personal psychology, and nothing to do with bile. At this point, though, we've moved rather far away from a physicalist criterion, and onto something else entirely. 5.53

5.54 The present point can be put as an objection to the physicalist criterion. Start by assuming the physicalist view: you are a physical organism. Now suppose that your brain and body become separated, as in the case of brain transplantation. Either your brain is the closest physical continuer of you or your body is. It seemed wrong to suppose that your body was the closest physical continuer. However, the only reason to believe that your brain, and not the rest of your body, is your closest physical continuer is that it is your brain that preserves your psychology. If your kidneys preserved your psychology, then they would be your closest continuer (and, after division, be you). So it's not the *organ* that really matters for your survival—what matters is the continuation of your mental life, your mind, memories, and personality. That suggests that you're not to be identified with any particular group of cells, heap of molecules, or particular bodily organ. You're not a physical object at all. You're a mind.

The Psychological Criterion

5.55 The idea that the solution to the problem of personal identity has to do with one's psychology goes back to the seventeenth-century English philosopher **John Locke.**[18] Locke obviously believed that he had a physical body, and Locke even believed that there were supernatural souls. Yet he didn't think that either one of them explained the nature of the self. Locke pondered the problem of **sameness,**[19] just as we have. What, he wondered, made him the same person as a particular person who saw the River Thames flood last winter? Locke's answer was that he had the same consciousness as the person who saw it overflow. Locke's sure that he's the same person who just sat down at his desk because he is conscious of just doing it; he remembers doing it. He gives the exact same reason for believing that he is the same person who saw the Thames overflow last winter. The present Locke is connected backwards through time to the person who saw the river flooding through continuing consciousness.

5.56 Locke's psychological criterion is a true alternative to the theories we have so far discussed; it isn't simply a disguised version of physicalism, or another soul view. As far as personal identity goes, it's irrelevant where we locate your consciousness—it doesn't matter whether your consciousness is in a brain, or a soul, or whatever. In Locke's words, "place that self in what substance you please"—consciousness is the essential thing, since "without consciousness, there is no person." All you have is a dead carcass.

Closest psychological continuer relation

The psychological criterion is analogous to the physicalist criterion in certain respects. For both a person at a moment in time is to be identified with some particular collection. Under physicalism, that collection is the heap of physical parts. A person's parts may change over time so long as the closest physical continuer relation connects them. For the psychological criterion, a person at a moment in time is a bundle of psychological qualities, a certain collection of beliefs, ideas, thoughts, and sensations at that time. A person's psychology changes over time as they have new sensations, have new ideas, different beliefs and emotions, and so on. Yet so long as each person is connected to each preceding one by a *closest psychological continuer* relation, then they are the same person at different moments in time. 5.57

What is the closest psychological continuer relation that is the key to the answer to the problem of sameness? Is it no more than memory? While Locke's official view is that continuing consciousness is the answer, he emphasizes the importance of memory, and many of his early interpreters took him to be insisting that we are the same persons over time because we remember our earlier experiences and thoughts. Locke is the same person as a particular witness to the Thames flooding because he remembers the flood at that specific point in time, from that particular point of view. So one idea is that previous incarnations of you are really you because you remember being that person. The image is something like Figure 5.5. 5.58

Each backwards arrow indicates what you can remember. When you have new ideas, you can remember your old ideas. When you have newer ideas, you can remember your new ideas and your old ideas. When you have your newest ideas you can remember your newer ideas, your new ideas, and your new ideas. The person-shaped collection of mental properties farthest to the right depicts you at the present moment, when you can remember the ideas, thoughts, sensations, etcetera, that you just had, and you can remember what it was like for you before that time, and what it was like the time before that one. At each moment you can remember all of your previous moments. 5.59

First objection to the memory interpretation of the psychological criterion 5.60
One obvious objection to the view just related is that we all sleep, and when we sleep we don't remember anything about ourselves. Certainly in dreamless sleep there's just no memory of any sort going on. Do we then go out

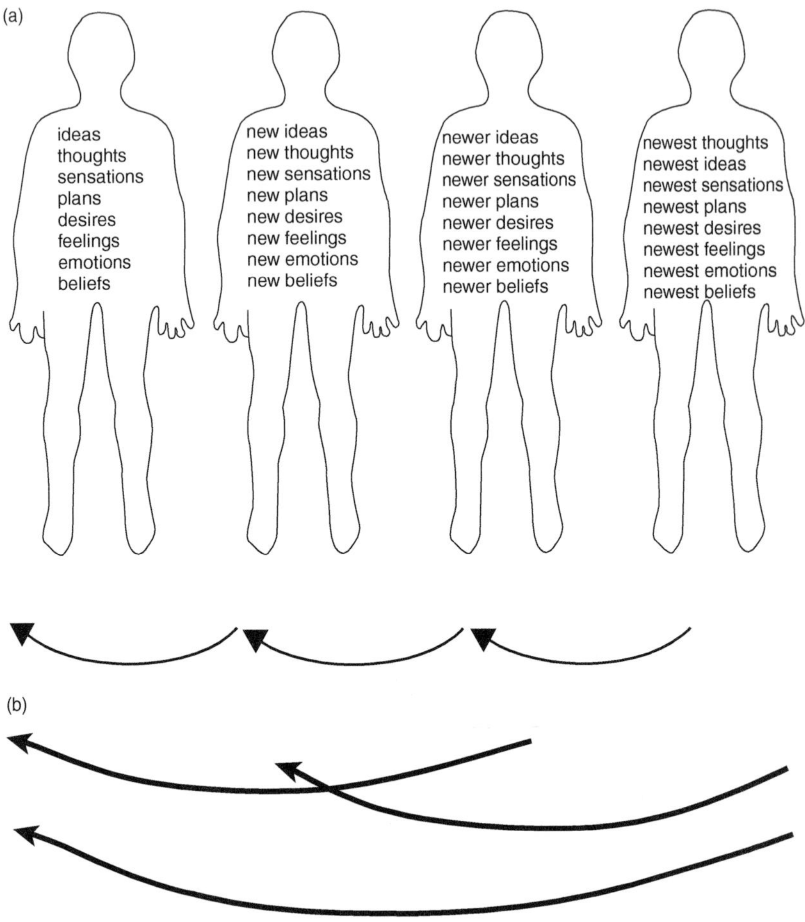

Figure 5.5 Psychological continuity depicted as remembering every preceding moment

of existence? Are those previous selves not earlier versions of you because you can't remember them?

5.61 We needn't panic just yet. Locke's idea isn't the rather silly notion that at every moment our minds are filled with the recollections of every preceding moment in our lives. No one is actively remembering everything that ever happened to him or her at every moment. It's that we *could* remember those earlier stages. We are *capable* of remembering them—that's what makes those persons in the past previous incarnations of ourselves. Even this softened view faces a rather serious, and equally obvious objection.

Second objection to the memory interpretation of the psychological criterion 5.62
Who can remember all that stuff? You don't remember what you had for breakfast two days ago, much less anything from when you were a baby. Which means that you were never a baby—you don't remember it. The sort of incredibly strong memory requirement depicted in Figure 5.5 just can't be right. It demands far too much to solve the problem of sameness.

The eighteenth-century Scottish philosopher **Thomas Reid**[20] devised a 5.63
clever argument along these lines that has come to be known as the brave officer **paradox.**[21] Reid imagines a boy who is flogged for stealing apples (Reid wrote back in the day when flogging fruit-loving children was the norm). Later in life he becomes a military officer and performs a brave deed. As an officer he still remembers the flogging. Still later the officer becomes a general. The general recalls being the brave officer, but has completely forgotten the youthful flogging. Reid argues that this simple tale, when added to Locke's requirement that memory is the key to identity through time, generates a contradiction.

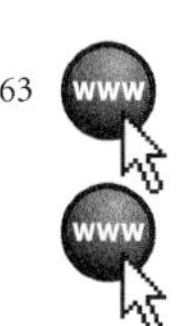

1. Someone is identical to an earlier person if and only if they can remember being that person.	(Locke's memory criterion)
2. The officer = the boy.	(from 1, and the officer can remember being the boy)
3. The general = the officer.	(from 1, and the general can remember being the brave officer)
4. Therefore, the general = the boy.	(from 2, 3, and the transitivity of identity)
5. The general ≠ the boy.	(from 1, and the general does not remember being the boy)
6. Since (4) and (5) contradict each other, the primary assumption in (1) is false.	(*reductio ad absurdum*)

In other words, treating Locke's psychological criterion of personal identity as a memory requirement leads to a contradiction—thus proving that his theory must be mistaken.

5.64 Reid thought the brave officer paradox was the killer objection to the memory idea, and it is a pretty clever one. It can be answered, though, by easing up on the memory requirements as follows: you are the same person as a person of a few moments ago because you can remember being that person. In other words, you can remember what just happened. If you can remember further back, good for you. It's a bonus. But to be a continuing person through time only requires that you can remember what just happened the immediately previous time, and at that previous time you can remember what just happened before that. And so on back through time. Those are all the memory links that are needed to be a persisting, continuing person. Each link in the chain only needs to be attached to the preceding and succeeding links; it doesn't need to be attached to every link in the chain. Figure 5.6 depicts the new proposal.

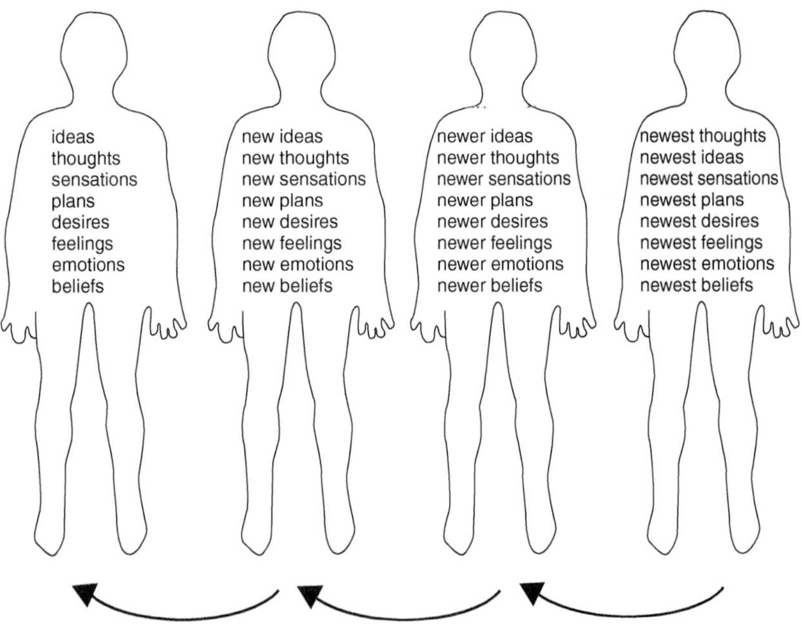

Figure 5.6 Psychological continuity depicted as remembering the immediately preceding moment

The general can remember being the brave officer, the brave officer 5.65
can remember being the boy. No problem. If the general's memory is so good that he also remembers being the boy, that's nice, but not a requirement. The new-and-improved model can accommodate Reid's forgetful general. The backwards links of memory tie together all the earlier editions of the same man, without demanding superhuman feats of mental recall.

Third objection to the memory interpretation of the psychological criterion 5.66
The final objection to the idea that memory is what makes us the same persons over time was raised by **Joseph Butler** in an appendix to a 1736 book of his on religion.[22] Personal identity was a sort of afterthought for Butler, but he came up with an intriguing argument. Butler's objection is that the memory idea actually builds in a self-defeating circularity. That is, the memory interpretation assumes the very thing that it is supposed to establish—a logical no-no. Here's the argument.

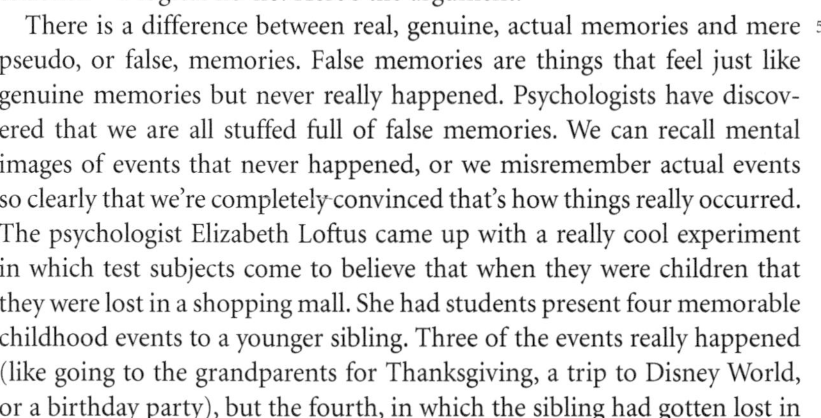

There is a difference between real, genuine, actual memories and mere 5.67
pseudo, or false, memories. False memories are things that feel just like genuine memories but never really happened. Psychologists have discovered that we are all stuffed full of false memories. We can recall mental images of events that never happened, or we misremember actual events so clearly that we're completely convinced that's how things really occurred. The psychologist Elizabeth Loftus came up with a really cool experiment in which test subjects come to believe that when they were children that they were lost in a shopping mall. She had students present four memorable childhood events to a younger sibling. Three of the events really happened (like going to the grandparents for Thanksgiving, a trip to Disney World, or a birthday party), but the fourth, in which the sibling had gotten lost in a mall, was completely made up. Each of the events was presented in paragraph-length detail and the test subject (the younger brother or sister) was asked what they recalled about each of the episodes.

When asked what they remembered about getting lost in the mall, the 5.68
subjects spontaneously filled in details like how they got lost in a toy store, and were really scared, until that old man in the flannel shirt found them crying, then Mom was so relieved when they were returned to Sears, and so on. Loftus's subjects were completely sincere in their "recall" of these fictitious events, and from their perspective the shopping mall false memory was every bit as real as the other things they remembered from childhood. It's absurdly easy to instill false memories in people, and there is little doubt

that many of the images you can recall from your childhood are really inventions of your mind, created in response to hearing your parents and others relate your younger exploits.

5.69 All right, there are false memories and genuine memories. The difference is easy to state: real memories recall things that really did happen to you, and false memories do not. The test for something's being a genuine memory is that it really happened to you. But what's the test for someone's being you? According to the memory interpretation of the psychological criterion, it is the presence of genuine memory! False memories don't connect you to anyone in the past, but genuine memories connect the present you to the past you. However, the notion of a genuine memory *presupposes* that we already know how to identify which individual in the past is you. That wouldn't be so bad, except that if genuine memory is the glue that holds you together as a persisting person over time, it means that the concept of *you* presupposes that we already know what genuine memories are. The concept of *you* is logically prior to the concept of genuine memory, and the concept of *genuine memory* is logically prior to the concept of you. Butler's objection is that this makes the memory view completely circular and unhelpful.

5.70 A defender of the psychological criterion has a ready reply to Reid and Butler: you guys are making the mistake of thinking that memory is the only thing that matters. Give that up and your objections evaporate. Looking at memory alone is much too narrow a way to think about what it is to be psychologically connected to earlier past versions of oneself. There are many overlapping strands of psychological connection: personality, tastes, beliefs, memories, interests, preferences, desires, and intentions, to name a few. These are woven together like the strands in a rope. No thread continues from one end of the rope to the other. While the fibers that compose a rope are relatively short, they overlap, interlock, and twist together so that the rope itself is strong and whole. The same is true of your psychological history; it is the time-spanning rope that ties together the different times of yourself. In Figure 5.6, imagine the arrow that connects instances of yourself back through time as not just a single strand of memory, but as a thick hemp rope.

5.71 *Objection: Severe psychological disruption* Just as a rope can become so frayed and damaged that one section is only tenuously attached to the next, so too a person's psychology can become so damaged that there are only the slimmest of threads connecting them back in time to earlier selves. In

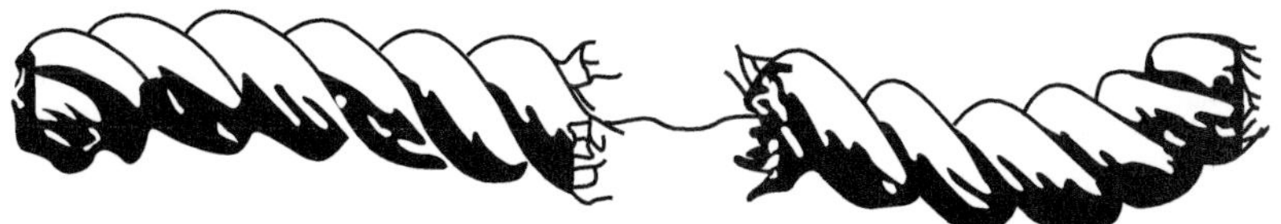

Figure 5.7 Two different ropes connected by a thread, or one rope severely frayed in the middle?

the rope case we may well doubt that a rope so damaged is still one *rope*, as opposed to two ropes connected by a thread (see Figure 5.7).

How much psychological damage can someone endure before we are 5.72
ready to say that they are literally not the same person, that one person has died and a new person has come into existence? Here are two famous cases of such damage that are quite different from each other, both in terms of organic cause and in terms of which strands of the mental rope are broken.

The case of Clive Wearing Clive Wearing was one of London's leading choral 5.73
conductors and had an enviable reputation in the field of classical music as one of the world's experts in the Renaissance music of **Orlando Lassus.**[23] He served as chorus master of the London Sinfonietta, as well as being director of the London Lassus Ensemble. In 1985, Clive suffered brain damage as the result of viral encephalitis brought on by the *Herpes simplex* virus (the kind that usually just causes cold sores), and now has a dense, irreversible amnesia. The disease destroyed both of his hippocampi, located in the temporal lobes, and also a portion of his left frontal lobe. As a result, he is unable to store new long-term memories, and his short-term **memory** is 10 minutes long.[24] If his wife Deborah is gone for more than 15 minutes, Clive greets her return as if she has been missing for 20 years, with a tearful, heartwrenching reunion.

In fact, Clive lacks episodic memories of any kind, although he retains 5.74
a kind of semantic memory that allows him to possess basic facts about the world. For example, Clive knows that he has children, although he cannot remember ever having them. He also retains a procedural memory—that is, Clive remembers how to do things, like speak English, play the organ, conduct the choir, sing, and read Latin, even though he is completely unaware that he knows how to do these things, and is repeatedly surprised to find that he has these abilities.

In Clive's own view of himself, he constantly feels that he is in the twi- 5.75
light zone between sleep and consciousness, and that he is just waking up

at every moment, with the dream world of the past rapidly slipping into nothingness. When interviewed, he repeatedly insists that he is just now conscious for the first time, that he has been asleep, that he has been blind, deaf, dumb, with no sense of taste, touch, or smell. He has never been visited by anyone before. All of his senses, in the moment he is aware of them, have just been "switched on." When he views himself conducting a choir on TV, Clive declares that the person on TV is not *himself*, that the person "is not conscious to me . . . no connection to me at all." Most hauntingly, Clive steadfastly maintains that he has been dead, and just now, in the present moment, lifted out of the abyss of nonexistence. When Clive looks at earlier entries in his diary, written minutes ago in his own hand, he angrily crosses them out or revises them, and has insisted that "these entries were written by other people."

5.76 Taking Clive literally, viral encephalitis killed Clive Wearing. What has been left is a succession of related but non-identical Clives: Clive$_1$, Clive$_2$, Clive$_3$ . . . They are different pieces of rope connected by a thread. On the other hand is the view of Clive's wife, Deborah Wearing. She interprets his claims about being dead to be a simile—that Clive's condition is *like* death. She states that despite his catastrophic memory loss, the "Cliveness of Clive remains." His memories may be gone, but, for the most part, his personality and abilities are intact. The preservation of those things is, in her mind, sufficient psychological continuity to affirm that Clive survives, in a diminished, weakened sort of way, but he is still one persisting person through time. It is clear that both Clive and Deborah accept the psychological criterion of personal identity. They just disagree about the level of psychological connectivity that is required to be one person who persists through time.

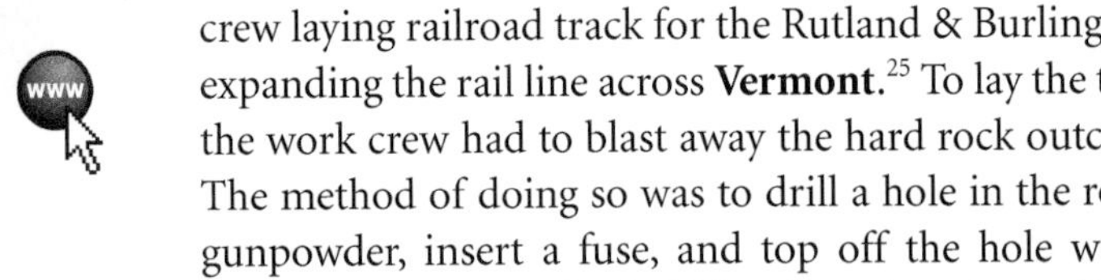

5.77 *The case of Phineas Gage* In 1848 Phineas Gage was the foreman of a work crew laying railroad track for the Rutland & Burlington Railroad company, expanding the rail line across **Vermont.**[25] To lay the track level and straight, the work crew had to blast away the hard rock outcroppings in their path. The method of doing so was to drill a hole in the rock, fill it halfway with gunpowder, insert a fuse, and top off the hole with sand. Then a man pounded a three-and-a-half foot long iron bar called a tamping rod onto the sand to pack it in tight. The sand was crucial—when the fuse was lit, the packed sand forced the explosion down into the stone to be cleared away.

5.78 One hot summer afternoon, the crew had drilled a hole and poured in the gunpowder. Gage instructed his helper to top it off with the sand. Then someone called to Gage, who looked away, distracted. He turned back, and began to tamp the sand with the iron rod. But the sand had not yet been poured in, and Gage struck iron against gunpowder against stone. It immediately sparked and exploded, firing the tamping rod like a missile. The 13-pound iron rod shot through Gage's left cheek, through his skull and the front of his brain, and out the top of his head. Astonishingly, he never lost consciousness, and was even able to walk and speak coherently afterwards, despite the obliteration of his prefrontal cortex.

Before the accident, Gage had been a reliable, responsible person. Not 5.79
only was he the foreman of the crew, but his bosses described him as "the most efficient and capable" man they had. Gage had been sober and hardworking, so serious about his trade that he had had his tamping iron custom-made for him by a blacksmith. After the accident, however, his personality underwent a 180-degree change. While unknown at the time, the prefrontal cortex is essential to sociability, understanding practical interactions, deliberative planning for the future, and a sense of responsibility. All of that was demolished in Gage. In the words of his physician, Dr John Harlow, Gage was "fitful, irreverent, indulging at times in the grossest profanity which was not previously his custom, manifesting but little deference for his fellows, impatient of restraint or advice when it conflicts with his desires, at times pertinaciously obstinate, yet capricious and vacillating" (Damasio, 1994, p. 8). Women were advised to avoid Gage, and he was incapable of holding down a job.

Clive Wearing lost his memories, but his personality remained largely 5.80
intact. Phineas Gage was the exact opposite: his memories were untouched by the accident, but his personality and character were destroyed. Gage's friends and acquaintances thought that Gage was no longer Gage. The philosophical question is how literally to take that. Was the psychological disruption so severe that we should conclude that the tamping iron killed Gage and left a different person in his body? If you are inclined to say yes, then the post-accident person, $Gage_2$, is not a sufficiently close psychological continuer of pre-accident $Gage_1$ that under the psychological criterion $Gage_1$ and $Gage_2$ count as the same person at different times.

You might naturally think that nothing is as sharp and precise as the 5.81
moment of your death. Death is a bright boundary between a world that contains you and a world that does not. Dying might be quick, or drawn out, painful or painless, but the instant of death, *that* is but the work of a moment. Or so it seems. The objection to the psychological criterion lurking in the cases of Clive Wearing and Phineas Gage is that it fails to

give a precise account of the boundaries of personhood. That is, there seems to be no exact matter of fact as to when someone goes out of existence, because there is no objective way to determine when there is such inadequate and broken psychological continuity that the original person has ceased to exist.

5.82 At some future time you will be dead. Given the psychological criterion there will be future times at which we cannot definitely say whether you are dead or alive—we could declare that a future piece of rope is only connected by a thread to an earlier piece, or we could insist that there is only one continuous rope stretching into the future, just badly frayed in spots. But either way, it's completely arbitrary which one we choose. The psychological criterion was supposed to solve the problems of difference and sameness, but suddenly it looks incapable of solving either one. Is $Gage_2$ a different person from $Gage_1$, or the same person? Is $Clive_2$ different from or the same as $Clive_1$? There's no way to tell.

5.83 The final major solution to the problem of personal identity attempts to make lemonade out of the lemons of the vague boundaries of existence. It is a proposal as ancient as classical Buddhism, as recent as contemporary neuroscience, and endorsed by the greatest philosopher to write in the English language. It is also the most radical and shocking view of the self we have yet discussed.

The Bundle Theory

5.84 Both the physicalist criterion and the psychological criterion face the problem of division. We saw that for the physicalist that the brain could be divided from the rest of the body, and then the puzzle was how to identify the closest continuer of the pre-division self. Are you the body or the brain? The most intuitive answer was "the brain" because that is the seat of your consciousness, which in turn motivated giving up the physicalist view in favor of a purely psychological account. But division rears its ugly head for the psychological view too. Not only can your physical body be split into parts, but so can your mind. Such mental division happens in cases of split-brain surgery.

Split-brain surgery

5.85 Patients with severe epilepsy can have frequent, nearly continuous, electrical storms in their brains known as seizures. With seizures, the brain's

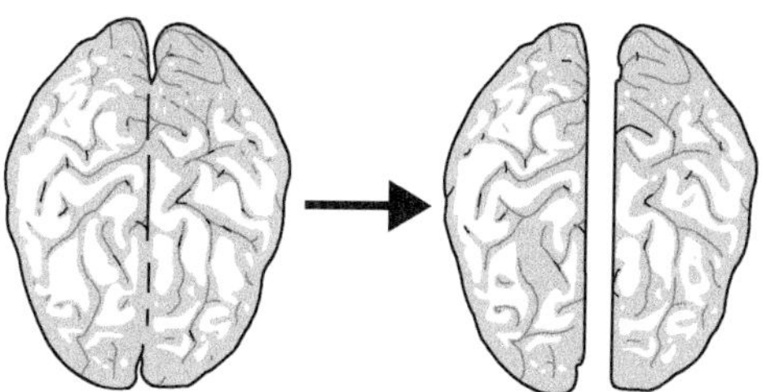

Figure 5.8 Split-brain surgery

electrical activity is caught in a kind of feedback loop and it builds and builds into a chaotic frenzy, an unhealthy state that can ultimately cause death. In such extreme cases, one medical approach is to sever the corpus callosum, the highway of nerves that connects the two hemispheres of the brain, in a procedure called a commisurotomy or split-brain surgery (see Figure 5.8). When that band of nerves is cut, the two hemispheres cannot fire electricity back and forth in a seizure storm, and so the surgery prevents future epileptic attacks. However, it also means that the hemispheres are completely and permanently unable to communicate with each other.

Brain hemispheres are not redundant. Each is somewhat specialized, 5.86
with the left brain more focused on grammar, vocabulary, and linear reasoning, and the right brain more directed to sight, hearing, and perceptual recognition. The right brain does have some language functions, though, and certain activities, such as performing music, need the whole brain.

Starting in the 1960s, neuroscientists began to study patients who have 5.87
undergone **split-brain surgery**, and discovered some astonishing things.[26] Once separated, the hemispheres can, simultaneously, have different emotions, beliefs, and interests. One **split-brain patient** would put a cigarette in her mouth with her right hand (controlled by the left hemisphere) and before she could light it, her left hand (controlled by the right hemisphere) would pull the cigarette out of her mouth.[27] The patient reported feeling that her left hand was not under "her" control, and that it was an alien, separate entity. Other researchers have reported that the hemispheres can feel contrary emotions at the same time. Simply by covering one eye, which prevents one hemisphere from receiving optical information, the emotions of their patients changed. Traumatized patients who felt depressed, agitated, or anxious with one eye covered, reported feeling calmed and more relaxed when their other eye was covered instead. Separated hemispheres may not even believe the same things; the neuroscientist V. S.

Ramachandran recently studied a patient whose right hemisphere believed in God, and whose left hemisphere was an **atheist**.[28] This patient was apparently of two minds about God.

5.88 Split-brain cases suggest that within each of our brain hemispheres is a distinct mind, with its own personality and beliefs. Or, more modestly, each hemisphere becomes its own mind after the corpus callosum is cut. So where is all this are we? If you have split-brain surgery, what happens to *you*? If your mind itself divides, is one mind you and the other not? Which one is the real you, and how could you tell?

5.89 The right answer to these questions, according to the bundle theory, is that strictly speaking, there is no you. There never was. The mistake all along was to think that you are anything more than a loosely unified confederation of interests, motivations, beliefs, sensations, and emotions. The subconscious is a roiling sea of ancient decision-making algorithms and drives inherited from our pre-human ancestors. The feeling of consciousness is a latecomer to the party. In terms of computer programmers, there are reams of "legacy code" buried in our wetware that may serve no purpose in the modern world and yet are hidden and untouchable by consciousness. For example, your body evolved to not feel full for about 20 minutes after a meal, a fine adaptation in the Pleistocene when abundant food was only an occasional treat and overeating once in awhile helped pack on fat that could be used by the body during leaner times. Now that there are loads of high-calorie foods about, the old programming leads to obesity. But we can't command our bodies to feel full right away, and it is very difficult to stop eating delicious food even when you consciously know you have consumed sufficient calories. Parts of "you" want to cut back on food consumption, parts want to keep eating. Perhaps some parts of you, like Ramachandran's patient, are atheists and others theists. But where are *you* in all of this?

Buddha and Hume

5.90 Perhaps nowhere. The **Buddha**[29] promoted the concept of *anatta*, the view that there is no self. The self, he thought, is a fiction, a mere name to describe a collection or aggregate of what is truly real, the *khandhas*. There are five khandhas in Buddhism: *matter*, the material world, including the physical body; *sensation*, particularly whether an experience is pleasant or unpleasant; perception, in the sense of the cognition and recognition of objects; *mental formations*, such as intentions, ideas, thoughts, and dispositions; and *consciousness*, which for the Buddha had vitalist connotations of an animating force. These changing elements composed what we consider the self. The self, however, is just a manner of speaking regarding these components. In one text, the Buddha gives an analogy of a chariot—a chariot is made out of parts that are in a sense more real than the chariot, which is just a **convention**, a name we give to a certain assemblage of those parts.[30]

In the eighteenth century, David Hume offered the first modern defense 5.91
of the Bundle Theory. Hume wrote that no matter how much he introspected himself, he could never detect any sort of soul-like entity, but would

> always stumble on some particular perception or other, of heat or cold, light or shade, love or hatred, pain or pleasure. I can never catch *myself* at any time without a perception, and can never observe anything but the perception. When my perceptions are remov'd for any time, as by sound sleep; so long am I insensible of myself, and may be truly said not to exist. And were all my perception remov'd by death, and cou'd I neither think, nor feel, not see, nor love, nor hate after the dissolution of my body, I should be entirely annihilated, nor do I conceive what is farther requisite to make me a perfect non-entity. (Hume, 1739, bk. 1, pt. 4, sec. 6)

Hume insists that he is no more than "a bundle or collection of different perceptions, which succeed each other with an inconceivable rapidity, and are in perpetual flux and movement." He describes the mind as a theater, the space in which these ever-changing perceptions and thoughts "make their appearance, pass, re-pass, glide away, and mingle." Genuine identity over time he thought to be a fiction and an act of the imagination; we identify persons over time out of custom, without a more profound or defensible philosophical reason.

To be sure, the bundle theory sounds strange at first. But reflection on 5.92
other sorts of weird objects can remove some of the feeling of strangeness about it. Think about the constellation Orion. Is it a real object? You might be inclined to say that it is not real, just a fanciful way that people group stars together, just patterns drawn in the night sky. Constellations are no more than a way to talk about a particular collection of stars, but it's the stars that are actually real objects. Or consider a club, like a sports team, an army, or a rock band, all of which change their members over the years, disband, and reform, sometimes with new leaders and new names.

The Sex Pistols

5.93 Consider a band like **The Sex Pistols**.[31] They formed in 1975 with members Johnny Rotten, Steve Jones, Paul Cook, and Glen Matlock. In 1977 Sid Vicious replaced Matlock. The band broke up in 1978, and the next year Sid Vicious died of a heroin overdose. In 1996, Rotten, Jones, Cook, and Matlock assembled under the name "The Sex Pistols" for a reunion tour. Was it the same band? Here are some options:

1. The Sex Pistols went out of existence in 1978 and came back into existence (briefly) in 1996.
2. The Sex Pistols never went out of existence. They just stopped playing music together for 18 years.
3. "The Sex Pistols" is no more than a conventional name for a group of people who played music together, but is not a real entity in its own right.
4. The 1996 Sex Pistols was a different band than the 1977 Sex Pistols who released *Never Mind The Bollocks, Here's The Sex Pistols* (the group's only album) because by 1996 Sid Vicious was long dead. In other words, "The Sex Pistols" was used as the same name for two different bands that overlapped in parts.

Or how about bands with even more complicated histories, like **Journey**?[32] The band was originally formed in 1973, replaced its members repeatedly over the years, broke up in 1984, and reformed a decade later. Only one person, guitarist Neal Schon, has been a continuous member of Journey, barring, of course, the ten years that the band did not exist. We can ask whether later incarnations of Journey or The Sex Pistols are the same bands as earlier bands with the same name, but the question seems empty. It's a purely arbitrary decision to vote one way or the other. Will The Sex Pistols exist 20 years from now, with all new members, and play easy-listening soft rock? We can know all the facts about Johnny Rotten, Sid Vicious, Steve Jones, Paul Cook, and Glen Matlock, know all the facts about rock-and-roll, and still not have an objective, definitive answer to this question. As Hume said, it's just a verbal dispute, an argument over words.

5.94 According to the bundle theory, you are like bands, clubs, armies, and teams—at any given moment there is some collection of thoughts, ideas, and perceptions that makes you up. And there are psychological and causal links back in time to what are typically regarded as earlier versions of yourself and forward in time to future yous. The elements of the bundle all change over time, from the molecules that compose your body to the thoughts make up your mind, as we have seen. At some time in the future we can ask "Is that future person *you*?" and there is no answer. This is perhaps the most shocking feature of the Bundle Theory: when you go out of existence is vague. There are times in the future when there is no fact of the matter whether you are alive or dead.

The bundle theory's answer to the problem of difference is fairly straight- 5.95
forward: at any given moment in time, the bundle that composes you is different from the bundle that composes anyone else. The solution to the problem of sameness is so radical that many reject the theory entirely because of it. According to the bundle theory, persistence over time is a myth; there is no genuine continuity, no true personal identity that stays the same despite change. All we have is a kind of pragmatic identification, where we just declare that the baby that existed 20 years ago is the same person as you, or that Journey in the present year is the same band as Journey in 1973. But there's no deep metaphysical fact to discover; it's simply a matter of decision. That's not to say that the decisions about our identity over time are all that easy to revise. Our brains are relentless unifiers whose overarching mission is to put everything together in a coherent way. It is only in the fascinating cases at the borderlands of neuroscience—split brains, stroke-induced anosognosia, left side neglect, temporal lobe seizures, confabulation, and the like—that we lift the curtain to see the haphazard machinery that produces the sense of self.

Conclusion

The problem of how it is possible for anything to change over time while 5.96
also remaining the very same thing is a puzzle for shoes and ships and sealing-wax, for cabbages and kings. It is a quite general metaphysical puzzle with roots to the ancient Greeks. In some respects the problem of identity is especially acute for persons, because we, unlike ships and cabbages, have minds. Our conscious self is a vivid and ever-present feature of our lives. And we *feel* that we are the same over time, no matter how much we may age, wrinkle, sag, droop, or forget. Our minds build a seamless narrative, the story of our lives in which we each are the hero. The question is whether our powerful feeling of unity over time tells us anything about reality.

5.97 In this chapter we have considered four very different solutions to the problem of personal identity: the soul criterion, the physicalist criterion, the psychological criterion, and the bundle theory. The soul criterion is the least popular option among philosophers, ever since Locke (who nevertheless thought souls existed) ditched it back in 1690. The bundle theory is also less common, despite its defense by some very prominent scholars, because it leads to such a radical view of the self. While the physicalist criterion is enjoying a bit of a renaissance in contemporary philosophy, the psychological criterion remains the most popular view. Still, all are quite live options and each is hotly contested. Since each theory leads to surprising and counterintuitive consequences, no matter which turns out to be the best way to understand personal identity, you can be fairly confident of one thing: *you are not what you think you are.* That may be the most surprising result of all.

Annotated Bibliography

Butler, Joseph (1736) *The Analogy of Religion*, full text available at www.earlymoderntexts.com/pdfbits/butdis2.pdf, accessed May 16, 2012. In the first appendix, Butler gives his circularity objection to Locke's psychological criterion.

Damasio, Antonio (1994) *Descartes's Error: Emotion, Reason, and the Human Brain* (New York: G. P. Putnam's Sons). A fine, accessible discussion of brain science, written by a neurologist. It contains many fascinating neurological case studies, including an in-depth discussion of Phineas Gage.

Dollar, John (director) (1986) *Prisoner of Consciousness*. A video documentary about Clive Wearing that originally aired on the British TV show Equinox. The interviewer/host is Jonathan Miller, MD, and the film contains penetrating discussions of personal identity.

Harris, Maurice H. (1901) *Hebraic Literature: Translations from the Talmud, Midrashim, and Kabbala* (Washington and London: M. Walter Dunne), full text available at www.sacred-texts.com/jud/hl/index.htm, accessed May 16, 2012. The source for the tale of the luz bone.

Hobbes, Thomas (1655) *Of Body*, full text available at www.philosophy.leeds.ac.uk/GMR/hmp/texts/modern/hobbes/decorpore/decorp2.html#c11, accessed May 16, 2012. In chapter 11, paragraph 7, Hobbes offers a succinct and penetrating discussion of the ship of Theseus puzzle.

Hume, David (1739) *A Treatise of Human Nature*, full text available at www.earlymoderntexts.com/pdfbits/humtr14.pdf. Hume's epoch-making masterpiece, accessed May 16, 2012. Book 1, part 4, section 6 contains his presentation and defense of the Bundle Theory.

Locke, John (1690) *An Essay Concerning Human Understanding*, full text available at www.earlymoderntexts.com/pdfbits/lo24.pdf, accessed May 16, 2012. Book 2, chapter 27 contains Locke's presentation and defense of the psychological criterion.

Loftus, Elizabeth and Katherine Ketchum (1994) *The Myth of Repressed Memory* (New York: St Martin's Press). Chapter 7 gives the details on the shopping mall experiment to induce false memories.

McDaniel, Kris (forthcoming) *This is Metaphysics: An Introduction* (Oxford: Wiley-Blackwell). A comprehensive entrée to metaphysics that delves further into issues of change, identity through time, and vagueness.

Perry, John (1978) *A Dialogue on Personal Identity and Immortality* (Indianapolis: Hackett). Contains a nice discussion of whether souls will solve the problem of personal identity. It is the source for the chocolate example.

Plato (c. 375 BCE) *Phaedo*, full text available at http://classics.mit.edu/Plato/phaedo.html, accessed May 16, 2012. Plato's seminal discussion of the immortality of the soul.

Plutarch (c. 100 CE) *Lives of the Noble Greeks and Romans*, full text available at www.gutenberg.org/ebooks/674, accessed May 16, 2012. The chapter on Theseus contains the first discussion of the famous ship of Theseus problem.

Reid, Thomas (1785) *Essays on the Intellectual Powers of Man*, full text available at www.earlymoderntexts.com/reip.html, accessed May 30, 2012. Essay 3, "Of Memory," Chapter 6, contains the Brave Officer Paradox, which Reid presented as a criticism of Locke.

Treays, Jane (director) (2005) *The Man with the Seven-Second Memory*. A later TV documentary about Clive Wearing. Slicker and more professionally produced than *Prisoner of Consciousness*, but it does not highlight the philosophical issues as well.

Wearing, Deborah (2005) *Forever Today: A Story of Love and Amnesia* (London: Doubleday). A detailed history of Clive Wearing's illness, by his wife.

Online Resources

1 A discussion of buzkashi, a form of polo played with a headless goat carcass over a period of days. It is the national sport of Afghanistan: http://en.wikipedia.org/wiki/Buzkashi
2 Information about gamelan, the traditional music of Indonesia: http://en.wikipedia.org/wiki/Gamelan
3 An in-depth discussion of the life and works of G. W. Leibniz, a great polymath who made "deep and important contributions to the fields of metaphysics,

epistemology, logic, philosophy of religion, as well as mathematics, physics, geology, jurisprudence, and history": http://plato.stanford.edu/entries/leibniz/
4 A detailed discussion of the principle of the identity of indiscernibles: http://plato.stanford.edu/entries/identity-indiscernible/
5 The full text of *Hebraic Literature: Translations from the Talmud, Midrashim, and Kabbala*. The source for the story of the luz bone: www.gutenberg.org/files/14368/14368-h/14368-h.htm
6 The Jewish Encyclopedia's entry on "luz": www.jewishencyclopedia.com/articles/10200-luz
7 A well-informed discussion of Plato's theories of the soul: http://plato.stanford.edu/entries/ancient-soul/#3
8 A synopsis of the film *Ghost*, a typical film portrayal of the Hollywood conception of souls: www.allrovi.com/movies/movie/ghost-v19626
9 A history of vitalism and its dismissal by contemporary science: http://en.wikipedia.org/wiki/Vitalism
10 A discussion of the German chemist Friedrich Wöhler, the first person to synthesize urea: http://en.wikipedia.org/wiki/Friedrich_W%C3%B6hler
11 The nature of the soul according to the Catechism of the Catholic Church: www.vatican.va/archive/ENG0015/__P1B.HTM
12 The Hindu conception of the true self, or Atman: www.hinduwebsite.com/atman.asp
13 A discussion of the gryphon, or griffin, a legendary creature with the body of a lion and the head and wings of an eagle: http://en.wikipedia.org/wiki/Griffin
14 Research using twin studies to understand the heritability of schizophrenia: http://psychology.wikia.com/wiki/Schizophrenia_-_Twin_studies
15 Homer Simpson sells his soul to the devil for a donut and is sent to the ironic punishment lab to suffer: www.youtube.com/watch?v=X3ZcZ2h4Ths
16 The legends of Theseus, the mythical founder of Athens: http://en.wikipedia.org/wiki/Theseus
17 A video of the first neuroscientist to remove a brain from a body and keep it alive: www.youtube.com/watch?v=8On7rktFZME
18 The life and works of John Locke, British philosopher, physician, government official, economic writer, and revolutionary: http://plato.stanford.edu/entries/locke/
19 Book II of John Locke's *Essay Concerning Human Understanding*: www.earlymoderntexts.com/pdfbits/lo24.pdf
20 A discussion of the thought of Thomas Reid, one of the seminal figures in the Scottish Enlightenment: http://plato.stanford.edu/entries/reid/
21 An in-depth discussion of Reid's thoughts on personal identity and memory: http://plato.stanford.edu/entries/reid-memory-identity/
22 The life and works of Bishop Joseph Butler: www.iep.utm.edu/butler/

23 A discussion of amnesia victim Clive Wearing: http://en.wikipedia.org/wiki/Clive_Wearing
24 A synopsis and reviews of *Memento*, a film about an amnesia victim trying to sort out the puzzle of his own past: www.rottentomatoes.com/m/memento/
25 More information about the case of Phineas Gage: http://neurophilosophy.wordpress.com/2006/12/04/the-incredible-case-of-phineas-gage/
26 A documentary on split-brain patients with Alan Alda and Dr Michael Gazzaniga, one of the leading researchers on commisurotomy patients: www.youtube.com/watch?v=lfGwsAdS9Dc
27 A discussion of a split-brain patient with alien hand syndrome: www.bbc.co.uk/news/uk-12225163
28 Neurologist V. S. Ramachandran explains the case of a split-brain patient with one theist hemisphere and one atheist hemisphere: www.youtube.com/watch?v=PFJPtVRlI64
29 A detailed discussion of the life and thought of the Buddha: http://plato.stanford.edu/entries/buddha/
30 A Buddhist nun who offered a succinct explanation of the bundle theory of the self: http://en.wikipedia.org/wiki/Vajira
31 The official website of the seminal punk rock band The Sex Pistols: www.sexpistolsofficial.com/
32 The complicated biography of the band Journey: www.journeymusic.com/pages/bio

6

MIND

The Rare and Mysterious Mind

You see the words on this page and you have certain sensations: sensations of color (grey, black, white), shape (of the letters), patterns (of the words and sentences). Look around you and you have even more sensations of colors and shapes. You hear the birds outside the window, or music on your iPod, high and low pitches, with complex intervals and varying amplitudes. You taste the coffee and it has a *flavor*. You think, wonder, puzzle, daydream, believe, doubt, fantasize, worry, love, fear, rage, learn, remember, drowse, and desire. You itch, ache, burn, tickle, feel cold, and have orgasms. You feel jealousy, happiness, pride, relief, horror, envy, remorse, surprise, and awe. You (and other sentient creatures) are filled with sensations, emotions, and thoughts, in a word: consciousness. Your consciousness is the single most amazing feature of your life. 6.1

Almost nothing else in the entire universe is conscious. In fact, practically everything in the universe is either hydrogen (90%) or helium (10%). The other 90 naturally occurring elements, including everything that composes Earth, every species on it, and you yourself, exist in such trace amounts that they're hardly worth mentioning. Just a cosmic rounding error. Where did all those larger elements come from, then? They are the byproducts of thermonuclear fusion, the engine that powers the stars. When a star runs out of fuel and dies, it collapses on itself and then explodes in a spectacular supernova, as bright as a billion suns. In its death agony, the star spews forth a blizzard of particles that seeds solar systems across its galaxy. All those elements in your body that are bigger than helium were once manufactured inside a star. You are, literally, stardust. 6.2

This Is Philosophy: An Introduction, First Edition. Steven D. Hales.

6.3 That's quite a cool **fact** about you (and one undiscovered until 1957[1]), but the most astonishing and bizarre fact is that somehow all that solar debris came together and made a conscious mind. The vast majority of Earth's mass is not conscious at all. Mostly the planet is just rock and water, yet a little bit of it is alive, growing in the dirt or crawling across the surface of the globe. Even among living things, consciousness is quite rare. About half of the Earth's entire biomass is bacteria and other single-celled **micro-organisms**.[2] Nearly all the rest is some form of plant life. A third of the land animal biomass is made up of **ants and termites**.[3] The more sophisticated animals like mammals are big and noticeable, but a small part of the whole. Consciousness is just about the least common thing there is.

6.4 Mentality is not only rare, but profoundly mysterious. This fact may be hard for you to see at first because thinking and feeling are the most familiar everyday facts of your existence. You are confronted with your own mental life every waking moment (and some of your sleeping moments too). As the great Cambridge philosopher Ludwig Wittgenstein once wrote, "the aspects of things that are most important for us are hidden because of their simplicity and familiarity. One is unable to notice something—because it is always before **one's eyes**."[4]

6.5 Viewed from the impersonal mathematical perspective of physics and chemistry, the idea of some fleshy bits of matter feeling pain or hearing sounds is perplexing. The fundamental forces of nature, like electromagnetism, the strong and weak nuclear forces and gravity—they seem incapable of explaining what happens in your mind. Atoms swerving in the void somehow made music, love, and art. Consciousness viewed this way seems like magic glitter sprinkled over certain small, slow animals, elevating them beyond their natural station.

6.6 Nearly all living things are not conscious—at least the plants and all that bacteria—and managed to evolve, survive, and reproduce just the same. Why couldn't human beings have been like they are? Why were we not merely unconscious meat robots that nevertheless perform all the same tasks, act in all the same ways, that we do now? The present chapter considers this very mystery—the puzzle of your conscious mind.

First Theory of the Mind: Substance Dualism

6.7 In the seventeenth century, French philosopher René Descartes proposed one of the most famous—and boldest—solutions to the puzzle of the mind. How is it possible for unthinking bits of matter to come together and form beings with full technicolor consciousness? According to **Descartes**, it's not![5] Now, he doesn't deny that we are conscious, that we have minds and mental lives and so forth. Instead what Descartes denies is that minds are in any sense *physical.*

Physical and mental substances

Descartes held that reality had two kinds of substances in it. 6.8

- *Physical substance.* This is regular physical, material, corporeal matter, the domain of scientific investigation. Your body is built of this stuff, for example.
- *Mental substance.* This is what ideas, thoughts, and sensations are composed out of. Your mind is, or is made out of, a mental substance. Your brain is a physical thing, but your mind is not.

Descartes thought substance dualism was true primarily because he thought there was an essential fact about physical things that's not true of mental things. Physical substances are extended. That is, physical objects like the book you're reading, your eyes, and the chair you're sitting in all occupy a portion of space. They are spread out in space, and consume a certain volume. To be extended in Descartes's sense is just to have a spatial size and location. Extension is an essential characteristic of physical things; if a material substance doesn't take up any room—zero, none whatsoever—then it's not really something physical after all.

Thoughts, on the other hand, don't seem to have any particular location. 6.9
Perhaps you might vaguely say that they are in the head, but that's rather weird, since they certainly don't take up space. If you have a really big idea, that's just a metaphor; you don't have a spatially large idea, or one so huge that it crowds out other ideas, or one you couldn't completely pack into your cranium. If you feel a pain, what size is it? How large (or small) is your happiness? What shape? Those questions are nonsensical. Ideas, feelings, sensations, none of them have a size; they are not extended. Descartes concluded that there had to be two different kinds of substances: physical substances that have extension, and mental substances that do not.

Descartes's conceivability argument for dualism

Descartes pushed his point even further, arguing that he himself was 6.10
a mental thing, he was a mind. He thought it was conceivable—that is,

something he could coherently imagine—that he could think and have thoughts and yet there is nothing at all material or extended. Some of his reasoning on this point ties in with his reflections on radical skepticism, and is discussed in Chapter 7 on knowledge. The basic idea here is that since ideas aren't extended, therefore minds aren't extended either. From there it is a short hop to imagine that reality might contain minds but nothing physical at all. Of course that's no proof that there is nothing physical; it's merely *conceivable* that everything's mental.

6.11 For Descartes, and many other thinkers of his time, whatever is conceivable is possible. The motivation for such a connection is clearer if you think about it in reverse: the impossible is inconceivable. You can't very well imagine a circle that is 3" high and 4" wide, can you? Nor can you imagine that you are further away from your neighbor than your neighbor is from you. It is inconceivable that a two-year-old is an adult. All of those things are impossible, which is why you can't even imagine or conceive of their truth. So, reasoned Descartes, if you *can* conceive of something, it must be possible. Coupled with the reasoning in previous paragraph, we can conclude that it is *possible* that everything is mental. It is possible that you think and nothing is extended. How can we get from here to the conclusion that in fact you're not extended, that you are just an immaterial mind?

6.12 Well, one thing you can be sure of is that if you think, then you exist. In Descartes's famous formulation, *cogito ergo sum* (I think, therefore I am). You can tell directly that you are thinking, and if you are, then you must exist to be doing that thinking. You don't *necessarily* exist, since you might not have existed, and there will come a day when you do not exist. But it's necessarily true that if you think, then you exist. Added to the previous conclusion that it's possible that you think and nothing is extended, it follows that it's possible that you exist and nothing (including you) is extended.

6.13 Anything that is a physical substance, an extended material object, *must* be extended. The book you are reading is physical, and couldn't fail to be physical; it just couldn't shrink down to a zero-dimensional point with no extension and still be a book. Likewise ideas and sensations, which have no length, width, or breadth, couldn't suddenly become voluminous. Ideas *can't* become three-dimensional objects that occupy space. In other words, if something is physical then it must physical, and if it's not, then it can't be.

6.14 Here's the kicker. Descartes had already argued that it's possible that you have thoughts and ideas and yet you're not a physical thing. Now he's added that anything physical must be physical. If you are physical then you couldn't possibly be some unextended mental thing. But since you could *possibly* be some unextended mental thing (watch closely here, as the rabbit comes out of the hat), you're not physical at all! Physical substances *have* to be physical. You don't have to be a physical object, which means in fact you're not one.

It is difficult to overestimate the powerful influence of Descartes's argu- 6.15
ment for substance dualism. It held sway in the philosophy of mind for 300 years after he thought of it. Since then, however, it has come under serious attack. Here are three of the most prominent criticisms.

Objections to substance dualism

Objection 1: Conceivability and possibility A key premise of the argument 6.16
for dualism is that if you can conceive of something, then that thing is possible. If you can imagine that you are an immaterial mind, then it's at least possible that you are one. Yet why should we believe that conceivability is a good guide to what's possible? Admittedly, there are impossible things that are unimaginable. We can't imagine something that's red all over and blue all over at the same time, and sure enough, such a thing is impossible. But perhaps there are impossible things that we *can* imagine, or at least it feels like we can conceive of them. If there are, then we can't count on what we can frame in our imagination to deliver real possibility.

Can you conceive of a time before the Big Bang? If you've ever asked 6.17
"What came before the Big Bang?" then you presumably think it makes sense to imagine some time prior to the first moment of the universe. However, that's a physical impossibility; according to physics, time didn't exist before the Big Bang, so there were no earlier times. There was nothing before the Big Bang because there was no "before." Cambridge physicist **Stephen Hawking**[6] has commented that asking what happened before the Big Bang is like asking "What's north of the North Pole?" It's a senseless question, because the North Pole is the defining limit of north. Perhaps you can conceive of a time before the Big Bang. If you can, then you are conceiving of something physically impossible.

Have you ever imagined what your life would be like if you had been 6.18
born into a different family? It seems perfectly conceivable that if you had been born to the Queen of England, then you would be a prince or a princess. The problem here is that it is a metaphysical impossibility for you to

have been born into a different family. A child born of different parents couldn't possibly be *you*. You have your parents essentially. When Dave Matthews sings, "Could I have been your little brother? Could I have been anyone other than me?," the answer is most definitely "no." You can't be other than who you are, for the simple reason that someone else isn't you. This sort of imagining is familiar from childhood:

- If I were God, I'd do things differently around here!
- I wouldn't do that, if I were you.
- If I were King Arthur, I'd keep a closer eye on Guinevere.

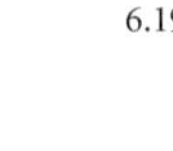

Nevertheless, all those imagined scenarios are impossible ones. You couldn't possibly be God, King Arthur, or anyone other than who you are. Likewise, it is conceivable that water turned out to be some chemical compound other than H_2O, or that lightning was something other than electrical discharges, but those things are impossible too. A **substance** that's not H_2O couldn't possibly be water.[7] An atmospheric disturbance that doesn't involve an electrical discharge can't be lightning.

6.19 On the flip side, some people have thought that certain scenarios were inconceivable (and hence impossible) only for later generations to discover that they were not only possible, but real. For example, in 1862 the great physicist Lord Kelvin wrote, "it is impossible to conceive a limit to the extent of matter in the **universe**."[8] While he may have found it impossible to conceive of such a limit, later physicists have managed the trick. The contemporary standard model of the cosmos says that the universe has a definite, finite size containing a fixed amount of matter. Wittgenstein found traveling to the moon inconceivable, writing, "We all believe that it isn't possible to get to the moon; but there might be people who believe that it is possible and that it sometimes happens. We say: these people do not know a lot that we know. And, let them be never so sure of their **belief**—they are wrong and we know it."[9] Ironically, while Wittgenstein's thoughts were written around 1950, they weren't published until 1969, the same year that Neil Armstrong and Buzz Aldrin took a **stroll** in the Sea of Tranquillity.[10]

6.20 People have managed to conceive of impossible things, and others couldn't conceive of things that really are possible. Perhaps there is a special kind of conceiving that reliably picks out the genuinely possible, but, if there is, the defender of substance dualism needs to explain exactly what it is, and how we can tell when we're using the trustworthy kind of conceiving and not the unreliable kind.

Objection 2: The mind–body problem **Princess Elizabeth** of Bohemia,[11] 6.21

one of Descartes's philosophical correspondents, offered a second objection to substance dualism. Her concern has turned out to be one of the most intractable and thorny problems for mind–body dualism. It's obvious that your thoughts cause what you do. You intend to wave goodbye, and the next thing you know, your hand is fluttering in the air. You want to change the channel, and that's followed by your fingers pressing buttons on the remote. It's no coincidence—your wants and desires, which are purely mental goings-on—cause your body to move. You should think before you speak, precisely because your thoughts control what you say. It works the other way too. You take a bite of pizza and you have taste sensations as a result. You step on a tack and it causes a sharp pain, you drink too much alcohol and your thinking is impaired. In short, the mind causes the body to do things, and stuff that happens to your body causes sensations in your mind.

Elizabeth wanted to know how on earth any of these perfectly obvious 6.22
and mundane facts could possibly be true given mind–body dualism. The puzzle is this. Physical events cause other physical events to occur. For example, when the car behind you skids on the ice and crumples your bumper, we can explain this completely in terms of mass, inertial forces, steel strength, elasticity, and the surfaces of objects coming into contact with each other. In the same way, the neurons in your brain send out signals along the nervous system to the rest of your body and your arm moves. Or you stub your toe and the pain signals travel along the nerves to your brain, where various neural processing then happens. Excited nerves pass along electrochemical signals to other parts of the nervous system; an entirely physical process.

Nonphysical things, on the other hand, don't have any effects on material 6.23
objects. Think about the number π. You can't put that in your pocket, throw it at someone, or cover it in whipped cream (that's a different kind of pie). π is a handy abstraction for mathematics, but that's about it. It has no interaction with the physical world of molecules, cells, trees, and stars. Yet according to substance dualism, your mind is no more physical than π is; minds are much more similar to abstract things such as numbers than they are like brains. So how it is possible for this mental thing that's literally

nowhere in physical space to have any causal commerce whatsoever with the physical world? An immaterial mind can't pull the levers of your brain any better than π can.

6.24 Elizabeth's mind–body problem can be summed up as follows:

1. The mind causes things to happen in the body, and things that happen in the body cause thoughts and sensations in the mind.
2. If substance dualism is true, those commonplace interactions are impossible.
3. Therefore, dualism is false.

6.25 *Objection 3: Other minds* A third objection to substance dualism is that if dualism is true, it apparently has the implication that it is impossible for us to know anything about the minds of other people. But we do often know what others are thinking, or how they are feeling, or what they intend to do. Therefore dualism must be mistaken.

6.26 Why does dualism mean that we can't know anything about the mental life of other people? Descartes suggests that you consider how you know you own mind. You know what your thoughts and sensations are through introspection. Often you can silently reflect and know straightaway whether you have a headache, hear music, feel energetic, are thirsty, and so on. You don't need to observe your behavior or do any kind of empirical investigation. There is an immediacy and directness about this sort of inward vision. You can just see, with the mind's eye, what your mental states are, and you can be absolutely certain of them. You might be mistaken that the car you are looking at is really brown, but you can't be wrong that it *looks brown to you*. You have a kind of special, privileged access to the contents of your mind that you don't have to anyone else's.

6.27 You might reasonably argue that sure, we don't have the same kind of privileged certainty that we have to our own minds, but we can make reasonable inferences about what others are thinking and feeling on the basis of their behavior. If you see Juan put his hand on a hot stove and then jump about yelling and shaking his hand, we can know that he is in pain. We know something about the contents of Juan's mind. It is a generalization from your own experience: every time you've touched a hot stove, you were in pain, and that's how you acted. So you infer that there is a similar correlation between Juan's "pain behavior" and some actual pain happening in his mind, which you can't directly observe or feel. In other words, to some extent we *can* know what the contents are of someone else's mind, what they are feeling, experiencing, or even thinking, even though it is by observation and inference.

While initially plausible sounding, there's a serious difficulty with the preceding argument. In fact, there is reason to think that *you can't have any idea at all* what is going on in someone else's mind. To keep it simple, let's just focus on one mental state, although the point is easily generalizable to other mental states too. Consider pain. The implicit argument of the previous paragraph is: 6.28

1. When you are in pain, you exhibit certain pain behavior (for example, you jump up and down, curse, yell, grimace, and so on).
2. When other people show the same pain behavior, they are in pain too.
3. If (2) is true, then you can know when other people are in pain—you can know something about their minds by observing their behavior.

Here's the problem. There is no way to give any evidence for (2). That is, you can formulate the hypothesis that so-called "pain" behavior in other people really is indicative of actual pain, but there's no way to prove it. You might ask, "Hey Juan, are you in pain? Did you burn your hand?" And Juan could say "Of course! Don't you see me jumping around and yelling?" But Juan's response is just more behavior, namely verbal behavior. So to test whether Juan's behavior showed he was in pain, you only looked at more of Juan's behavior. That's not going help. It is analogous to wondering if Mary is lying to you about already being busy on Saturday night, and deciding that asking her would settle the issue. "Say Mary—are you lying to me?" "Of course not!" she replies. Are you more convinced of her honesty? You shouldn't be. Maybe she's still lying. You can't test Mary's honesty by asking her, and you can't test whether Juan's behavior indicates pain by looking at more of Juan's behavior.

Not only is there no way to give positive evidence for (2), but here's a reason to think that (2) is out-and-out false: acting. When an actor pretends to be in **pain**,[12] he shows all the same pain behavior that someone really suffering would show. Yet of course the actor isn't really in pain; it's all make-believe. Pain behavior isn't proof of real pain, and more generally no behavior guarantees any particular mental state. 6.29

Wittgenstein gave a nice illustration of the idea that behavior is no proof of **mental states**.[13] Imagine that every person has a small box that they can look into. We can each see into our own boxes, but can never peer into someone else's box. Everyone calls the contents of their own box "a beetle." 6.30

I know that there is a beetle in my box, of course, since I can look right into it. Admittedly, you say the same words, "There is a beetle in my box too." But how can we be sure that we are using the word "beetle" to mean the same thing? Maybe there is a marble, or a coin, or a Cheez Doodle in your box, and you call it a "beetle." You might think the same thing about me—I'm calling what's in my box a "beetle" but you have nothing more than my words to go on. We have no way to *confirm* what's in each other's boxes. In fact, there might be nothing at all in your box, and you call your empty box a beetle.

6.31 In just the same way, you call a certain sensation that you have when you burn your hand "pain," and Juan uses the same word when he touches a hot stove. But, like Wittgenstein's beetle, you have no way of telling whether you and Juan are having anything remotely like the same sensations. Generalizing the problem, you have no way to determine whether Juan has the same kinds of mental states that you do, or even whether he has a mind at all (there might be nothing in Juan's box, but he still calls it a "beetle"). The other minds problem is especially acute for substance dualism. Remember, dualists think that minds are immaterial things that you can't see, touch, smell, feel, or taste. They are inherently private; the only way you can tell what's going on in your own mind is through introspection. You can only look inside your own box.

Second Theory of the Mind: Behaviorism

6.32 In the first half of the twentieth century, philosophers and psychologists widely disparaged substance dualism as requiring a mysterious "**ghost in the machine**."[14] Given all the problems with dualism, they started looking for a different account of the mind. An alternative approach came out of the other minds problem just discussed. If the only evidence you have about anyone else's mind is what they say and how you see them act, then let's just focus on behavior and forget about looking for invisible ideas and sensations. It could be that behavior is all we need to understand mentality.

Explanation of the theory

6.33 Consider the meaning of "beetle." Perhaps "beetle" means nothing more than the way in which people use the word. Like all words, it may be used with more precision or less, or it could be ambiguous and have more than one meaning. We learn the meaning (or meanings) of "beetle" by seeing how others use the word, just as we learn all words by observing how our parents and teachers use them. If we learn meanings only through our experiences of how words are used, then it looks like a short step to the additional claim that the meaning itself is to be found in use. That is, not only do we learn meanings through the verbal behavior of others, but there is nothing more *to* meaning than that behavior. Behavior is all we have to go on, and positing invisible agency behind that behavior—like dualism does—leads to all kinds of problems, as we've seen.

Now apply this meaning-as-use idea to the words for mental states. If 6.34
the meaning of words is just behavior, then that works for "pain," "blue," "happy," "pensive," "belief," and all the rest as well. "Pain" means no more than certain motions and noises, and "sweet tasting" refers to other motions and noises. We can take a sentence that is about mental states, for example:

- Paul has a toothache.

And translate it into a sentence that only refers to various sorts of behavior, like this one:

- Paul complains about his tooth, holds his hand to his jaw, moans, chews his food very slowly and gingerly, and so on.

The behaviorist idea is that the second sentence tells us everything that the first sentence did, without using any words that appear to be about private mental states, like "toothache." Toothaches just become ways of talking about what we observe. They are sort of like sunrises and sunsets. We talk about the sun rising in the sky, but we all know that the sun isn't really moving relative to a stable Earth. We're really the ones moving, and the whole sun rising business is an optical illusion. Nevertheless, it's handy to talk about the sun rising or setting, even when we know that it does no such thing. Likewise it's convenient shorthand to talk about toothaches and other supposedly "mental" states, even when we know that such talk really refers to behavior. In reality, mental states are no more real than sunrises.

That troublesome mental language is thereby ditched in favor of nice 6.35
wholesome talk about behavior. For behaviorists, mental states are publicly observable facts, not the hidden, private beetles of dualism. Minds are right out there in the open, and no more or less observable than anything else

in the natural world. We might need some sort of theory to tie together the observations of behavior that we make, but that's no different from what is done in the rest of science.

Objection: Mental states without behavior

6.36 According to behaviorism, talk about mental states is just a way of speaking about behavior, in the same way that "sunrise" is a way of speaking about the earth's rotation and present position relative to the sun. This idea is only going to work out if every sentence that seems to be about a mental state can actually be replaced—without any loss of truth or meaningfulness—with a sentence about behavior. We saw above how this idea would work with "Paul has a toothache." But how about more complicated or sophisticated mental states? Consider these sentences:

- Einstein believes that $E = MC^2$.
- Todd is planning to go skiing, unless it gets too warm and the snow melts, in which case he will go cycling.
- Sarah is secretly in love with John.
- Philby, a double agent, knows to which country he is loyal, and to which he is feeding false information.

What kind of behavior are these sentences really about? The behaviorist must insist Einstein performs some sort of behavior equivalent to (and conveying all the same meaning as) believing that $E = MC^2$. It is not easy to see what that might be. What behavior is equivalent to Todd's making plans, so that we are not committed to a mental state of "planning"? Seeing what Todd does after the fact, whether he went skiing or cycling, tells us nothing about him when he is planning for the future. You might be tempted to say that the right behavior to look at is verbal behavior. Einstein *says* that "$E = MC^2$." Saying something is, of course, a kind of behavior. So we don't need to talk about what Einstein believes at all; in good behaviorist fashion, we can just refer to what he says or writes.

6.37 The problem with the verbal behavior move is that Einstein doesn't merely *say* that "$E = MC^2$"; he also *asserts* it. A five-year-old can say that "$E = MC^2$," but a five-year-old can't assert it because she has no idea what it means. Einstein's got something that the five-year-old does not—he understands what he's saying, and that's part of what it is to make an assertion. Looking at verbal behavior alone can't distinguish between just saying words that you don't understand and actually asserting something. The problem is that the behaviorist is in no position to claim

- Einstein believes that $E = MC^2$ = Einstein's verbal behavior (he says $E = MC^2$) + Einstein understands and asserts what he is saying.

Remember, the behaviorist's whole plan is to eliminate any reference to those unobservable mental states (like belief) by only talking about observable behavior. Once we do that, then we can write mental states out of our scientific psychology. However, making the vital distinction between saying and asserting requires sneaking a mental state—namely, understanding—back into the picture.

In the case of Sarah and her secret love for John, if Sarah's love really is 6.38
completely secret, presumably she isn't doing anything that indicates her feelings for John. At the very least her actions are ambiguous; they could be interpreted as loving, but perhaps they are just respectful, friendly, admiring, or the like. The secretiveness problem goes double for Philby. As a double agent, Britain's evidence about his behavior shows that Philby is their man, spying on the Soviets while pretending to be a Soviet agent who spies on Britain. But the Soviets have the same behavioral evidence, and they think he is a British agent they've turned to be a **Soviet mole**[15] in **MI6.**[16] There's surely some objective fact of the matter, having to do with the information Philby has, the disinformation he is spreading, and his loyalties and plans. If Philby is a really excellent double agent, then the KGB and MI6 can't tell his mental states (where Philby's loyalties really lie, what he knows, and what his intentions are) from his actions alone, which means that his mental states must be more than mere behavior.

Even the toothache example might not do as much as behaviorists hope. 6.39
Imagine two people with toothaches: Paul, who moans, groans, holds his jaw, and complains relentlessly, and Saul, a silent tough guy who stoically swallows his pain. Since Saul exhibits no pain behavior whatsoever, the behaviorists must insist that Saul is not actually in pain at all. But by hypothesis he *is* in pain. He just toughs it out. The behaviorist has little recourse but to rather lamely insist that either the hypothesis is impossible and Saul couldn't exist, or abandon real behavior in favor of dispositions to **behave.**[17] Maybe Saul doesn't exhibit pain behavior, but he *would* if he *were not* so stoic. Now the behaviorist has given up looking at Saul's actual behavior, and is instead talking about what Saul woulda, shoulda, and coulda done. Behaviorism's street cred depends upon its claims to be

robustly empirical, grounded in observations of the physical world. Once it is reduced to identifying mental states with merely possible behavior, that credibility starts to fade away.

6.40 Behaviorism apparently promises more than it can deliver. There's more to your mental life than just behavior—your behavior may often indicate what's on your mind, but that's about the best it can do. We might be able to salvage this core idea out of behaviorism, though: mental states are in some way physical. Mental states may not be behavioral states, but they still could be material or physical; we aren't yet driven back to Cartesian ghosts in the machine. Instead of looking at your behavior, let's look at your brain.

Third Theory of the Mind: Mind–Brain Identity Theory

6.41 Your brain is a moist, densely packed, pinkish-beige forest of neurons (the worker bees of the brain) and **glial cells** (the support staff).[18] It's about three pounds and the consistency of Jell-O. It's also the most complex object in the known universe. Your brain is not a uniform mass, but has large-scale structural parts like left and right hemispheres and various chunky bits, such as the cerebral cortex, the cerebellum, and the brainstem. The cerebral cortex itself is further divided into the temporal, frontal, occipital, and parietal lobes. While there is some overlap and redundancy, the various regions of the brain are rather specialized. For example, vision involves the occipital lobe, whereas hearing involves the temporal lobes. The ability to speak is connected with a tiny part called Broca's Area, in the inferior frontal gyrus. Fortunately, there's a certain amount of plasticity in the brain, where one section can take over the duties of another section, should the latter get injured on the job and go on disability.

Explanation of the theory

6.42 What does all this fancy brain business have to do with mental states? Consider seeing a yellow banana. Various wavelengths of light pass through your cornea and hit the cells of your retina. The receptor cells are the rods and cones. There are three types of cones, with overlapping sensitivities to shortwave, mediumwave, and longwave light between 700nm and 400nm. The energy from the photons causes these cells to fire excitedly. Depending on the light hitting the cones, sometimes the shortwave cones will fire more than the longwave cones, and the middlewave cones, or the middlewave cones will fire more, and so on. There will always be some ratio among the firing of the cones. The information about this firing ratio is transmitted to the ganglion cells and then along the optic nerve fibers to the visual cortex in the occipital lobe of the brain. There the information is processed into the visual sensation of a yellow banana. Disrupt any of these steps and you won't see a thing.

Visual sensations in your mind clearly have a great deal to do with visual 6.43
processing in your brain. According to the mind–brain identity theory, that's because they are exactly the same thing. A pattern of neural activity in the visual cortex just *is* seeing a yellow banana. Some particular event in your brain is identical with the sensory event of seeing a banana. After reading Descartes's argument for dualism, you may find the identity theory puzzling or off-putting. But identity theorists are quick to point out that science makes all sorts of similarly surprising discoveries.

- Lightning is identical to an electrical discharge.
- Gold is identical to atoms with 79 protons, 118 neutrons, and 79 electrons.
- The stars the Greeks called Hesperus and Phosphorus are really the same celestial object, the planet Venus.
- The grape varieties Syrah and Shiraz are genetically identical.
- Heat is the mean kinetic energy of molecules.

It took real investigation to sleuth out these facts; physics, astronomy, and biology all had roles to play. Each of these discoveries went against centuries of misunderstandings, wild speculations, and misinformation. Science has unpacked the mysteries of the fire of the stars, the origin of time, the evolution of life, and how to **transmute lead into gold**.[19] Is it really such a surprise that wonder, knowledge, love, sight, and sound turn out to be no more than physical events? The mind–brain identity theorist claims that what DNA testing did to settle the score about wine grapes, neuroscience is in the process of doing to explain the mind. Every mental event is really a physical event—just sit back and wait for the brainiacs to fill in the details.

Objections to the mind–brain identity theory

Objection 1: The subjectivity of experience A prominent objection to the 6.44
mind–brain identity theory is that it fails to capture the most essential fact

about our mental lives, namely that they have a *feeling* to them, a quality that brain events do not. Neurons and synapses are described in the cold, objective language of science—we're told about their biological structures and given mathematically precise accounts of their electrochemical interactions. Yet you *see* the yellowness in the banana and *taste* its sweetness. Where is yellowness and sweetness in the electrical activity of the synapses of your brain? Where is the feeling of your memories and your passions? Those subjective sensations, the way they feel to you, are somehow missed by objective science.

6.45 Can you imagine what it is like to be a whale, or a dog, or a bat? Vision dominates the way in which human beings experience the world around us (our visual cortex is much larger than our olfactory cortex) but the reverse is true for dogs. Dogs are able to **discriminate odors** at concentrations nearly 100 million times lower than humans can.[20] The world is a complex, textured mosaic of smells for a dog, the indicators of distance, the passage of time, and the movements of friends and foes. It's not just that dogs are sort of like you when it comes to the power of smell, only more so. The fundamental way in which they understand and map reality is through scent.

6.46 Or consider bats. Their primary method of sensing the world is with a sense that human beings don't have at all—echolocation. Try to imagine singing a note as loud as a jet engine, but so high in pitch that it is beyond the range of human hearing. You listen carefully for the echo from the objects around you, sensing the **Doppler shift** of sound as the echoes come bouncing back.[21] From these echoes you construct a 3D mental map of your environment. Now imagine doing all that while weighing less than a pound, flying zigzag through the air, and snatching mosquitoes you've spotted by echolocation. What is it like to be such a creature? How does it feel from the inside? There just doesn't seem to be any way for **human beings** to know.[22]

6.47 But if there is no way to know what it is like to have those subjective mental states, then no matter how much the mind–brain identity theorist tells us about bat brains or dog cortexes, no matter how many details science provides about olfactory receptors or ultrasonic echoes, we still won't understand the mental lives of dogs and bats.

6.48 *Response* Here's how mind–brain identity theorists reply to the subjectivity objection. Many of the other identifications that science has made go against, or ignore, our subjective sensations. For example, you would naturally think that temperature has something to do with how hot or how cold things feel. Yet according to science, temperature is just the mean kinetic energy of a group of molecules; the scientific definition completely ignores those subjective feelings. Should we conclude that thermodynamics is just plain wrong about the nature of temperature? Of course not. When a snowball feels cold and a campfire feels hot, all that means is that our bodies are responsive to temperature, that the feelings of hot and cold are a way to get some information about the temperature of snowballs and campfires. Touching something isn't nearly as accurate as a thermometer, but it is a way of learning about temperature. None of that means that temperature is in some important way related to whether things feel hot or cold. Your sensations *indicate* temperature, but they do not *constitute* it.

There are different pathways or routes to the same facts. Touch is one 6.49
way to get at the facts of temperature, using a thermometer is another. People who suffer from congenital insensitivity to pain with **anhidrosis** (**CIPA**) can't feel pain, heat, or cold.[23] They can't touch something to learn about its temperature. Nevertheless, the snowball is still cold, and its temperature is objectively measurable with thermometers, even if a CIPA sufferer can't feel it. Using a thermometer is one way to arrive at temperature facts, touching is another. People with CIPA can't use touch to figure out the temperature, but they *can* use thermometers. Just because every mental event is really a physical event doesn't guarantee that knowing all the relevant physical processes provides every possible route to understanding the facts about the mind. The neuroscience of bat brains and the physics of sound waves *can* tell us everything there is to know about what it is like to use echolocation, even though you would need to be a bat to have certain ways to access those facts. Bats have a way to understand echolocation that humans do not. Nevertheless, we can know every fact there is about bat echolocation. Likewise, objective science can tell us all the facts about the mind.

Response to the response Just to sum up the discussion so far, the identity 6.50
theorist says that mental states are identical with brain states. The subjectivity objection is that the identity theory fails to explain the feeling, the what-it's-like of mental states. The identity theorist's response is that internal sensations are only one way to know the facts about mental states. Objective neuroscience is another perfectly valid and equally good way to know all the same facts. The subjectivity objector isn't finished yet, though. Here's his rejoinder, known as the knowledge **argument.**[24]

Imagine a super-smart neuroscientist named Mary. Mary has been raised 6.51
and lived her entire life in a black-and-white room. All her knowledge of

the wider world comes from a black-and-white TV. Nevertheless, she has become one of the world's foremost experts on how the brain processes visual information. Mary knows everything there is to know about the optical ganglia and the neurons of the visual cortex. According to the identity theory, Mary knows all the facts about color, even though she has never seen any color other than black, white, and shades of gray. Now suppose that the door to her monochromatic room is finally opened, and she steps out into the **multicolored world**.[25] Here's the question: did Mary learn anything when she saw colors for the first time?

6.52 The Mary example is a famous philosophical thought experiment, but there's a real-life medical case that poses exactly the same issue. Sue Barry is a professor of neurobiology, and is an expert on visual processing, binocular vision, and **stereopsis**.[26] Barry was born cross-eyed, which meant her eyes were not properly aligned with each other and couldn't focus on the same point in space. The result was that she lacked the depth perception that ordinary noncross-eyed people have. If you cover one of your eyes and see how flat and two-dimensional the world looks with just one eye, you'll have a sense of what her vision was like. In 1996 Barry was asked by the neurologist Dr Oliver Sacks if she knew what **stereoptic vision**—the sense of depth produced by having two eyes separated from each other but focused on the same thing—was like.[27] She insisted that she did know, on the basis of her extensive scientific knowledge, and could imagine stereoptic vision quite well, even though she had never experienced it.

6.53 After 1996 Barry began to have problems with the fine muscles of her eyes, and sought help with an optometrist who recommended a new kind of visual physical therapy. This therapy taught Barry how to fixate both eyes on the same point in space, so that the images of the world delivered by each eye were fused together by the brain into a three-dimensional picture. Once she had learned to do so consistently, objects "popped out" at her—her subsequent diary is filled with poetic astonishment at the depth and texture of the world. In 2004 Barry wrote to Dr Sacks to say, "You asked me if I could imagine what the world would look like when viewed with two eyes. I told you I thought I could . . . But I was wrong" (Sacks, 2010, p. 124). Sue Barry had no idea what she had been missing.

6.54 Now, the identity theorist is compelled to insist that in fact Mary already knew all the color facts before she walked through that door. She didn't learn anything new. The same for Sue Barry. She did know everything about stereoptic vision before being able to see that way, and it could not have been a revelation. But that response seems very strange. Intuitively, Mary *did* learn something, and Barry herself insists that her scientific knowledge didn't add up to knowing what seeing properly with two eyes really was like. Yet according to the identity theory, neither of them learned a thing; at most they acquired a new way to access facts that they already possessed. If you think that is the wrong way to think about it, then you may want to reject the identity theory.

Objection 2: Multiple realizability Here is another objection to the mind– 6.55
brain identity theory. According to the identity theory, mental states are identical to brain states. In a fully developed neuroscience of the mind, we'll get statements sort of like these:

- John sees yellow = the lateral geniculate nucleus relays the cellular excitation information from John's retinal cells to such-and-such neurons in the primary visual cortex, which fire in such-and-such patterns.
- Maria hears an A-flat = hair cells in the epithelium of Maria's inner ear trigger nerve impulses along the eighth cranial nerve which travel to the primary auditory cortex in the temporal lobes, where such-and-such nerves fire.

Every possible mental state will spelled out in terms of what's happening in the brain. *Planning to go shopping, feeling amused by a joke, looking for Mr Goodbar*, and *waiting for Superman*, will all be given neural equivalents. You might be doubtful about such a promise—if it is kept at all, it will be pretty far into the scientific future. Current neuroscience is nowhere close to pulling this off. In some sense that's just a practical or technical problem, not a reason to think that the mind–brain identity theory isn't right in principle. However, here's a reason to think that no matter what amazing things future neuroscience does, it will never show that mental states are identical to brain states as sketched above.

We have to take seriously the idea that John's seeing yellow is *identical* 6.56
to—the very same exact thing as—some complicated story about his retinal cells and visual cortex neurons. Just to keep it simple, let's say that seeing yellow = brain state Y (with the understanding that brain state Y is just shorthand for some very detailed neurological story about human brains). What this means is that if anything else is going on in John's brain besides brain state Y, it is not the experience of yellow. Nothing can have the experience of yellow unless it is in brain state Y, because that's just what the experience of yellow *is*. The way to think about it is that since water = H_2O,

nothing is water unless it is made out of two hydrogen atoms and one oxygen atom. Other things can be wet, drinkable, and good for washing, but they are not water.

6.57 Here's the problem. There is excellent, universally accepted experimental evidence that **honeybees** can see in color.[28] Their color vision is somewhat shifted from our own, though, as they are unable to see red, yet can see into the ultraviolet range, which we can't. However, honeybees *can* see yellow, despite the fact that their **brains** are the size of a sesame seed and have no structural similarity to our own.[29] In fact, bees and humans only share 30 percent of their genes. All of which means that honeybees cannot be in brain state Y; their miniscule brains don't have the right parts, design, or genetics. Nevertheless, they can still see yellow, which implies that seeing yellow is not identical to brain state Y. Bees can be in a yellow-seeing brain state, but it is not the same as the human yellow-seeing brain state. Thus seeing yellow is not identical to any particular brain state.

6.58 The point about seeing yellow can be generalized to other mental states as well. Mental states are *multiply realizable* by different kinds of physical things. All kinds of different actual and possible creatures can have sensations, or make plans, or feel emotions, despite having brains radically unlike our own. Honeybees are just one example.

6.59 Here's the argument in brief:

1.	Mental states are identical to brain states.	(mind–brain identity theory)
2.	Therefore, seeing yellow = brain state Y.	(from 1)
3.	Honeybees cannot be in brain state Y.	(premise)
4.	Therefore, honeybees cannot see yellow.	(from 2, 3)
5.	Honeybees can see yellow.	(premise)
6.	(4) and (5) contradict, therefore the assumption in (1) must be false. Mental states are not identical to brain states.	(*reductio ad absurdum*)

The multiple realizability argument has been very influential, and has driven philosophers away from the identity theory. So where do we go from here? The central physicalist idea is that you need something physical in order to have thoughts and sensations. The lesson of the multiple realizability argument is that you don't need anything in particular. Perhaps the mind isn't a sort of hardware at all—maybe it's *software*. Just as a computer program or application might run on all kinds of computing hardware that are built out of various semiconductor chips and have an assortment of logic board designs, so too mental states might run on brains as different as humans and honeybees. The mind as software is the idea behind functionalism.

Fourth Theory of the Mind: Functionalism

Functionalism takes from substance dualism the insight that the mind is an abstract, immaterial object, and it also accepts the physicalist demand that the mind must be connected to material objects. There are no disembodied minds for functionalists, but at the same time minds aren't just brains either. One analogy is that of music. 6.60

Explanation of the theory

When **Texas bluesman Blind Lemon Jefferson**[30] made his first recording in 1925, he played and sang directly into a conical horn, with his natural sound alone powering a cutting stylus to engrave a wax disc. This disc was then used as the master for fragile shellac resin records, which were played back at 78 revolutions per minute (rpm). Later this same recording would have been reproduced on more durable long-playing vinyl records that played at 33 rpm. Still later Jefferson's original recording was copied onto magnetic tape, in the form of compact cassettes, reel-to-reel, and 8-track. Now his music is in the digital domain, and you can get it on CD, or buy from iTunes. The point is that it's irrelevant what encodes "Matchbox Blues" or "See That My Grave's Kept Clean"—an antique 78, an old cassette, or brand new MP3. They are still the very same songs, kept in existence by various media. It's still Jefferson's voice and six-string guitar coming through the speakers. No matter what the technology of the future is, so long as blues lovers make sure there are recordings of Blind Lemon Jefferson in that format, his music still lives. 6.61

Functionalism holds out the same promise of immortality. According to functionalism, your brain is no more than an old wax master that encodes your mind. It may be that other kinds of hardware could also contain your mind, and if your thoughts, memories, and personality can get perpetually transferred onto the latest medium, then your mind too can live forever. 6.62

A natural question for functionalists is if the mind is just a sort of software that can run on all kinds of hardware, could it run on a computer? 6.63

Not the biological, wet-ware computer of your brain, but a computer of the dry, digital, silicon variety? Something as puny and simple as a honeybee brain can see colors, smell flowers, learn language (the **waggle dance**[31]), form memories, and navigate the world—surely a computer could do the same. Perhaps no existing computer is up to the task, but let's consider the possibility that we could, in principle, build one that has mental states. From the point of view of functionalism, it is hard to see why we couldn't.

6.64 Suppose Apple came out with the new iBrain—the first computer that thinks and feels just the same as you do! Would you believe their claims? What would be good, acceptable evidence that the iBrain really does live up to the Apple hype? In 1950 the British cryptologist and logician **Alan Turing**[32] gave the first and most famous answer to this question. Start by thinking about why you believe that other human beings have a mind like you do. You might want to say that it's because of how others look, or how they behave. A little reflection shows that can't be right, though; after all, you believe that you are engaged with a human mind just by talking with someone on the phone, or by emails, or instant messaging. The evidence that there's a real person on the other end is that they *respond* to you in perfectly sensible ways. What they say isn't crazy talk, but just an ordinary, everyday conversation. If instead you got a lot of nonsense or gibberish in response to your comments, you might start to wonder whether you're really IM'ing with a real person.

6.65 Turing argued that if you were to engage in a conversation with a computer and you couldn't tell whether you were talking with a computer or a real human being, then you would have perfectly good evidence that the computer has a mind every bit as much as a human being. The evidence that the computer has a mind is exactly the same evidence you use to conclude that the unseen being on the other end of an IM chat has a mind—the things they say and how they respond to you. Sometimes Turing has been charged with being a behaviorist about the mind on the grounds that he equates mentality with verbal behavior. But that criticism is wrongheaded. Turing argues that human level linguistic behavior is good, sufficient *evidence* of mentality, not that it is the very same thing as mentality. Turing's proposal is known as the:

> ***Turing Test***:[33] A thing has a mind if you can talk with it as sensibly as you can a human being.

No one has ever built a computer that can pass the Turing Test. Lots of people have tried, though, and the attempts get better every year. There's an international competition, the **Loebner Prize**,[34] in which programmers compete to design a computer that can best pass the Turing Test. The Loebner judges have online chat sessions with both computers and human beings. They aren't told in advance which is which, and have to figure it out based upon the responses. The best annual entry receives a bronze medal and $4000. If a computer persuades two or more judges into thinking it is human, that wins $25,000 and a silver medal. No computer has yet won this prize. The top honor, to go to a computer—well, to its programmers—that fully passes the Turing Test (the Loebner Prize requires that the winning computer respond appropriately to visual information too) is $100,000 and a solid gold medal.

All existing computers fail the **Turing Test**, although there are some quite clever attempts to pass it.[35] However, that all attempts so far have failed does not show that the functionalist theory of the mind is wrong, or that Turing's behavioral test for minds is misguided. The real question is whether it is possible *in principle* to design such a computer. It might be just a matter of time before technology catches up and someone wins the gold medal. If that happens we need to be prepared—have we created a true thinking machine, a microchip person, a new form of life? 6.66

Objections to functionalism

Objection 1: Emotions, feelings, and sensations You might be inclined to argue that even if Apple's iBrain could pass the Turing Test, all that really shows is that the computer can communicate like a human being does. But at most it will be like Star Trek's **Lt Commander Data**—an emotionless android that feels no pain, experiences no joy, and never loves, hates, worries, or laughs.[36] Without the full suite of human emotions and feelings, a computer will never have a human-like mind. At most it will be a kind of pale **imitation**,[37] a faded and imperfect copy. 6.67

Replies Here are two replies to the "no emotions" objection. First, the demand that computers are able to have feelings or emotions is too strong. There are human beings who suffer from psychopathy, autism, and other disorders that leave them emotionally blind. They may be unable to read the emotions of others, or feel certain emotions themselves. Nevertheless such people still have minds. **Helen Keller** was deaf and blind,[38] and so couldn't sense the world very well, but her lack of sensation didn't prevent her from thinking, learning language, and communicating. So even if it is true that computers have no feelings or emotions, that is irrelevant to the 6.68

issue of whether they can think or have minds. It may be possible for a creature to have thoughts, make plans, formulate ideas, and possess beliefs even if they have no sensations or feelings. Even if objection 1 is granted, it misses the mark. Failing to have a human-style mind does not mean failing to have a mind at all.

6.69 The second reply is that the only reason you have to think that human beings have feelings, emotions, and consciousness, is the way they behave, talk, and interact. You can easily conclude that one of your friends is unhappy when she texts you "**He told me they were just razor bumps**!"[39] or that she is flattered when she texts you "I just walked into a room at this party and someone yelled '**dibs**!'"[40] There's no reason that a computer couldn't tell you just the same things. A computer capable of passing the Turing Test should be fully capable of all the same verbal behavior that conveys emotions. In that case, you'd have no more reason to deny that a computer has feelings than you do to deny that other human beings have feelings. If observing behavior is a good enough reason to believe humans feel, then observing behavior is a good enough reason to believe machines feel. If it is not a good enough reason, then we are led to doubt that other humans really have emotional minds. The evidence in both cases is just the same.

6.70 *Objection 2: Creativity* In the mid-nineteenth century, the English mathematician **Charles Babbage** designed the first computers.[41] His original conception was an intricate mechanical device capable of arithmetic calculations to 31 digits. Babbage called this device the Difference Engine. The Difference Engine only existed on paper until a working model was made from his blueprints over 100 years after his death. Babbage also designed, again, only on paper, a machine called the Analytical Engine, which could be programmed using punch cards.

6.71 Few people at the time saw Babbage's designs as anything more than practical calculators, a sort of a cotton gin for number nerds. One far-sighted correspondent was the mathematician **Ada King**,[42] better known as the Countess of Lovelace. Lady Lovelace is credited with writing the first computer program, a method of designing punchcards for the Analytical Engine that would calculate a series of **Bernoulli numbers**.[43] She also foresaw the idea that computing machines might eventually be seen as intelligent because of their calculating power. In Lady Lovelace's view, machine intellect could never rival the minds of human beings, on the grounds that machines cannot learn, or do anything truly original. Here's her argument.

1. The output of a computer is strictly a predictable function of input by human programmers.
2. Humans, on the other hand, do not have this limitation; we are fully capable of originality and creativity.
3. Thus no matter what mighty powers of computation a computer might display, it will never rival the thought of human beings.

If Lady Lovelace's objection is right, then either the Turing Test is wrong or it is impossible to build a computer that would pass it.

Reply Three computing innovations illustrate why the first premise of this 6.72
argument is doubtful. The first is IBM's chess-playing computer **Deep Blue.**[44] Deep Blue was capable of evaluating 200 million possible chess moves per second, and could learn from its own mistakes. Deep Blue was a far superior chess player than any of its human programmers, and developed its own strategies during the course of play. None of its programmers knew in advance what moves Deep Blue would play, and they had no way of finding out other than to watch and see what it did. After the computer beat world chess champion Garry Kasparov in 1997, Kasparov declared that he had seen deep intelligence and creativity in Deep Blue's moves and promptly accused the programmers of cheating by allowing human intervention in the game. Kasparov, like Lady Lovelace, couldn't imagine that a machine could be authentically creative.

A second example is **Experiments in Musical Intelligence** (**EMI**).[45] 6.73
Musicologist and composer David Cope fed the works of numerous great classical composers such as Mozart, Beethoven, Mussorgsky, and Bach into a computer. He then programmed the computer to find commonalities among, say, all 371 Bach chorales, and distill Bach's signature style. The resulting program, EMI, could then write its own chorales in the style of **Bach.**[46] While some of these compositions have been good enough to fool classical music aficionados, on the whole they are distinctly second-rate. But being second-rate to Mozart or Bach hardly means there is no musical merit there, or that the compositions are not creatively original. They are. All musicians have their influences and yet no one denies that their works are still original creative works. Cope, like the programmers of Deep Blue, has no idea what music EMI will compose, and no way to predict it ahead of time. There is no reason to suppose that EMI is any less inventive or innovative than human composers who may be heavily influenced by their predecessors. "**Last Train to Clarksville**"[47] is an original Monkees song, even though without the Beatles there would be no Monkees.

6.74 The third example is another IBM machine, **Watson.**[48] Watson was designed to play the game show Jeopardy. In the show, the host gives various answers, and contestants must guess the correct questions, in the format of "What is . . . ?" Playing Jeopardy is harder than playing chess or writing sonatas in this way: winners have to have an incredibly broad knowledge of every area of human activity and inquiry, not just one narrow pursuit like chess or music. Not only that, but contestants have to recognize puns, wordplay, contextual clues, and linguistic trickery. Here's some sample Jeopardy answers and questions that Watson got right:

- Nearly 10 million YouTubers saw Dave Carroll's clip called this "friendly skies" airline "Breaks Guitars." (answer: What is United Airlines?)
- Aeolic, spoken in ancient times, was a dialect of this. (answer: What is ancient Greek?)
- A recent bestseller by Muriel Barbery is called this "of the Hedgehog." (answer: What is *The Elegance of the Hedgehog*?)
- You're just a little stiff! You don't have this painful mosquito-borne joint illness with a Swahili name. (answer: What is dengue fever?)

Watson wasn't connected to the Internet. It is a completely stand-alone, autonomous machine jam-packed with millions of books, including dictionaries, encyclopedias, and the entire content of Wikipedia, among other things. It is capable of finely parsing language, reviewing its colossal database, generating hypotheses as to the correct answer, and assigning probabilities to each of those hypotheses. It can do all this in a microsecond. In game play, it crushed Ken Jennings and Brad Rutter, the two greatest (human) **Jeopardy champions.**[49] Afterwards, Jennings quipped, "I for one welcome our new computer overlords."

6.75 There's no question that Watson is an amazingly impressive machine; like Deep Blue and EMI, it is no mere pocket calculator. It may not pass the Turing Test, but is still a landmark in the development of **artificial intelligence.**[50] Even so, you may wonder whether Watson actually *understands* what it is saying, whether it *comprehends* the answers that it gives. When Watson reviews a million books in a second and issues a probability report, does it actually know what it is doing, or is it no more than the whirr and clank of a mindless machine that only imitates a mind? A famous objection to functionalism argues that no computer can ever do more than manipulate symbols, no matter how much it looks from the outside that it understands language.

Objection 3: The ***Chinese room***[51] Perhaps the best-known objection to artificial intelligence (and by extension, functionalism) comes from the Berkeley philosopher **John Searle.**[52] Imagine that you are a native English speaker (which you probably are, if you're reading this book) and that you don't know a word of Chinese. You can't read Chinese or speak it, and Chinese ideograms look like so many meaningless squiggles to you. Now suppose that you get a job that requires you to sit alone in a room with two fat books. In one of these books is nothing but long lists of Chinese symbols. You look on the spine and it reads *Database.* The other thick tome is in English, and contains nothing but rules about how to manipulate ideograms; that is, how to correlate certain Chinese symbols with other Chinese symbols. On the spine it says *Program.* Your new boss tells you to expect slips of paper with Chinese writing on them, and to follow the rules in the *Program* book. The slips of paper start coming in (let's call these the input) and you consult the *Program* book for what to do. It tells you how to look up the input symbols in the *Database* book and, on the basis of the rules, write down other symbols. You write down the new symbols on a fresh sheet of paper (let's call this the output) and send it out of the room to your employer. 6.76

Unknown to you, the input contains questions in Chinese, and the output that you return is the answers, again given in Chinese. If you are efficient and accurate in using the *Program* book, then from the perspective of someone outside of the room, you are indistinguishable from a native Chinese speaker. What they see are Chinese questions going into the room, and correct Chinese answers coming back out. So from the outside perspective, it looks like you understand Chinese. But you don't—you don't understand the language at all. You don't even understand what you're doing with your symbol manipulations, or why. You only know *how* to use the *Program* and *Database* books to look up input squiggles and write down different output squiggles. You understand the syntax (how to manipulate symbols according to rules) but not the semantics (the meaning) of your actions. 6.77

While you effectively implement a Chinese-language program, you still don't understand Chinese. A computer is no better off than you are. The fact that it might run a program so that, from the outside, it looks as if it understands questions that are posed to it, and it can give correct and cogent answers, does not show that it has any awareness of what it is doing. Which means a computer could pass the Turing Test without having any cognitive states at all. It could receive English-language input in the form 6.78

of questions and deliver sensible English-language in the form of answers, but it is simply manipulating symbols. It does not have a mind. Here is a summary of the Chinese Room argument:

1. In the Chinese room you do not understand Chinese, even though you are a perfectly competent syntax-crunching symbol manipulator.
2. Computers are just like the Chinese Room.
3. Therefore, computers are just syntax-crunching symbol manipulators with no understanding or awareness of what they are doing. (from 1, 2)
4. Therefore, at best, computers only simulate minds.
5. The Turing Test can't distinguish between real minds and simulated minds.
6. Therefore it isn't an adequate test of whether computers are capable of having minds.

None of this is to suggest that minds aren't machines or essentially connected to them. After all, the brain is a kind of machine. If functionalism is right and thought is something abstract or immaterial, then it should be able to be implemented in lots of different formats, just like musical recordings. The Chinese Room argument seems to show that thought has to be something more than just mathematically manipulating symbols. Thinking is more like photosynthesis or lactation—computers can model or simulate those processes, but you're never going to get milk out at the end. Lactation isn't some abstract, formal procedure; it's an organic causal process that requires the right kind of biology. Thinking requires the right kind of biology too, just like lactation. Yet if thought and understanding really does require the brain's biochemical wetware, then the mind isn't like a piece of music, as functionalism contends. Thought isn't essentially abstract like "Matchbox Blues," and so isn't something transferable from format to format. In the end the mind does require the brain, but not in the way functionalism says. Thus functionalism isn't the correct theory of the mind, and we're back to square one.

Conclusion

6.79 There is no received view of the nature of the mind, or a well-established explanation of consciousness. We have reviewed some of the leading contenders: substance dualism, behaviorism, mind–brain identity theory, and functionalism. Each of these has contemporary supporters, and has been developed in increasingly sophisticated ways. Functionalism is probably the most commonly accepted theory, and functionalists have developed a considerable literature on ways to escape the Chinese Room and other objections to functionalism that cannot be treated here.

Still, the mind remains a deep and vexing puzzle, one that is so intrac- 6.80
table that some philosophers have thrown in the towel and declared that explaining the nexus between the mind and the body is beyond the power of **human reason**.[53] How can nonconscious bits of matter come together to build a conscious mind? How can mental events cause physical events (and vice versa)? How can the stimulation of our nerves produce sensations like sound, color, and taste? Do mental properties emerge out of the purely physical properties of objects or do even atoms have rudimentary mental qualities that when properly assembled become minds? Why aren't we unconscious zombies who shuffle through the world without any mental states at all? These are open questions that philosophers of mind and cognitive scientists continue to grapple with. The fact of your subjective experience is at once boringly commonplace and yet a glittering faceted diamond—hard, rare, unbroken.

Annotated Bibliography

Bisson, Terry (1990) "They're Made Out of Meat," *Omni*, full text available at www.terrybisson.com/page6/page6.html, accessed May 17, 2012. A marvelous one-act play in which sci-fi writer Terry Bisson makes vivid the strangeness of thinking meat. Seriously, you should read this.

Descartes, René (1641) *Meditations on First Philosophy*, full text available at www.earlymoderntexts.com/pdfbits/dm3.pdf, accessed May 17, 2012. In the Sixth Meditation, Descartes gives his classic argument for substance dualism.

Kean, Sam (2010) *The Disappearing Spoon and Other True Tales of Madness, Love, and the History of the World from the Periodic Table of the Elements* (New York: Little, Brown). Everything about the history of the periodic table that you didn't learn in chemistry class, with loads of anecdotes, personalities, and intrigue. Chapter 4 contains a nice discussion of stellar nucleosynthesis—how exploding stars made all the elements in your body.

Mandik, Pete (forthcoming) *This Is Philosophy of Mind: An Introduction* (Oxford: Wiley-Blackwell). A more in-depth discussion of various theories of the mind, including views not discussed here such as epiphenomenalism, anomalous monism, solipsism, and eliminativism. Mandik also addresses mental phenomena such as perception and intentionality.

Nagel, Thomas (1974) "What's it Like to Be a Bat?" *Philosophical Review* 83:4, 435–450, full text available at http://organizations.utep.edu/portals/1475/nagel_bat.pdf, accessed May 31, 2012. A fantastically influential article in which Nagel gives the subjectivity of experience objection to mind–brain identity theories.

Place, U. T. (1956) "Is Consciousness a Brain Process?" *British Journal of Psychology* 47, 44–50, full text available at http://home.sandiego.edu/~baber/analytic/Place1949.html, accessed May 31, 2012. A seminal defense of the mind–brain identity theory.

Putnam, Hilary (1960) "Minds and Machines," in Hook, Sidney (ed.), *Dimensions of Mind* (New York: New York University Press), pp. 148–180, full text available at www.csun.edu/~tab2595/PutnamMAM.pdf, accessed May 17, 2012. One of the first arguments for functionalism.

Ryle, Gilbert (1949) *The Concept of Mind* (London: Hutchison), full text available at http://archive.org/details/conceptofmind032022mbp, accessed May 17, 2012. Ryle denounces dualism as a "ghost in the machine" and defends a form of behaviorism about the mind.

Sacks, Oliver (2010) *The Mind's Eye* (New York: Alfred A. Knopf). A warm, humane, literate, and insightful series of case studies by a famous neurologist. Chapter 5 is about Sue Barry, the woman who gained three-dimensional vision late in life.

Searle, John (1999) "The Chinese Room," in Wilson, Robert Andrew and Frank C. Keil (eds), *The MIT Encyclopedia of the Cognitive Sciences* (Cambridge, MA: MIT Press), pp. 115–116. A succinct statement of Searle's Chinese Room argument and some common responses.

Smart, J. J. C. (1959) "Sensations and Brain Processes," *Philosophical Review* 68, 141–156, full text available at http://philosophyfaculty.ucsd.edu/faculty/rarneson/Courses/SMARTJACKphil1.pdf, accessed May 17, 2012. Another early and influential defense of the mind–brain identity theory.

Turing, A. M. (1950) "Computing Machinery and Intelligence," *Mind* 59:236, 433–460, full text available at http://mind.oxfordjournals.org/content/LIX/236/433.full.pdf+html, accessed May 17, 2012. Turing's discussion of the possibility of thinking computers was ahead of its time, and the Turing Test continues to be important in cognitive science, philosophy of mind, and artificial intelligence.

Wittgenstein, Ludwig (1953) *Philosophical Investigations*, trans. Anscombe, G. E. M. (Oxford: Basil Blackwell). Section 129 contains the quotation about how we often fail to notice things that are right before our eyes.

Online Resources

1 A discussion of the Nobel Prize-winning scientific article that established stellar nucleosynthesis: http://en.wikipedia.org/wiki/B%C2%B2FH
2 A scientific paper on the massive amounts of microbes on the Earth: www.pnas.org/content/95/12/6578.full.pdf
3 A brief note on how much of the biomass is composed of ants and termites: www.madsci.org/posts/archives/2001-05/989366143.En.r.html
4 The life and works of the twentieth-century philosopher Ludwig Wittgenstein: http://plato.stanford.edu/entries/wittgenstein/
5 The complete text of Descartes's *Meditations on First Philosophy*: www.earlymoderntexts.com/pdfbits/dm3.pdf
6 The official website of Cambridge cosmologist Stephen Hawking: www.hawking.org.uk/
7 An overview of Saul Kripke's book *Naming and Necessity*: http://en.wikipedia.org/wiki/Naming_and_Necessity
8 A paper by Lord Kelvin, in which he claims that a universe of finite size is inconceivable: http://zapatopi.net/kelvin/papers/on_the_age_of_the_suns_heat.html
9 The complete text of Wittgenstein's *On Certainty*. He discusses the impossibility of lunar travel in section 286: http://web.archive.org/web/20051210213153/http://budni.by.ru/oncertainty.html
10 NASA's detailed account of the first moon landing: www.nasa.gov/exploration/home/19jul_seaoftranquillity.html
11 The life of Princess Elizabeth of Bohemia, who raised the mind–body objection to Descartes's substance dualism: http://en.wikipedia.org/wiki/Elisabeth_of_Bohemia,_Princess_Palatine
12 A death scene from the film *Platoon*, demonstrating faked pain behavior: www.youtube.com/watch?v=9HzIVc2vwVE&feature=fvst
13 A scholarly article entitled "The Uses of Wittgenstein's Beetle: *Philosophical Investigations* §293 and Its Interpreters": www.uiowa.edu/~phil/documents/TheUsesofWittgensteinsBeetlePI293.pdf
14 The complete text of Gilbert Ryle's *The Concept of Mind*, the book in which he criticizes "the ghost in the machine": http://archive.org/details/conceptofmind032022mbp
15 A discussion of clandestine spies, the long-term sleeper agents known as "moles": http://en.wikipedia.org/wiki/Mole_(espionage)
16 The official website of the British secret intelligence agency, MI6: https://www.sis.gov.uk/

17 A sophisticated discussion of dispositional properties, such as solubility and fragility: http://plato.stanford.edu/entries/dispositions/
18 An animated tour of the human brain, describing its parts and functions: www.youtube.com/watch?v=9UukcdU258A&feature=grec_index
19 A brief note on the physics of transmuting lead into gold: http://chemistry.about.com/cs/generalchemistry/a/aa050601a.htm
20 A note on the power of scent in canines: http://en.wikipedia.org/wiki/Dog#Smell
21 An explanation of how the Doppler shift works: http://science.howstuffworks.com/radar2.htm
22 A video of a rare instance of human echolocation: www.youtube.com/watch?v=YBv79LKfMt4
23 The clinical description, cause of, and treatment for congenital insensitivity to pain with anhidrosis: http://en.wikipedia.org/wiki/Congenital_insensitivity_to_pain_with_anhidrosis
24 A discussion of the Mary the colorblind scientist thought experiment and various critical responses to it: http://en.wikipedia.org/wiki/Mary's_room
25 Willy Wonka's multicolored world of pure imagination: www.youtube.com/watch?v=RZ-uV72pQKI
26 A discussion of how stereoptic vision works: www.vision3d.com/stereo.html
27 Neurologist Dr Oliver Sacks talks with Sue Barry about how she gained the sense of 3-D vision after a lifetime without it: www.youtube.com/watch?v=308-n1_tBUk&lr=1
28 Facts about color vision in honeybees: http://en.wikipedia.org/wiki/Bee_learning_and_communication#Color_Discrimination
29 Information about bee brains: http://phys.org/news123927986.html
30 The life and music of Texas bluesman Blind Lemon Jefferson: http://en.wikipedia.org/wiki/Blind_Lemon_Jefferson
31 A discussion of the dancing language of bees: http://en.wikipedia.org/wiki/Waggle_dance
32 A detailed account of the sad, fascinating life of Alan Turing, and his enduring legacy: http://plato.stanford.edu/entries/turing/
33 A close analysis of Turing's thoughts on the Turing Test for machine mentality, along with its critical reception: http://plato.stanford.edu/entries/turing-test/
34 The home page of The Loebner Prize in Artificial Intelligence, to be awarded to the first computer to pass the Turing Test: www.loebner.net/Prizef/loebner-prize.html
35 A fun interactive artificial intelligence program called Evie: www.existor.com/
36 All you ever wanted to know about Lt Commander Data from *Star Trek: The Next Generation*: http://en.memory-alpha.org/wiki/Data

37 *Star Trek: The Next Generation* episode "The Measure of a Man," in which the mental life of the android Data is addressed, and the Turing Test applied: http://en.memory-alpha.org/wiki/The_Measure_Of_A_Man_(episode)

38 The inspirational story of Helen Keller, blind and deaf from infancy: http://en.wikipedia.org/wiki/Helen_Keller

39 User-submitted text messages from people who have generally made questionable decisions: www.textsfromlastnight.com/Text-Replies-11287.html

40 User-submitted text messages from people who have generally made questionable decisions: www.textsfromlastnight.com/Text-Replies-3012.html

41 Charles Babbage, the English mathematician, philosopher, inventor, and mechanical engineer who originated the concept of a programmable computer: http://en.wikipedia.org/wiki/Charles_Babbage

42 A biography of Ada Lovelace, the English mathematician and daughter of Lord Byron who is considered the first computer programmer: http://en.wikipedia.org/wiki/Ada_Lovelace

43 A mathematical introduction to Bernoulli's numbers: http://numbers.computation.free.fr/Constants/Miscellaneous/bernoulli.html

44 The history of the chess-playing IBM computer Deep Blue: http://en.wikipedia.org/wiki/Deep_Blue_(chess_computer)

45 Composer/programmer David Cope's account of his music-writing software, Experiments in Musical Intelligence: http://artsites.ucsc.edu/faculty/cope/experiments.htm

46 A video interview with David Cope about Experiments in Musical Intelligence: www.youtube.com/watch?v=yFImmDsNGdE&feature=related

47 A music video of the Monkees' song "The Last Train to Clarksville": www.youtube.com/watch?v=VUUSdvwEC_Y

48 A discussion of the architecture, development history, and capacities of IBM's Jeopardy-playing computer: http://en.wikipedia.org/wiki/Watson_(artificial_intelligence_software)

49 A video of Watson competing on Jeopardy with Ken Jennings and Brad Rutter: www.youtube.com/watch?v=WFR3lOm_xhE

50 A detailed overview of research in artificial intelligence: http://plato.stanford.edu/entries/logic-ai/

51 An in-depth discussion of the Chinese room argument, the principal responses to it, and how it fits into larger philosophical issues: http://plato.stanford.edu/entries/chinese-room/

52 An overview of the philosophical work of John Searle: http://en.wikipedia.org/wiki/John_Searle

53 A succinct summary of Colin McGinn's view that the mind–body nexus is unknowable: www.consciousentities.com/mcginn.htm

7

KNOWLEDGE

Epistemology is the theory of knowledge. Knowledge, evidence, arguments, truth, and belief are the meat and potatoes of epistemologists. While these topics may initially sound abstract or remote, the issues of what you ought to believe and why affect every part of your life. The questions of how we can come to have knowledge, and how far our knowledge can extend, are so basic that epistemology is considered one of the most fundamental philosophical enterprises. Let's start off with a question that, like many so far discussed in this book, is deceptively simple on the face of it. 7.1

The Value of Truth

Do you have a right to your own opinion? It's a safe bet that you are ready to indignantly insist that of course you have a right to your opinion. Like most questions in philosophy, though, a little reflection shows that that it's more complicated than it first appears. One way to understand the question is this: do you have the right to express your own opinion? Put this way it looks like a mere matter of law. In the United States you mostly do have a right of free expression (thanks to the First Amendment to the Constitution). In other countries expression may be curtailed in various ways. In Germany it's illegal to declare your love for the National Socialist Party, in Saudi Arabia it is unlawful to insult the prophet Muhammad, in France it is illegal to boo the national anthem. The issue of expressing your opinions is largely a matter for governments and lawyers, not philosophers. There's 7.2

This Is Philosophy: An Introduction, First Edition. Steven D. Hales.

a way to understand the question of whether you have a right to your own opinion which is clearly philosophical, though:

- Is it OK to believe whatever you want?

Regardless of whether the government might crack down on you for expressing your beliefs, is it all right for you to believe whatever you choose to in the privacy of your own mind? Before you answer, consider the following question, which looks awfully similar:

- Is it OK to do whatever you want?

The answer to this question is obviously *no*. It's not OK to do whatever you want. The reason is obvious: some things are *wrong* to do, there are things you should not do. You could still do those wrong things—perhaps no one's stopping you—but you would be making a moral mistake. Chapters 1 and 2 on ethics in the present book deal with the ins and outs of what you shouldn't be doing. Analogously, maybe there are things that you should not believe. You could believe those wrong things anyway, but by doing so you would be making a mistake. Not a moral mistake, perhaps, but at least an intellectual one.

The rational principle

7.3 So what kinds of things would be the wrong thing to believe? How about this: *false* things. It's an intellectual mistake to believe false things; you shouldn't believe them. Instead (hold onto your hat!) you should believe true things. Perhaps that doesn't sound too radical to you. Let's formulate it as a principle.

> *The rational principle*: You should gain truth and avoid error.

In other words, we should do whatever we can to have only true beliefs; we don't want any false beliefs. As rational thinkers we should prune our garden of beliefs, weeding out the false, the mistaken, the erroneous, the bogus and foolhardy. Instead we keep what is right, true, and real. Now, you may well ask how we can tell the difference between the true and the false, how we can tell the flowers from the weeds. That's an excellent question. But let's hold off on that a bit; we'll get to it shortly.

You might think that the rational principle isn't right, since sometimes mistakes are useful and by messing up we can figure out what the right thing really is. In which case we shouldn't avoid error at all. Making errors is a useful step along the road to the truth. It's like if you're learning to play tennis—you hit a lot of shots out before you learn to hit them in consistently. 7.4

Well, sometimes things work that way, but often people believe ridiculous things and never get one inch closer to giving them up and finding the truth. If we stop caring about avoiding errors, that's a recipe for giving up an active search for truth entirely and instead just passively hoping that we'll eventually see our mistakes in the fullness of time. Supposing that we will always see our mistakes for what they are, the principle still holds: we don't *want* to make errors, even if they are inevitable. The goal is to get rid of false beliefs and gain true beliefs. The tennis example is the right one. The first commandment of tennis is *you should hit your shots in and not hit them out*, a mighty fine principle to adopt, even if you're going to miss a lot of shots as you learn the game. A more serious challenge to the principle that you should gain truth and avoid error we'll call the hedonist's challenge. 7.5

The hedonist's challenge

The rational principle looks cold and puritanical, just the sort of boring edict you'd expect from friendless eggheads. We're each going to kick around on the planet for 80 years or so—who cares whether what we believe is true or false? If you want to believe in space aliens, worship the **Flying Spaghetti Monster**,[1] think that there are energy chakras, or admire talk-show hosts for their insight and wisdom, knock yourself out. It just doesn't matter. If believing something makes you happy, if it gets you through the day, then go for it. If hunting down the truth floats your boat, then go for that instead. But if you prefer the tabloids to ***The New York Times***,[2] that's just as good. 7.6

The hedonist principle: You should believe whatever makes you happy.

Hedonists aren't opposed to the truth, they're merely indifferent to the truth. The key difference between the rational principle that you should gain truth and avoid error and the hedonist principle that you should believe whatever makes you happy has to do with what the value of truth is supposed to be. A little philosophical joke will help illustrate this difference. (There aren't a lot of philosophical jokes; we need to enjoy all the ones we have).

> Socrates was widely lauded for his wisdom. One day the great philosopher came upon an acquaintance who ran up to him excitedly and said, "Socrates, do you know what I just heard about one of your students?"
>
> "Wait a moment," Socrates replied. "Before you tell me I'd like you to pass a little test. It's called the Test of Three."
>
> "Test of Three?"
>
> "That's right," Socrates continued. "Before you talk to me about my student let's take a moment to test what you're going to say. The first test is Certainty. Have you made absolutely sure that what you are about to tell me is true?"
>
> "No," the man said, "actually I just heard about it."
>
> "All right," said Socrates. "So you don't really know if it's true or not. Now let's try the second test, the test of Goodness. Is what you are about to tell me about my student something good?"
>
> "No, not really, Socrates."
>
> "So," Socrates continued, "you want to tell me something bad about him even though you're not certain it's true?"
>
> The man shrugged, a little embarrassed.
>
> Socrates continued. "You may be able to tell me though, because there is a third test, that of Usefulness. Is what you want to tell me about my student going to be useful to me?"
>
> "No, not really."
>
> "Well," concluded Socrates, "if what you want to tell me is neither Certain nor Good nor even Useful, why tell it to me at all?"
>
> The man was defeated and ashamed. This is the reason Socrates was a great philosopher and held in such high esteem. It also explains why he never discovered that his wife was stepping out with Plato.

What is the value of truth, or the value of attaining it? There are two possibilities.

1. The value of truth is *intrinsic*. Truth is valuable in itself, for its own sake, regardless of whether knowing it produces happiness or any other valuable thing.
2. The value of truth is *instrumental*. Truth is valuable insofar as knowing it allows us to survive, achieve our goals, and makes us happy. That is, the truth is no more than a useful tool to help us get what has

> intrinsic value. The Socrates joke treats truth as instrumentally valuable only (the test of Usefulness). Socrates was not harmed in any way by his false belief in his wife's fidelity. The truth doesn't really matter so long as there is no downside to false belief and believing makes you happy. There's no point in caring about truths that lead to unhappiness; in fact in those cases it's better to believe in a nice soothing lie.

There's no doubt that truth does have instrumental value. When considering medical treatment, it is best to know the truth about your condition, and know whether your surgeon trained at **Johns Hopkins**[3] or at Hollywood **Upstairs Medical College.**[4] If you're standing in the middle of a highway, you'd be better off possessing the truth that the truck seems to be getting larger because it is rapidly bearing down on your position, instead of believing the falsehood that sometimes trucks grow rapidly in size. When picking mushrooms for dinner, knowing how to spot the differences among chanterelles (delicious), amanita phalloides (poisonous), and amanita muscaria (hallucinogenic) is a valuable skill to have. The question is whether the *sole* value of truth is instrumental; if truth also has intrinsic value, then we should covet it for its own sake. We should want the truth, in the German philosopher **Fichte's** clarion cry, "even though the heavens fall."[5]

The hedonist principle takes the value of truth to be solely instrumental, 7.7
whereas the rational principle assumes that truth also has intrinsic value. "Gain truth and avoid error" advises pursuing the truth regardless of what it might do for you, or whether it would benefit you somehow. "Believe what makes you happy," on the other hand, recommends the truth only occasionally, just in those cases where it is a nice pleasant truth to have. Otherwise, forget it. How shall we decide which way to go?

Let's consider the following thought experiment and see whether you 7.8
think that truth has intrinsic value as well as instrumental.

Suppose that your boyfriend or girlfriend is cheating on you. Often. 7.9
Further imagine that there are two possible paths the future might take. Path 1: You find out about the cheating. The usual recriminations, crying, accusations, arguments, blowups, and breakups ensue. Path 2: You never find out about the cheating and nothing bad ever happens. Let's be as clear as possible—no one gets an STD, no one gets pregnant, there are never any rumors or suspicions, and from your perspective, everything is going just fine in your relationship.

7.10 Which path do you want to take? Do you want to find out about the cheating or not? If you do want to know, consequences be damned, then you believe that the value of truth is intrinsic. The case was specifically designed so that there was no downside to remaining cheerfully ignorant, and learning the truth only led to unhappiness. If you wanted the truth about your cheating partner anyway, it was not because it made you happy. It was because, to quote **Emil Faber**,[6] knowledge is good. If you preferred the second path, in which your partner keeps on cheating and your never find out about it, then you think that the value of truth is solely instrumental; it is only good to have the truth if it produces something useful or valuable for you have, like happiness. Like Socrates in the joke, if there is no good payout for learning the truth, then forget about it.

7.11 If you are like most people, then you would want to know if your partner is cheating on you. Which means that you think that possessing the truth has intrinsic value. Thus the rational principle is right about our intellectual duties: we should gain truth and avoid error. Even if the rational principle is correct, that doesn't mean that you are necessarily interested in every topic under the sun, or care about what's true in every area of human inquiry. Do you care who will win the next World Cup or American Idol? Do you care whether **Goldbach's conjecture** is true?[7] Does it matter how many angels can dance on the point of a **needle**?[8] Maybe not. Nevertheless, there may be value in things that hold no personal interest for you. As the fidelity example above illustrates, some of that value is intrinsic.

7.12 But how can we pursue this goal? How can we tell whether our beliefs are true or false, or when we should go ahead and believe some claim or proposal?

The Value of Evidence

7.13 In the 1980s **Michael Shermer** was a professional marathon cyclist.[9] In the **Tour de France**, cycling's most famous race, riders churn out up to 140 miles in a single day.[10] Marathon riders do more than twice that distance, for days on end. Shermer once completed the **Race Across America** (3100 miles) in 10 days, 8 hours.[11] Only Iron Man triathletes and ultramarathon runners approach this level of relentless, body-punishing competition. Shermer and his fellow marathon cyclists were ready to try anything to improve their performance, and keep them strong in the saddle. After all, reasoned Shermer, what did they have to lose? If someone had a theory, why not take it on faith and try it out?

Fraud and quackery

Shermer once fasted for a week on a diet of nothing but a potion made 7.14
of water, cayenne pepper, garlic, and lemon. Halfway through a long ride he collapsed, violently ill. He went out to a health spa for a mud bath that was supposed to suck the toxins out of his body, and found his skin was dyed red for a week. Shermer set up a negative ion generator in his bedroom that would charge the air to give him more energy. It only turned the walls black with dust. An iridologist studied the irises in his eyes, and told him that the little green flecks meant there was something wrong with his kidneys. Shermer's never had a kidney problem before or since. He set up a pyramid in his apartment to focus energy, and only got strange looks from guests. Shermer then had a Rolfing massage, which is a really deep tissue massage, and it hurt so much that he never went back. During one race, he slept under an "Electro-Acuscope" which was promised to measure his brain waves and put him into an alpha state for better sleeping, rejuvenate his muscles, and heal his injuries. Instead it did nothing he could detect. Finally, a nonaccredited "nutritionist" advised taking handfuls of assorted vitamins and minerals every six hours during the Race Across America. They were so disgusting that Shermer could barely choke them down. But he did, and wound up with nothing but the most expensive and colorful urine in America. It was then that he decided maybe he should not believe every extravagant claim and snake oil salesman that came his way. He went back to college and ultimately earned a Ph.D. in the philosophy of science, starting a second career promoting critical thinking.

The entire history of medical fraud and quackery is based upon sick folks 7.15
who don't look into the scientific rationale for the claims that people make and instead choose to believe in remedies because they sound good, or conform to their own prejudices, or are slickly marketed. Pleasure is no proof of truth, though. In the nineteenth and early twentieth centuries, trained medical professionals used the electric vibrator to cure "female problems" like hysteria, nervousness, and weakness, by causing hysterical paroxysm (i.e. orgasms). In its advertising copy, the manufacturers of the **White Cross Electric Vibrator**[12] claimed that:

> Vibration is life. It will chase away the years like magic. Every nerve, every fibre of your whole body will tingle with the force of your own awakened powers. All the keen relish, the pleasures of youth, will throb within you. Rich, red blood will be sent coursing through your veins and you will realize

> thoroughly the joy of living. Your self-respect, even, will be increased a hundredfold. (Maines, 1999, p. 108)

Even earlier, the elixirs of patent medicines usually contained at least one of the following ingredients: alcohol, opium, or a laxative. All three of these had immediate effects of one sort or another, thus assuring the user that the medicine was "working." For example, Lydia Pinkham's Vegetable Compound, chiefly marketed to women, contained some useless vegetable root extracts and was 19 percent (38 proof) alcohol. This of course, was not mentioned in their advertising, which claimed "for all weaknesses of the generative organs of either sex, it is second to no remedy that has ever been before the public, and for all diseases of the kidneys it is the greatest remedy in the world." Needless to say, if you spent the afternoon knocking back some Lydia Pinkham's and going a few rounds with the White Cross, you'd feel a lot better. But that's a far cry from actually curing a disease or improving your lasting health.

7.16 Many quack remedies were, and are, downright dangerous. Consider the Testone Radium Energizer, which was produced and sold around 1900. Radium had only been recently discovered, and the principles of radiation were badly understood, especially by nonphysicists. The Testone Radium Energizer was essentially a jockstrap laced with 20 micrograms of refined radium, 200 times the tolerance dose set for workers at the Manhattan Project. Yet according to the advertising copy, it

> is a scientific means of applying the ENERGIZING GAMMA RAYS to the male gonada, or testes—those fountain-head of Manly Courage and Vigor . . . The Radium Pad comes into direct contact with the testes and completely envelopes them. In this manner, these vital sex glands may be KEPT CONSTANTLY under the strengthening influence of the radium rays—truly a greatly desired benefit . . .

Sounds great, right? Radium has a lot of energy, energy is good for you; it will put some pep in your step. Besides which, the company guaranteed the product. What could go wrong?

7.17 In the list of the world's worst inventions, the Testone Radium Energizer has to rank right up there; sterility, radiation poisoning, cancer, and death are likely side effects. It may not be as bad as the hydrogen bomb, but it's a good thing the Energizer was outlawed before Michael Shermer could buy special Testone Radium cycling shorts. They would surely give new meaning to saddle sores.

Ways we can go wrong

Quack medicine and fraudulent solutions to problems never go away. 7.18
Loads of people have gotten rich through Internet sales of **penis-enlargement creams** and supplements, despite the fact that none of their products work in the slightest.[13] The same thing is true of fad diets and various lotions, minerals, and massagers that are claimed to eliminate **cellulite.**[14] Newspapers regularly recount the plight of victims of stock market and investment scams. There are scores of ways in which we can wind up believing the wrong thing. We can

1. be taken in by swindlers and con artists
2. just look at one-sided evidence
3. refuse to consider the evidence against what we already believe
4. believe in something because we really want it to be true
5. be prone to psychological biases.

There are all kinds of ways that we might mess up in forming our beliefs, and the field of critical thinking is essentially applied epistemology, in which one learns the scientific method, studies how to assess evidence, and examines how to be on guard against shoddy reasoning and our own psychological foibles. For our purposes here, we can at least note this: *evidence matters.* Our rational goal is to gain truth and avoid error, and the best strategy is to look at the evidence. To be sure, there will be plenty of times that our evidence is incomplete, or misleading, and we will wind up believing something false, just as a novice gardener may sometimes pull up flowers instead of the weeds. There are no guarantees. Nevertheless, evidence is the signpost on the road to truth.

How Much Evidence Do We Need?

Part 1: We need a lot

Just how much evidence for a claim do we need before it becomes rational 7.19
to believe that claim? In the late nineteenth century, the English mathematician and philosopher **W. K. Clifford** considered this question and proposed a striking, and firm, answer.[15] Clifford declared that:

> *It is wrong always, everywhere, and for anyone, to believe anything upon insufficient evidence.*

It's not enough to have *some* evidence for a claim. Not just any old reason will do to make a belief a reasonable one. Clifford thought that only *sufficient* evidence was enough to justify believing. Admittedly, just what sufficient evidence means isn't completely clear, but minimally he means that you need considerable evidence to believe something; the evidence needs to obviously point to one thing before believing that claim to be true is the right choice. When there's no credible evidence, or the data is incomplete, or the arguments seem to lead to all sorts of different conclusions, then the smart action is to suspend belief until the evidence is in and we can tell what really is the most reasonable thing to believe.

7.20 Clifford offers a thought experiment. Imagine a shipowner who is about to send out an emigrant ship, carrying several families over the ocean to a new home. The ship he is sending out is rather old, and has a lot of nautical miles on her. People had raised some doubts about her seaworthiness, and suggested that maybe the ship should be dry-docked, inspected, and overhauled before going out again. The shipowner considered these suggestions, but managed to convince himself that the ship was fine and ready to go. He put out of his mind any ungenerous suspicions about the integrity of shipwrights and contractors, and told himself that the ship has already made so many successful voyages that surely the Lord will see the emigrant families safely to their new home. With this sort of reasoning, the shipowner convinced himself that the ship was sound and seaworthy.

7.21 The shipowner was not deceitful or dishonest. He sincerely believed in the soundness of the ship. It's just that his belief was not grounded in actual evidence (like one might get from an impartial inspection); instead he was engaged in rationalization and self-deception. Clifford gives two different endings to this case: in the first the ship sinks at sea with a loss of all hands. In the second the ship makes it safely over the ocean to port. Clifford argued that, from the point of view of rational belief and intellectual integrity, it didn't make a bit of difference whether the ship sank or not. The shipowner did the wrong thing by forming his belief on the basis of self-deception and wishful thinking instead of on the basis of evidence. So whether the shipowner fulfilled his intellectual duties had nothing to do with the truth or falsity of his beliefs about the ship. Instead it had everything to with whether his beliefs were based upon sufficient evidence, good reasons, and cogent arguments. The shipowner needed a lot of evidence to believe that the ship was seaworthy, and he didn't have it.

7.22 You might object that it didn't matter if the shipowner thought that the ship was sound. His beliefs were irrelevant—all that mattered was whether he inspected the ship before sending it out. He could have believed that the ship was fine and still gone through the process of inspecting it. The problem with this approach, as Clifford himself notes, is that if you have already decided what the truth is before looking at the evidence, you aren't going to be impartial. Prejudice hinders rational assessment, which is why defense attorneys question prospective jurors before a trial (during ***voir dire***[16]) and dismiss those who already have an opinion about the defendant's guilt or innocence. Clifford advises keeping an open mind until all the evidence is in.

Another objection you might raise is that beliefs are essentially a private 7.23
matter. Duties and obligations are to other people, not to ourselves; the very idea of an *intellectual* duty is senseless. We might have moral duties to act in certain ways, but that just underscores the idea that it's actions that matter, not what we believe in the privacy of our own minds. The shipowner did something wrong when he sent out a dodgy ship, but what he believed or didn't believe is irrelevant. So he didn't need any evidence at all to form his beliefs; beliefs are just a personal choice.

The problem with this objection, according to Clifford, is twofold: first, 7.24
our beliefs invariably influence our actions. Letting careless reasoning and ignorant beliefs off the hook when they lead to negligent actions like that of the shipowner is about like letting a gunman off the hook and putting all the blame on the bullet instead. Second, and more important, we have an obligation to posterity to pass down the best beliefs we can. What we teach our children is the most important legacy that we can leave them, and we should do everything we can to make sure that we pass along the best knowledge of our time. We can fill our children's minds full of prejudice and superstitions or we can educate them and provide what wisdom we can. To be sure, what counts as knowledge to one generation may be overthrown by the discoveries of the next. But we should make sure that our successors do not have to start with nothing.

Clifford makes no distinction between beliefs like the shipowner's, which 7.25
mattered considerably to the welfare of others, and insignificant, trivial beliefs that affect no one. He thought that no beliefs are truly trivial. Having unjustified beliefs leads to the bad habit of not caring about evidence and reason, and this habit only paves the way for more unjustified beliefs. It's like a lawman who decides that he'll take only small bribes to look the other way on minor crimes. Once that line has been crossed, small bribes have a way of growing until complete corruption sets in. Crooked cops undermine a civil society based on the rule of law, and sloppy, dishonest thinking

leads to losing reverence for truth and honesty. Not caring about the evidence, not caring about how to reliably find the truth, only means that you don't really believe in the intrinsic value of truth after all.

7.26 Getting things right is so important that not only must we insist on evidence for what we believe, but we need a lot of evidence. To believe, to make a judgment, is to enter into a sacred intellectual trust—it is not something to be done lightly. You've got to make sure that you've done everything you can to get it right.

Part 2: Go on, take a chance

7.27 The philosopher and psychologist **William James** mounted the biggest challenge to Clifford's view that we should only believe if we have sufficient evidence to do so.[17] James and Clifford agree in some important ways; both confirm that:

- Our goal as rational thinkers should be to gain truth and avoid error.
- If nearly all the evidence supports some claim P and there is practically no decent evidence against P, then the rational thing to do is believe P. P is most probably true.

Where they differ is in cases where the evidence is less than sufficient, where the evidence is mixed or ambiguous. For example, suppose that you're wondering whether it will rain later today. You check one newspaper in the morning and it says that it will rain. You look at another newspaper and it says that the rain will pass to the south and miss you completely. So you turn on the TV and the Weather Channel says that in fact the rain is going to hit you after all. But the weatherman on the local news channel reports that the rain will be elsewhere and you'll stay dry. There is credible evidence that it will rain on you this afternoon, and equally credible evidence that it will not rain on you this afternoon. Clearly you want to believe that it will rain if and only if it is actually true. So what should you do?

7.28 In any case where there is mixed evidence for some claim P, there are three possible choices.

1. Withhold belief about P. Just refuse to either believe or deny P until more evidence comes in that clearly settles the matter about P and you can make a more informed decision.

2. Go ahead and believe P anyway.
3. Go ahead and deny P anyway.

Obviously the Clifford approach is to choose (1)—we should suspend judgment about P until we amass enough evidence that clearly points to the truth (or falsity) of P. Wait until we have sufficient evidence before believing anything at all about P. As James points out, Clifford sets very high standards for belief: don't believe anything until there is a ton of evidence for it. By setting such high standards, Clifford is excellent at avoiding errors. If you don't believe anything until there is a mountain of evidence for it, you won't be wrong very often. On the other hand, you won't be believing much at all, since there will be many things for which you just don't have enough evidence to lead you one way or another. Remember that our goal is to *gain truth and avoid error*. The Clifford approach of option (1)—withhold belief until the evidence shakes out—is terrific at half of this goal. Namely, it's great for avoiding errors. It's not so good at gaining truth, because if you don't believe very many things, it follows that you don't believe very many true things either.

In fact, suppose that you didn't care at all about gaining truth, and the 7.29
only thing you wanted was to avoid error. The best approach would be to believe nothing at all. You're never right, but you're also never wrong! Some of the **ancient philosophers**, like Sextus Empiricus, recommended this idea.[18] On the other hand, suppose that all you wanted was to gain as much truth as you possibly can, even if that means making a lot of mistakes. Then you should believe everything you hear. Believe contradictions if you can manage it. Sure, you'll be wrong a lot of the time, but by believing so much, you'll be sure to scoop up all the truths you can. Perhaps no philosopher has defended the extremely gullible view of believe everything you hear. The point is that the two parts of our rational goal pull in opposite directions. *Gain truth* advises believing everything, whereas *avoid error* advises believing nothing. How can we do both at once? Clifford and James both recommend looking to the evidence. Clifford sets a high evidential bar for believing, thus emphasizing the *avoid error* half of the goal. In other words, Clifford adopts the following risk averse principle:

> *Risk averse principle*: Better off to miss out on some truths rather than add more errors.

James's objection is this. OK, the risk averse principle is one way we might go, but why should we think it is any better than a more risk positive principle, one that promotes *gain truth* instead of emphasizing error avoidance? Such a principle is, he thought, just as rational to adopt as Clifford's risk averse principle.

> *Risk positive principle*: Better off to add more errors rather than miss out on some truths.

In a case of mixed and inconclusive evidence for P, the risk positive principle counsels us to go ahead and take a chance and believe that P is true. Yes, we will be wrong more frequently than with the risk averse principle, but we'll be right more often as well.

7.30 At this point you might well be saying that all these principles about belief, truth, and evidence sound awfully abstract and obscure; how could any of this stuff be relevant to your ordinary life? The answer is swift and perhaps surprising: you make decisions every day using analogues of the risk averse and risk positive principles.

7.31 Here's one example. Just like *gain truth and avoid error* is a good goal, so is *gain pleasure and avoid pain.* The problem is that many pleasurable things are risky or dangerous. Drinking a lot of alcohol may be fun, but there's the downside of hangovers. Skiing is a good time, but you could break your leg. Motorcycles, casual sex, cocaine, falling in love, gambling—all pleasurable, all with risks. If you only cared about avoiding pain, then you would sit on the couch, fasten your seatbelt, and take no chances. If you only cared about gaining pleasure, then you would stand naked on your head, popping a wheelie on your motorcycle at 100 mph down the highway while shooting China white. You're not going to go for either of those extremes. The two middle-of-the-road positions are:

> *Risk averse principle (pleasure/pain version)*: Better off to miss out on some pleasures rather than add more pain.

> *Risk positive principle (pleasure/pain version)*: Better off to add more pain rather than miss out on some pleasures.

So which will you, in general, prefer? Do you tend to avoid risk, or are you more willing to take some chances for a good time? There's not necessarily a right or wrong answer here, so much as a measure of your own personal attitude to taking chances. But, just as the twin goals of gain truth and avoid error are inversely proportional (you maximize one goal at the expense of the other), so too with pain and pleasure.

Here's another analogue, one that, like the pursuit of truth, has broader social ramifications than just your own pleasure and pain. One of the most fundamental objectives of the legal system is to *convict the guilty and set free the innocent*. As in the previous cases, the two parts of this goal are in conflict with each other. Clearly if we only cared about convicting the guilty, we would convict everyone charged with a crime, a plan sure to convict all the guilty parties. Yet if all that mattered was making sure that no innocent people were unjustly convicted, we would set everyone free, which would guarantee that no innocent person would go to prison. The middle positions are these: 7.32

> *Risk averse principle (guilt/innocence version)*: Better off to let some guilty go free rather than convict more innocent people.
>
> *Risk positive principle (guilt/innocence version)*: Better off to convict more innocent people rather than let any guilty people go free.

To ensure that we don't convict any innocent people, or as few as possible, we should set very high standards of evidence—the state should meet a robust and substantial burden of proof. By setting such high standards we won't be convicting very many innocent people, since it is hard to get that much evidence against someone who is in fact innocent. On the other hand, we will be letting many guilty people go free, because the prosecution just couldn't come up with enough evidence to sufficiently demonstrate their guilt. That's the risk averse principle.

To pursue the alternative aim of convicting the guilty we ought to lower our standards and make it easier to punish the accused; with a lower bar of evidence we'll be convicting more people, and therefore be convicting more guilty people. Of course, more innocent people will wind up in jail on the basis of flimsy or circumstantial evidence. That's the risk positive principle. 7.33

Which principle do you vote for in the guilt and innocence case, and why? If you're afraid of criminals harming you or your property, you'll likely opt for the risk positive version, to make sure that as many crooks as possible are behind bars. If you're more afraid of an omnipotent government robbing you of your civil liberties, then you'll want the risk averse principle, which will make it harder for an innocent citizen to get railroaded. There is no perfect solution that will maximize both objectives. 7.34

Recall that when it comes to gaining truth and avoiding error that Clifford defends the risk averse principle. James's point is not that the risk 7.35

positive principle is superior and that's the one we should adopt, but rather that the two are *equally rational*. There's no reason, in James's view, that we should privilege not screwing up over getting it right. We're entitled to believe anything "live enough for us" that it is tempting to believe; it's rational to be a little risky. If there is no evidence whatsoever for a hypothesis, that's beyond the pale; it's still wrong to believe something when there is nothing at all to back it up. But if there's some plausible evidence for a claim, even if it is inconclusive, then go ahead if you want—take a chance and believe it.

7.36 James's view does lead to some surprising results, though. If there is some evidence for and against some hypothesis or proposal P, then there is some evidence for and against not-P. The evidence that counts against P will count in favor of not-P, and vice versa. So on the risk positive principle, it would be just as responsible to go ahead and believe not-P as it is to believe P. James uses the example of "God exists" as a hypothesis he thinks there is some evidence for and some against, but neither conclusive. While James argues that it is rational to be risk positive and believe that God exists, it follows that it is just as rational to go ahead and believe that God does *not* exist when faced with conflicting evidence. So in the very best case, James shows that belief in P based on conflicting evidence is intellectually responsible. But he does not show that we ought to believe P when the evidence conflicts. Maybe we can't be criticized for believing P on grounds of reason and evidence, but we can't be criticized for denying P either. At the end we're left with a curious situation in which belief and disbelief are equally rational. At this point you might miss the good old option of suspending judgment and waiting for sufficient evidence.

7.37 Here's another odd result for James. Consider a case where there is conflicting evidence about some hypothesis. In fact, like our example above about whether it will rain this afternoon, let's suppose that the amount of evidence for and against is exactly the same. There are five data points, five good arguments, five equally decent reasons, (however you want to put it) both for the hypothesis and against it (Figure 7.1a).

7.38 In Case A, James is committed to saying that under the risk positive principle it is perfectly rational to believe that the hypothesis is true (there's evidence in its favor), and it is also completely rational to believe that the hypothesis is false (since there's evidence it is false). So far, no problem. But what about this case (Figure 7.1b)?

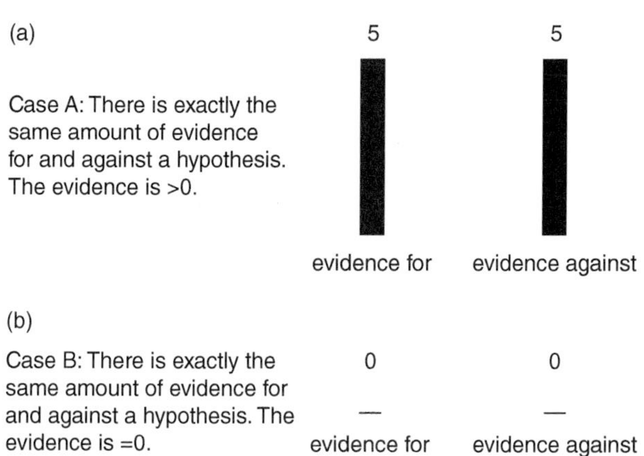

Figure 7.1 Balancing evidence

Suppose the hypothesis is that the next person who walks past you is wearing white socks. You can't see the color of their socks, or even whether they're going sockless. So you have no reason to believe that they're wearing white socks, and also no reason to deny it. Is it reasonable to go ahead and believe that they are wearing white socks? Presumably not; believing a claim on the basis of literally nothing whatsoever is surely the very essence of irresponsible belief. James might be willing to take some chances and believe things when the evidence is inconclusive, but believing when there is no evidence at all is something else altogether. So in Case B, the right call seems to be to withhold belief and suspend judgment until some actual evidence shows up that justifies believing one thing or the other. 7.39

Here's the problem: why not think that Case B and Case A really come to the same thing? That is, there's a sense in which the all the reasons to think it will rain this afternoon and the reasons to think it will stay dry *cancel each other out*. The scale of evidence is perfectly balanced in Case A, just as it is in Case B. So the mixed-evidence case is really the zero-evidence case after all. Which means that it's incoherent to think that belief is a rational choice in Case A, but irrational in Case B. Either you should think that you should withhold judgment in both cases, or it's fine to form a belief in both cases. This result is a predicament for James, who is fine with believing in the case of mixed evidence, but not in the case of zero evidence. So it could be that Clifford is right after all—high standards are the way to 7.40

go. Although then we're left with James's puzzle of why we should prefer to avoid error instead of gaining truth.

Sources of Evidence

Perception, testimony, memory, reason

7.41 Evidence for our beliefs can come from all sorts of places. You can gain evidence that James and Clifford once had a debate over the standards of beliefs by reading this chapter. Checking a site like www.weather.gov gives you evidence about **tomorrow's temperature.**[19] Your memory is evidence about what you need to do later; that is, you remember what your upcoming tasks are, and ground your beliefs in those memories. You might even have certain sorts of subconscious instincts or intuitions that are evidential. For example, you might instinctively know you can hit this fastball, or that you said something wrong to your girlfriend. And of course, your immediate perceptions can provide you with evidence—you know that the salsa picante is very spicy because you tasted it.

7.42 The traditional sources of knowledge include testimony (knowledge you get from good teachers and other reliable sources), memory (the things you directly recall to be true), and sensation. There is also the more abstract faculty of reason. For example, in the Sir Arthur Conan Doyle short story "A Scandal in Bohemia," Sherlock Holmes sees Dr Watson and tells him that he can see that Watson had gotten very wet recently, and has "a most clumsy and careless servant girl." Watson, constantly amazed at Holmes's powers of inference, asks how Holmes knew all this. Holmes replies,

> It is simplicity itself . . . My eyes tell me that on the inside of your left shoe, just where the firelight strikes it, the leather is scored by six almost parallel cuts. Obviously they have been caused by someone who has very carelessly scraped round the edges of the sole in order to remove crusted mud from it. Hence, you see, my double deduction that you had been out in vile weather, and that you had a particularly malignant boot-slitting specimen of the **London slavey.**[20]

Here Holmes uses reason to make an inference to the best explanation of what he observes about Dr Watson's shoe. This explanation, which is not the result of perception, memory, or testimony, takes the observation of the cut and damaged shoe and reasons backwards to its most likely cause. Watson quickly admits that Holmes is right.

Any of these sources of knowledge might be mistaken, and are no guarantee of truth. However, if you do have some knowledge, it's likely that it came from one of these sources. In 1690, John Locke argued that all of these—perception, testimony, memory, and reason—are grounded in one fundamental method, a sort of grand unification theory of knowledge. According to Locke, all of our knowledge ultimately comes from just one source, namely experience, or our sense perceptions. This is his theory of empiricism: there is nothing in the intellect that is not previously in the senses. The bumper sticker version is *no conceiving without first perceiving.* 7.43

Empiricism

Locke thought that when we are born our minds are a blank slate, or a *tabula rasa*. We have the capacity to learn, and the faculties for learning, but our minds are empty and waiting for nature to inscribe them. A more contemporary analogy than Locke's blank slate is that when you were born your mind was like a formatted, yet otherwise empty, computer hard drive. Then your experience of the world starts programming your head and filling it with information. When you remember something, you remember some earlier experience you had, some prior perception or sensation. When you rely on the testimony of others, you directly experience that testimony—for instance you read it in a newspaper, hear someone speaking, or look it up online. What's more, you assume that that the authority you've consulted has had direct experience of what they're talking about. If you believe that there was a car wreck on your commute because your friend told you about it, you assume that she saw the wreck herself, or, if she is just reporting what someone else said, that that person saw the wreck. It all goes back to someone's experience. 7.44

Even reason, like Holmes's inference to the best explanation above, is a matter of the mind assembling and rearranging the basic ideas given to it by experience. Nature programs your mind, but you are able to make connections among your ideas, draw inferences, and reason out new conclusions. You had no innate ideas, though. You weren't born knowing anything; knowledge must come from experience of one form or another. 7.45

Empiricism has been a vital step to developing the scientific method. Prior to the seventeenth century, knowledge was widely regarded as either 7.46

the product of pure reason alone or the result of religious revelation. In fact, a common medieval view is well expressed by Jorge of Burgos, a character in Umberto Eco's brilliant novel set in the fourteenth century, ***The Name of the Rose***, "There is no progress, no revolution of ages in the history of knowledge, but at most a continuous and sublime recapitulation."[21] After the fall from the golden age—whether Eden or the heights of classical Greece and Rome—there is no such thing as the advance of knowledge. Such a view is shocking only to us, heirs of empiricism and scientific inquiry, but not to Jorge's audience.

7.47 There have been many criticisms of Locke's empiricism. For one, it is hard to see how experience of the world leads to mathematical knowledge. Consider the Pythagorean Theorem: $A^2 + B^2 = C^2$. The length of the hypotenuse of a right triangle is the square root of the sum of the squares of the two sides. **Pythagoras** was reportedly so delighted when he discovered this theorem that he sacrificed several oxen to the gods.[22] But how could Pythagoras have discovered it empirically? No actual, physical, triangle has a perfect right angle or even perfectly straight sides, no matter how carefully you attempt to draw one. Therefore the Pythagorean Theorem can't be 100 percent accurate of any triangle in the world, even if it is 99.9 percent accurate. Yet all mathematicians regard it as an absolutely correct truth of Euclidean geometry. So if the theorem is true, it must be true of abstract, mathematically ideal triangles, not physical triangles that Pythagoras actually saw. Then how was his knowledge of the theorem grounded in empirical experience? It seems that it can't be.

7.48 More generally, there seems to be knowledge that, like knowledge of mathematics, is a priori. "A priori" is philosopher-speak for knowledge that is prior to experience, and independent from it. Consider ethical claims, like "you should keep your promises," or "capital punishment is immoral." Those might be true or they might be false, but either way it does not look like science, observation, and testing are going to sort it out. Philosophical reflection and argument, not empirical experience, is a more effective strategy.

7.49 Or how about these:

- All squares are rectangles.
- Everything that has a shape also has a size.
- Nothing completely red is completely blue.
- If anyone is a cyclist, then there are bicycles.
- All bachelors are unmarried.

You ask bachelor after bachelor for his marital status, and lo and behold, all tell you that they are wifeless. But you didn't have to do that—while experience can confirm that all bachelors are unmarried, you don't need to conduct such a poll to know that all bachelors are unmarried. Furthermore, no conceivable experience could undermine or refute the bulleted statements. They are true come what may; they must be true, they are *necessarily* true. Authentically empirical claims are not necessarily true. Consider these:

- The universe is 13.7 billion years old.
- Perpetual motion violates physical law.
- A meteor killed off the dinosaurs.
- My desk is 6 feet wide.
- Human beings share 98 percent of their DNA with chimpanzees.

Statements that are really empirical are contingent; they might be true or they might be false. We'll find out from experience, whether it is simple observation or a complicated scientific experiment, which it is. A priori statements are not contingent. If they are true, then they are necessarily true, and the most experience can do is to confirm the obvious, as in the bachelor example. If an a priori statement is false, then it is necessarily false. For example, "some circles have three corners" is necessarily false, and no matter how many circles you look at, you'll never find one with three corners. You don't even need to look at any to know that.

So one sort of criticism of Locke's empiricism is that there is knowledge 7.50 that is apparently not grounded in experience. Another criticism is that a priori knowledge has a quality of necessity about it, which empirical knowledge does not. Again this suggests that at best some of our knowledge is ultimately grounded in experience, but not all. But what is knowledge exactly? We have so far examined the value of the truth, the value of evidence, the matter of how much evidence we need to justify belief, and looked at little at some sources of evidence. Let's now ask about knowledge itself.

The Nature of Knowledge

In the film *Men in Black*, Agent Kay (played by Tommy Lee Jones) revealed 7.51 to Agent Jay (played by Will Smith) that there were extraterrestrial aliens secretly living in New York City. Afterwards, as they sat on a public bench, Agent Kay said,

> 1500 years ago everybody 'knew' the Earth was the center of the universe. 500 years ago everybody 'knew' the Earth was flat. And 15 minutes ago you 'knew' that people were alone on this planet. Imagine what we'll '**know**' tomorrow.[23]

Kay's point is that we often believe that we know things that we do not in fact know. It might have been the case that 1500 years ago that everybody thought that the Earth was the center of the universe, and, had you asked them, would have claimed to know it. But they were wrong. They knew no such thing, for the simple reason that the Earth is *not* the center of the universe. Likewise, before Agent Kay showed him the truth, Agent Jay would have claimed to know that there were no extraterrestrials living in Manhattan. In other words, Jay was wrong; he didn't know the truth about the aliens. Kay advises humility at the end of the quotation above: tomorrow we may well find out that we don't really know the things we think we do.

7.52 How can you discover that you don't actually possess the knowledge you think you do? Like Agent Kay, it is by finding out that you were wrong and that what you believed was mistaken. Actual knowledge requires the truth; to realize that you were in error is to grasp that you didn't really know what you thought you did. It follows that part of what it is to legitimately and authentically know something is to be in possession of the truth. Knowledge requires that you believe something, and it is true. Here is a first proposal for the nature of knowledge.

Analysis of knowledge, first attempt

Knowledge = true belief

7.53 That can't be entirely correct, though, because you might have a true belief by luck alone, and in that case it doesn't sound right to say that you have knowledge. For example, suppose that you buy a lottery ticket for Powerball. You're just feeling lucky, and you manage to convince yourself that this time you are definitely going to win. Let's imagine that by a stroke of incredible fortune, you beat the one in 175 million odds and actually take home the prize. Did you know that you were going to win? Well, you believed that you would win, and your belief was true. If knowledge is just true belief, then you did know. But that can't be right—no one knows that they will win Powerball. At best you could make a fortuitous guess, but then it is merely luck, not knowledge.

True belief is part of the story, but not all. What else do we need to convert true belief into knowledge? There needs to be something that *connects* your belief to the truth, some way in which belief is sensitive to the truth, and doesn't just stumble over it by accident. The traditional answer, going back to Plato, is that knowledge is true *justified* belief. Earlier we looked at the value of evidence in gaining the truth, and the idea here is that it is sufficiently strong evidence that knits belief and truth together into knowledge. How much evidence do we need before we can claim that a belief is justified? Well, this too was looked at earlier with the Clifford/James debate. Without returning to that thicket, let us just assume that there is some threshold of evidence that marks the boundary between beliefs that are justified and those that are not. 7.54

Note that a belief might be justified and still turn out false. Agent Jay's belief that there were no extraterrestrial aliens living in New York City was entirely justified on the evidence that he possessed. As Lisa put it to Homer in **The Simpsons** episode The Springfield Files, "It's just that the people who claim they've seen aliens are always pathetic low-lifes with boring jobs. Oh, and you, Dad."[24] But Agent Jay's belief that there were no aliens, while justified, was nevertheless false. Having good evidence does not guarantee that you'll hit the target of the truth. Thus a belief might be true but unjustified (the lucky guess), or justified but false. 7.55

Suppose you hit all three cherries on the slot machine: belief, justification, and truth. Do you win the payout of knowledge? Here's a revised conception of knowledge. 7.56

Analysis of knowledge, second attempt

Knowledge = justified true belief

The requirement of justification was added to escape the problem of luck, and for a very long time, philosophers thought it did the trick. It turns out, though, that epistemic luck is an insidious foe. Imagine a clock that is very precise and reliable—you depend on it frequently, and every time you've looked at it in the past, the clock has given you the right time. Unfortunately, while unknown to you, the clock has stopped working with its hands 7.57

left pointing to 3:00. You glance at the clock for the time, and as a result come to believe that it is 3:00. By sheer coincidence, you looked at the clock at exactly 3:00. Thus you believe that it is 3:00, it is true that it is 3:00, and you are justified in believing that it is 3:00 (since you came to have that belief on the basis of looking at a generally reliable clock). However, you don't *know* that it is 3:00—you can't know what time it is from looking at a stopped clock. You just got lucky that you looked at it at 3:00. It's the problem of epistemic luck all over again.

7.58 In the clock case you have a justified true belief, but you do not have knowledge. Therefore either knowledge is justified true belief plus some additional condition, or knowledge needs to be reconceived as something else altogether. There is no generally accepted view on the correct analysis of knowledge, although there are many creative and ingenious attempts. These are all beyond what can be addressed in the present volume. However, it is fair to say that justified true belief is generally regarded as being *close* to knowledge, even though not identical to it.

The Skeptic's Challenge

7.59 Whatever the standards are for evidence, no matter where we set the bar for justification, and regardless of the correct analysis of knowledge, there are those who think that it is *never* reasonable to believe anything, and that knowledge is perpetually elusive. Such people are known as skeptics. Before we get started on their arguments, it's important to note that "skepticism" can mean two different things.

Modest skepticism and radical skepticism

Modest skepticism. Modest skepticism is no more than critical thinking. It's the idea that you should demand evidence before you believe a claim, buy a product, join a religion, or vote for a candidate. And when you are offered reasons, you should scrutinize those reasons closely and consider opposing points of view. Make sure that the premises of the arguments you're considering really do support their conclusions, and that the premises themselves are acceptable ones. Be aware of the fact that smooth-talking charlatans will try to convince you of things that are dangerous, dumb, irrational, and all-around boneheaded.

Radical skepticism. We can neither avoid error nor gain truth. We're either incapable of eliminating error, invariably committed to circular reasoning, or should suspend judgment indefinitely. As far as the search for knowledge goes, we're basically screwed. If we have any true beliefs at all, we have them by accident. There's no trustworthy way to separate the true from the false, or, if there is, we can't figure out what it is.

Modest skepticism has been a theme so far in the present chapter: truth is 7.60
valuable, we should gain truth and avoid error, and getting some evidence is the best way to do so, even if there is debate about how much evidence justifies belief. The fun fact about radical skepticism is that just about no one agrees with the skeptical conclusion that knowledge is impossible. On the other hand, there's very little agreement about the best way to rebut the skeptic's ingenious arguments, or even if it is possible to do so at all.

So what are these arguments? There are many kinds of radical skepti- 7.61
cism, going back at least to Sextus Empiricus in the second century. The most famous skeptical argument attempts to show that there is an unbridgeable gulf between the truth about how the world really is, and any evidence we might marshal about it. The best known, and most discussed, of these skeptical arguments come from the French philosopher **René Descartes.**[25] In his little book *Meditations on First Philosophy*, Descartes offered some puzzling and disturbing thought experiments. Let's look at Cartesian-style skeptical reflections.

Dreamers, demons, and movies

Have you ever woken up in the morning, gotten out of bed, fixed yourself 7.62
some breakfast, brushed your teeth, and whatever else you do in the mornings, and then *really* woken up and realized that you had been just dreaming about having gotten up and starting your day? It's startling and disorienting, and for a while you're not sure what's real, whether you really have eaten a bowl of cereal or not. Now suppose that while you're trying to sort out your strange dream and get on with the morning, the exact thing happens—again you wake up and find yourself lying in bed. You had the same dream over again, just with the addition of a "waking-up" dream added to it. How many times would this have to happen to you before you wake up and say to yourself "All right, this is probably just another of those freaky waking-up dreams and in fact I'm still asleep in my bed." Of course, maybe you really did wake up for real this last time. How could you tell?

7.63 In fact, how can you ever tell if you're dreaming or awake? Dreams can be hyperrealistic, and, when you are in the middle of a dream, it feels as real as our waking lives. In our dreams we can be frightened, or amused, or sexually aroused. We have conversations with other people, and don't know what they are going to say next, just as we do awake. Sometimes you may be able to tell yourself "This is just a dream," and it really is. On the other hand, when some wonderful or terrible thing has happened to you in reality, you may tell yourself the very same thing ("I must be dreaming!"). Some people think that by pinching yourself you can determine if you are awake, a rather silly idea, since you could just as easily dream that you are pinching yourself.

7.64 In the movies, characters often dream and have no idea that they are dreaming. Dorothy's entire adventure in ***The Wizard of Oz*** is revealed at the end to have been nothing more than a dream that resulted from her being knocked unconscious by a tornado.[26] For Dorothy the dream of Oz was more vivid—and in brilliant Technicolor—than her drab real life in monochromatic Kansas. It never occurs to Dorothy, just as it rarely occurs to characters in other and-then-they-woke-up movie plots, that she has no reason to believe that Kansas is any more real than Oz. That is, the feeling of having woken up, and being surrounded by Auntie Em, Uncle Henry, and others could itself just be another dream. If the profoundly real-feeling Oz could have been just a dream, then the similarly real-feeling Kansas might be just a dream too. Even more, why wouldn't Dorothy think that vibrant, colorful Oz was reality, and thin, bloodless, sepia-toned Kansas was the shadow world of dreams?

7.65 In the fourth century BCE, the Chinese philosopher Chuang Chou (莊子, also known as Master Chuang, or Chuang Tzu; in pinyin, 莊子 is transliterated as **Zhuangzi**)[27] pondered the dream argument, and gave perhaps the first statement of it.

> Once Chuang Chou dreamt he was a butterfly, a butterfly flitting and fluttering around, happy with himself and doing as he pleased. He didn't know he was Chuang Chou. Suddenly he woke up and there he was, solid and unmistakable Chuang Chou. But he didn't know if he was Chuang Chou who had dreamt he was a butterfly, or a butterfly dreaming he was Chuang Chou. (Tzu, 1968, p. 49)

Master Chuang drew out the skeptical implications. If he couldn't tell whether he was a butterfly or a man, then he knew very little indeed.

> He who dreams of drinking wine may weep when morning comes; he who dreams of weeping may in the morning go off to hunt. While he is dreaming he does not know it is a dream, and in his dream he may even try to interpret a dream. Only after he wakes does he know it was a dream. And someday there will be a great awakening when we know that this is all a great dream. Yet the stupid believe that they are awake, busily and brightly assuming they understand things . . . (Tzu, 1968, p. 47)

Maybe you don't like the dream argument. Perhaps you think that there has got to be some sort of test to tell whether, at any given moment, you are dreaming. Pinching might not work, but surely there's something. Fine, says the skeptic. The dream argument is just one arrow in a vast quiver. There's no end to the skeptical scenarios that we can devise. Descartes himself offered another one, sometimes called the Demon argument. Here it is. Suppose there is an evil Marvel Comics supervillain called The Demon, who uses all his powers to delude you. The Demon is a trickster, an illusionist, a black magician who fools your senses with his powers of necromancy. What you see is unreal, what you hear is bogus, what you taste, touch, and smell is all a sham; everything your senses tell you is just an illusion conjured up by The Demon to keep you permanently deluded about how the world really is. The Demon never reveals himself, of course; he keeps his own existence as hidden as the real world.

Can you tell whether The Demon really exists or if he is just make- 7.66
believe? Can you tell the difference between reality and the deceptive illusions of The Demon? Presumably the answer to both questions is *no*. If The Demon exists and you are his victim right now, nothing changes for you—the world appears just as it always has. The difference is that, in fact, those appearances have nothing to do with reality, and you are massively deceived about what's real. If The Demon doesn't exist, and your senses genuinely are putting you in reliable contact with reality, then again, as far as you can tell, nothing changes. It's just that you do have knowledge about the world instead of being stuffed full of false beliefs by The Demon.

The skeptic is not claiming that The Demon really deceives you, or that 7.67
you really are dreaming at this moment. Rather, the claim is simply that you *might* be. You just can't tell. Since you might be massively fooled, and you have no way of telling, you can't actually claim to know anything about the world around you.

Once you see how to spin out these skeptical scenarios, it's easy to come 7.68
with any number of them. The film *The Matrix* is just another version of skepticism. In the movie, the reality perceived by humans is generated by

computers who feed it directly into the brains of captive humans used as power sources for the machines. Instead of sense organs delivering electrical impulses, which the brain then interprets as sight, sound, smell, taste, and touch, the computers provide the electrical impulses instead. The resulting perceived world is known as "The Matrix." It feels and seems 100 percent genuine, but the neural simulacrum world of the Matrix in fact has almost no relation to the real world. As Morpheus, one of the main characters in the film, states, "The Matrix is everywhere. It is all around us. Even now, in this very room. You can see it when you look out your window, or when you turn on your television. You can feel it when you go to work, when you go to church, when you pay your taxes. It is the world that has been pulled over your eyes to blind you from the **truth**."[28]

7.69 How can you tell whether you are living in the **Matrix** right now?[29] The skeptic's challenge is that you can't. Anything you might offer as evidence that the world as you perceive it is real, and that your beliefs about that world are true ones, could all be the result of malevolent computer programming.

7.70 The skeptic draws a sharp break between the sensations and perceptions inside your mind and whatever might be the cause of those sensations. Normally, you assume that if you see a chair, an actual chair outside of your mind that your perception somehow resembles causes your perception of a chair. The skeptic's strategy is to argue that your perception of a chair could have been caused by any number of different things—dreams, demons, the Matrix, etcetera. A real chair could even have caused it, as you believe. Who knows?

The theater of the mind

7.71 One way to think about the skeptic's argument is to think of the mind as a kind of theater. On the screen are all the images and sounds of a world. You experience the noises and flickering lights, interpreting them as people, places, and things. But the cause of the images on the screen is completely unknown to you—all your experience is on the screen.

7.72 In Figure 7.2, you (whatever you are; see the chapter on personal identity) are depicted by the stick figure on the left. Your perceptions, not only sight, but sound, taste, touch, and smell, are represented by the movie screen. It is all enveloping, the complete sense-surround system of your life, all your experiences and sensations are there. The projector is whatever is causing the images on your mental screen. But what is it exactly? What's

Figure 7.2 The theater of the mind

the cause of all your sensations? That is the great mystery. Here are some hypotheses about what the projector could be. The projector is:

1. A world of objects external to the mind that the images on the screen resemble.
2. Your own dreaming mind.
3. The Demon.
4. The malevolent machines in the Matrix.
5. Any number of other skeptical scenarios that we might think up.

You believe that the correct explanation of the projector is option 1, a world of mind-external objects that cause representations of themselves to happen in your mind. The skeptic's point is that there is absolutely no rational evidence whatsoever to believe that. For all you can tell, one of the other options is causing those sensations. You can never get past the screen to figure out the nature of the projector, because any evidence you might give is *on* the screen, not behind it. All we have to go on to figure out the nature of reality is the sensations in our minds, but the projector—the true nature of the world—is forever hidden from view.

Let's put the skeptic's argument another way. Take any ordinary belief 7.73
you have about the world: you have a body, you're reading this chapter, you're wearing clothes, you live on planet Earth, whatever. If any of those

ordinary beliefs are true, then no skeptical scenario is correct. If your ordinary beliefs are right, then you're not just dreaming that you have a body, or deceived by The Demon into believing you're reading this chapter, or wearing clothes provided by the Matrix. In other words, the truth of your ordinary empirical beliefs is incompatible with any skeptical scenario being true. Let's call this:

> *The metaphysical principle*: If any ordinary claim about the world is true, then no skeptical possibility (dreaming, Demon, Matrix, etc.) is true.

The metaphysical principle is extremely plausible; it essentially states that if the projector in the theater of the mind is a world of objects, then the projector isn't anything else, like The Demon. Hard to see how we might fault that rather obvious point. In fact, let's go ahead and claim that we *know* the metaphysical principle to be true. Since this is a claim about knowledge, let's call it:

> *The epistemic principle*: We know that if any ordinary claim about the world is true, then no skeptical possibility is true.

The epistemic principle just says that we know the metaphysical principle. All fairly straightforward so far. Now, says the skeptic, I've got you! Let's just imagine for a second that you know that you are reading this chapter. That's an ordinary, routine claim about the world. By the epistemic principle, it follows right away that you know no skeptical possibility is true. But, says the skeptic, that exactly what you *don't* know (since, you might be dreaming, deceived, and so on). Thus you don't know you are reading this chapter. Here's the argument in outline:

1.	You know that you are reading this chapter.	premise
2.	You know that (if you are reading this chapter, then you are not merely dreaming that you are reading this chapter).	epistemic principle
3.	Therefore you know that you are not merely dreaming that you are reading this chapter.	From 1, 2
4.	But (3) is precisely what you don't know, according to the skeptic.	premise
5.	Since the assumption of (1) led to a contradiction, it must be false. You don't know that you are reading this chapter.	3 & 4 contradict

The first premise is assumed for the sake of the argument and could be any modest thing that you think you know about the world—you know you're reading this chapter, you know that the sky is blue, you know that Domino's delivers, whatever. According to the epistemic principle, which we defended earlier, if you know one of those simple facts about the world, then you know that you're not just dreaming the whole thing. You can't very well *know* that you are reading this chapter if you're unable to rule out the possibility that you might just be dreaming it, or living in the Matrix or something. It follows directly in (3) that you *can* rule out those skeptical scenarios. Great, right? Not so much, says the skeptic. Skeptical possibilities are the very things that you can't just write off. You *don't* know you're not dreaming, or deceived by The Demon. In other words, having ordinary knowledge of the world implies that you can dismiss the skeptic; but since you can't legitimately ignore the skeptic, you don't have ordinary knowledge of the world after all.

Descartes himself gave one sort of response to the skeptic. Even if the 7.74 skeptic is right, and we don't know anything about the world outside of our minds, that does *not* mean that we don't know anything at all. There's still plenty that we do know. For example, you know that you exist. As Descartes famously wrote, "Cogito ergo sum." I think, therefore I am. In fact, try to imagine that you, right now, don't exist. Maybe you can imagine that there was a time before you existed, and a time after you cease to exist. But when you try to imagine that you don't exist right this minute, well, who's doing the imagining? You are! So you must exist. Another way to think about it is that you might be fooled or deceived about many things, but your existence isn't one of them. If The Demon tricks you, whom is he tricking? Again, it's got to be you. You have to exist in some manner to be the subject of deception. You can be certain, Descartes argued, of your own existence.

You know that you exist. But that's not all. Consider again the metaphor 7.75 of the theater of the mind. The skeptic's challenge is that you don't know the nature of the projector since all you have access to is what on your mental screen. Yet you do have immediate apprehension of what's on the screen, that is, the contents of your own mind. One sort of thing in your mind is *phenomenal states*, that is, sensations and feelings. You can be sure that you are having a noisy, red tractorish sensation, even if you have no idea whether a red tractor outside of your mind is really causing it or you are just dreaming the whole thing. You can know that you are feeling happy, blue, melancholy, cheerful, angry, wistful, jealous, disappointed, or excited even if you do not know the causes of these sensations, or are seriously mistaken about why you have those feelings. The Matrix may be able to fool you into believing you are eating a piece of steak, but cannot fool you about having a sensation of juicy deliciousness or being pleased about it. You are authentically having those sensations and feelings.

7.76 Besides phenomenal states, you also have *intentional states.* These are things like beliefs, hopes, desires, fears, wishes, loves, and hates. For example, you believe that you are wearing clothes right now. You might be mistaken about that (that's the skeptic's point), but one thing you are not mistaken about is that *you believe* that you are wearing clothes. You're not wrong about what it is that you believe. There is a subtle distinction to be made here—your beliefs can be wrong (you might be the victim of massive skeptical deception), but you aren't wrong about whether you have them. Suppose you believe that there is a Santa Claus. Your belief that there is a Santa is false (sorry), but your additional belief that *you believe that there is a Santa Claus,* that one's true. You might be afraid of spiders without there being any spiders, but you still know that you have that fear. You can know that you're in love with James Bond, despite the fact that he's fictional. These sorts of states are in your mind; they're on the mental screen, not behind it. The skeptic gets traction by proposing various hypotheses about the projector, but what's on the screen—that's something, Descartes thought, that you have direct, inerrant, access to.

7.77 Suppose that Descartes is right, and you do know the fact of your own existence, the nature of your phenomenal states, and your intentional states. That's not exactly an atomic pile driver move against the skeptic. All it really does is insist that despite skepticism we can still have knowledge of the contents of our minds, along with the fact that we have minds. The skeptic still holds the better hand, a straight flush against your pair of threes. You still know nothing about the projector behind the screen in the theater of the mind; you know nothing at all about the nature of extra-mental reality.

7.78 There have been many responses to Cartesian-style skepticism, as you might imagine. It is safe to report that none have been widely accepted as wholly convincing. A thorough survey of approaches to skepticism is well beyond the ambitions of the present book. Nevertheless, it's only fair to offer a little taste of how some have answered it. The English philosopher

G. E. Moore gave one well-known response to the skeptic.[30] Moore's argument is very easy to state, and reactions to it tend to fall into one of two camps. People either think that the argument is a brilliant, common sense response to skepticism that settles the issue, or they think that Moore's argument is childishly naive, and assumes the very thing it is supposed to prove. There isn't much of a middle ground. Here's the argument:

1. If skepticism is true, then we have no empirical knowledge.
2. But we do have empirical knowledge.
3. Therefore skepticism is false.

Simple, huh? What's more reasonable, Moore says, that you know that you have a hand, or that you know that the skeptic's scenarios really are possible or his reasoning is legitimate? We start with basic truisms like "I have a hand" or "I live on planet Earth." The rest of our knowledge rests on things like that. These truisms are what we know the best, says Moore, and we should be more confident in them than in anything the skeptic has to say. Yet the skeptic asks us to throw out our very starting point, the things that we know the best.

Essentially, the skeptic claims that the following are jointly inconsistent— 7.79
they can't all be true, and at least one has to be false.

a. *The epistemic principle*: We know that if any ordinary claim about the world is true, then no skeptical possibility is true.
b. We know ordinary claims about the world.
c. We do not know that no skeptical possibility is true.

The skeptic's answer to the inconsistency problem is to toss out (b). The epistemic principle is true, and it's true that we can't eliminate skeptical possibilities. The only choice is to admit that we don't know ordinary things about the world. Moore's response is to agree with the skeptic about the epistemic principle, but keep (b) and throw out (c). That is, Moore insists that we do know ordinary things about the world; he gives a long list of such things, such as "you know that you have a hand" and "you are, and have always been, very near planet Earth." It is far more reasonable, Moore thinks, to hold onto this commonsense knowledge than it is to concede that we can't summarily reject the skeptic's fanciful scenarios. If the choice is *deny that you know you have a hand* or *deny that you might be living in the Matrix*, Moore opts for the second. Therefore, we do know ordinary facts about an extra-mental world, and we know that skepticism is false.

You may well be persuaded by the theater of the mind, and think that 7.80
Moore is just missing the skeptic's point entirely. As noted, philosophers

are divided about his approach. But sometimes the best defense is a good offense.

The Counterfeit Detector

7.81 Skepticism of the sort just discussed leads us to the conclusion that we may be ignorant about the genuine nature of the world outside of our minds. There is a more comprehensive skeptical argument that aims to show that we know nothing whatsoever. It doesn't matter whether you are a fan of perception, introspection, or pure reason; no matter what method you use to gain your beliefs you will never be able to achieve knowledge. This conundrum is known as the problem of the criterion.

7.82 We're interested in getting some knowledge. Remember Faber's dictum from earlier: knowledge is good. But how can we tell whether we have a bit of knowledge, whether one of our beliefs achieves the exalted state of knowledge? In part the answer has something to do with whether we have the right evidence, and if we have enough of it to justify what we believe. No problem so far. But how can we tell whether we really do in fact have the right evidence and if we have enough of it to convert our true beliefs from a lucky accident into knowledge? That is, how do we know when to trust our evidence as authentically leading us to the truth? An example will help.

Genuine and counterfeit money

7.83 Imagine that you are in the **Secret Service**.[31] In the movies, Secret Service agents are always jumping in front of bullets to protect the president. To be sure, that's one of their jobs. But another one, and in fact the very reason that President Lincoln created the Secret Service, is to protect the nation's currency by tracking down phony bank notes and arresting counterfeiters. It's important to get funny money out of circulation because if there is enough of it floating around, it will lead to a devaluation of US currency and then to inflation. In a way, the presence of bad bills poisons the good ones.

7.84 Suppose someone hands you a $100 bill. How can you tell whether it is a fake? To tell whether a $100 bill is a counterfeit, you need some method of testing it. There are many ways we could try to tell the difference between legit $100 bills and phony ones. We could weigh them, for example, or we could see how they respond to certain chemicals, or we could judge money based on our personal impressions of the character of the owner. There are good methods and bad methods. A good method will reliably pick out the true $100 bills and also reliably winnow out the counterfeits. As you can see, this is another analogue of *gain truth and avoid error.*

The Secret Service has a method: there are certain features that they look 7.85
for to detect counterfeits. One of the things they examine is the paper used. **Crane and Co.** has made the paper for the Treasury since 1879,[32] and their proprietary paper contains "counterfeit deterrents, such as advanced security threads, watermarks, planchettes, security fibers, special additives, and fluorescent and phosphorescent elements." Other things to look for are the crispness and texture of the engraving, a watermark of Benjamin Franklin, and a color-shifting numeral 100. New notes also have a 3-D security ribbon that changes images as the bill is tilted and moved. In other words, the Secret Service has a whole system worked out to separate good money from bad.

Particularism and methodism

How can you be confident that the Secret Service method is a good one? 7.86
The answer is that the government makes the money—they buy the fancy paper from Crane and Co. and print it themselves at the Bureau of Printing and Engraving. So they have perfect examples of genuine $100 bills fresh off the printing presses, and can be completely certain that those bills are real. All that needs to be done is to compare any $100 note in circulation with the new ones the Secret Service is certain are genuine, and see whether they pass the test. In other words, to be a counterfeit detector, you start with a particular example of a true $100 bill and by studying it come to derive a method for spotting fakes. Let's call this approach *particularism.*

> *Particularism*: Start with some examples of what you are positive is real and then from those figure out a reliable method to separate the true from the false.

Suppose that someone hands you a bunch of $100 notes. You're always broke and have never held a $100 bill in your hands before, much less worked for the Bureau of Printing and Engraving or the Secret Service. You're in no position to derive your own method of counterfeit detection. So how can tell whether the notes you're holding are real? You don't want to be taken in by fakes. The solution is that you can just apply the methods discussed above—examine watermarks, the colors and engraving, the 3-D ribbon, etcetera. You're confident that the Secret Service knows what it is talking about and that those are good ways to check for fakes. The idea that to separate out the real from the phony you start with some method in which you're confident and just apply it is called *methodism*.

> *Methodism*: Start with some method you're sure is reliable and then use it to distinguish between the true and the false.

With particularism, you assume that you already have some examples of genuine $100 bills, and from there come up with a method for identifying fakes. Methodism works in the other direction. You start by assuming that you have a great method of identifying fakes and then use it to figure out which $100 bills are genuine. You may notice a bit of a problem here. Particularism assumes you can already tell the difference between real bills and phony ones. That's how you know you have some examples of genuine Benjamins. Which is to say, particularism works only by presupposing that you have some reliable method of picking out the true from the false. Methodism, on the other hand, presupposes that you already have some samples of real bills—that's how you're able to decide among different methods to detect counterfeits and figure out what system is the trustworthiest one. So particularism can work only if you already have a reliable method; in other words, methodism is logically prior to particularism. On the other hand, methodism will work only if you already have samples of bills you are positive are genuine; in other words, particularism is logically prior to methodism.

The wheel

7.87 The government has a way out of this circle (Figure 7.3): it prints the money. Therefore the $100 bills rolling off the assembly line are guaranteed to be genuine by federal decree. From there the method of detecting counterfeits can be developed. So far, so good. But suppose that instead of separating money into piles of real and fake, we have to separate our beliefs into two piles: true and false. As with currency, the bad beliefs tend to poison the good ones, so we need to identify, and throw away, the bad ones.

We don't make the truth like the Bureau of Printing and Engraving makes the money, so there is no independent guarantor of what's true. For

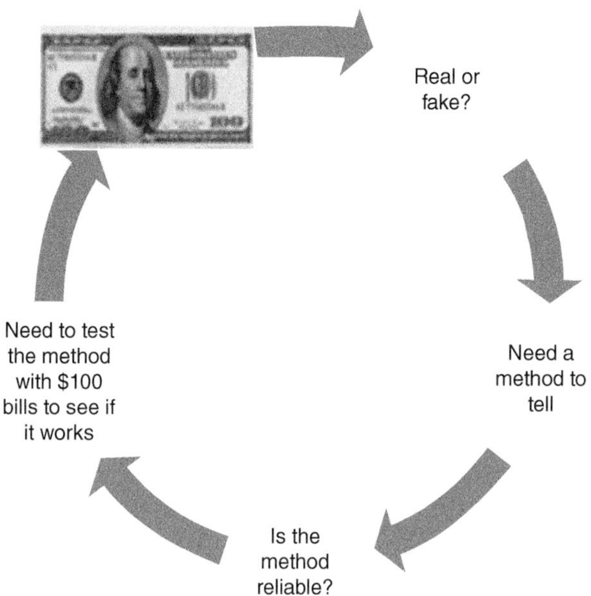

Figure 7.3 The wheel of money

any belief you care to offer, we can ask whether the belief is true or false. To figure it out we'll need a method of telling the true from the false. Of course, we want a trustworthy method that will reliably give us accurate results. Yet the only way we'll know whether our method is a reliable one is if it is correctly separating true beliefs from false ones, which requires that we *already* know which are which.

We are caught in the circle again (Figure 7.4). This time with no way 7.88
out. At least, there does not seem to be an escape that does not merely assume something for which we have no evidence. As we saw earlier, some philosophers, like Locke, hold that all of our knowledge ultimately comes from our senses and that the scientific method of experimentation and observation is the only way to get at the truth. Others maintain that it is through reflection on our own ideas and the analysis of concepts and their relations that we come to have knowledge. Both of these groups are methodists—they assume that they have the right method to separate truth out from error and then apply their belief-sorting strategy. Other philosophers claim that there are some facts that we know for certain (for example,

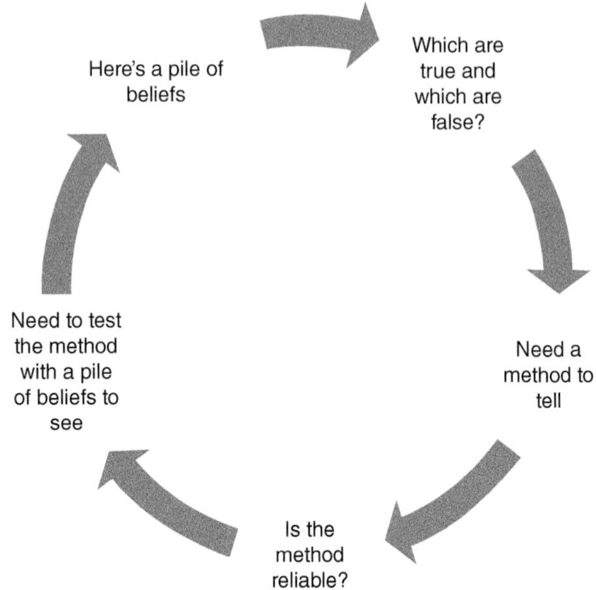

Figure 7.4 The wheel of belief

that you exist, that you have a body, that you are near the planet Earth, etc.) and, given that we know these things to be true, we can then figure out the best way to arrive at more truths. In other words, they are particularists. G. E. Moore was a particularist.

7.89 The problem is that both methodists and particularists simply assume that they have an answer to one of the stops on the wheel. That approach might have worked in the currency case, since the government creates the authentic bills, but, as we have already noted, it doesn't work here. Both methodism and particularism beg the question, that is, they assume the very thing that needs to be proved—a logical no-no. Yet it seems that there is no alternative except radical skepticism: since we cannot break out of the circle except by a sneaky, logically illegitimate move, we are never able to tell whether our beliefs are true or false. Genuine knowledge isn't possible.

7.90 Maybe radical skepticism isn't any better off than methodism or particularism, though. Here's why. The skeptic's position is:

> *The Wheel*: We can't know whether a belief is true unless we have some method to tell if it is true, but we can't know whether the method is a good

one unless we already know if it produces true beliefs. Each is logically prior to the other. Therefore we can't know either thing, and knowledge is impossible.

The skeptic is claiming that it is better to believe The Wheel than accept either methodism or particularism. If the skeptic claims to *know* that The Wheel is better, then the skeptic is offering The Wheel as an item of knowledge. If the skeptic is offering The Wheel as an item of knowledge, then the skeptic is a particularist. Therefore, the skeptic is a particularist. Or we can spin things around the other way. We can show that the skeptic is a methodist if she defends The Wheel by appeal to a general principle like this one: you can't know anything by **begging the question**.[33] This sets up nonquestion-beggingness as a requirement for knowledge, and is thereby a form of methodism. If the skeptic is *not* claiming to know that The Wheel is true, then there is no reason to fear it. Why should we worry about The Wheel if even its defenders don't claim to know it?

In the end, it might be that skepticism is not a real alternative to either methodism or particularism. Methodism vs. particularism may be the only real game in town. If that's right, then we are left with either assuming that we have some items of knowledge out of which we can build a method of inquiry, or we have to assume that we already have the correct procedure of gaining knowledge and then see what it gives us. 7.91

Now we have arrived at a deep mystery. Knowledge demands evidence. Yet we can't have knowledge unless we beg the question and accept either methodism or particularism without any evidence. We're therefore compelled to build our knowledge on something inherently and essentially impervious to evidence—surely a powerful motivation to accept extreme skepticism. Yet the claim of extreme skepticism, that The Wheel must be true, may not be an authentic alternative after all, as we've just seen in the last two paragraphs. Knowledge rests on paradoxical foundations indeed. 7.92

Annotated Bibliography

Chisholm, Roderick M. (1982) *The Foundations of Knowing* (Minneapolis: University of Minnesota Press). This collection contains Chisholm's explanation of the problem of the criterion, easily the best discussion of the problem in modern times.

Clifford, W. K. (1877) "The Ethics of Belief," *Contemporary Review* 29, full text available at www.infidels.org/library/historical/w_k_clifford/ethics_of_belief.html, accessed May 21, 2012. Clifford's classic defense of high evidential standards and why you should never form beliefs on insufficient evidence.

Descartes, Rene (1641) *Meditations on First Philosophy*, full text available at www.earlymoderntexts.com/de.html, accessed May 21, 2012. Descartes's most widely read work in epistemology, in which he worries about evil demons, dreaming, and presents the daunting problem of skepticism.

Gettier, Edmund (1963) "Is Justified True Belief Knowledge?" *Analysis* 23, 121–123, full text available at www.ditext.com/gettier/gettier.html, accessed May 21, 2012. A very short and lucid article with an incredible impact on subsequent epistemology. Gettier convinced everyone that the answer to his title question is "no."

James, William (1897) *The Will to Believe and Other Essays in Popular Philosophy* (New York: Longmans, Green). James's response to Clifford, and his defense of lowering one's standards for belief and taking some chances to gain more truths.

Littlejohn, Clayton (forthcoming) *This is Epistemology: An Introduction* (Oxford: Wiley-Blackwell). A more in-depth introduction to the theory of knowledge which examines perception, induction, testimony, justification, the analysis of knowledge, and how we might gain moral and religious knowledge.

Locke, John (1690) *An Essay Concerning Human Understanding*, full text available at www.earlymoderntexts.com/loess.html, accessed May 21, 2012. Locke's most famous work, in which he defends the view that all our knowledge comes from the evidence of the senses.

Maines, Rachel P. (1999) *The Technology of Orgasm* (Baltimore: Johns Hopkins University Press). The only published history of the vibrator, and a fascinating, scholarly look at one branch of medical quackery.

McCoy, Bob (2000) *Quack!: Tales of Medical Fraud from the Museum of Questionable Medical Devices* (Santa Monica, CA: Santa Monica Press). A constantly entertaining, yet very sobering, look at quack medical devices, products, and practices. Lots of excellent photos and old advertisements. There is a terrific chapter on radium "cures."

Moore, G. E. (1959) *Philosophical Papers* (London: George Allen and Unwin). This collection contains Moore's "A Defence of Common Sense," full text available at www.ditext.com/moore/common-sense.html, accessed May 21, 2012, and "Proof of an External World," his attempts to refute skepticism.

Pritchard, Duncan (2002) "Recent Work on Radical Skepticism," *American Philosophical Quarterly* 39, 215–257, full text available at www.philosophy.ed.ac.uk/people/full-academic/documents/RecentWorkonSkepticism.pdf, accessed May 21, 2012. Written for professionals, but a really fine overview of a variety of contemporary attempts to overcome radical skepticism.

Russell, Bertrand (1948) *Human Knowledge: Its Scope and Limits* (London: Allen and Unwin). Russell presents the stopped clock case on pp. 170–171, although he didn't realize that it was a counterexample to the justified true belief analysis of knowledge.

Shermer, Michael (1997) *Why People Believe Weird Things: Pseudoscience, Superstition, and Other Confusions of Our Time* (New York: W. H. Freeman). In the first chapter Shermer explains how he changed from a gullible cyclist to a critical thinker.

Tzu, Chuang (1968) *The Complete Works of Chuang Tzu*, trans. Watson, Burton (New York: Columbia University Press), full text available at http://terebess.hu/english/chuangtzu.html, accessed May 21, 2012. The writings of the fourth-century BCE Chinese sage.

Online Resources

1 The home page of the Church of the Flying Spaghetti Monster: www.venganza.org/
2 The home page of The New York Times, perhaps the major newspaper of record in the United States: www.nytimes.com/
3 Information about medicine at Johns Hopkins, one of the premiere medical schools and facilities in the United States: www.hopkinsmedicine.org/
4 Dr Nick Riviera from *The Simpsons*, the quack doctor who graduated from the (blessedly fictional) Hollywood Upstairs Medical College: http://en.wikipedia.org/wiki/Nick_Riviera
5 A detailed discussion of the life and philosophical work of Johann Fichte: http://plato.stanford.edu/entries/johann-fichte/
6 Allmovie's synopsis of *Animal House*: www.allmovie.com/movie/v60324
7 A discussion of a simple mathematical hypothesis that Christian Goldbach proposed in 1742: http://mathworld.wolfram.com/GoldbachConjecture.html
8 A sophisticated recent treatment of the issue of how many angels can dance on the point of a needle: www.scribd.com/sinnlos/d/74977227-Angels-Needle
9 A biography of cyclist, scholar, and skeptic Michael Shermer: http://en.wikipedia.org/wiki/Michael_Shermer
10 The official website of the Tour de France: www.letour.fr/us/index.html
11 The home page for the Race Across America: www.raceacrossamerica.org/raam/raam.php?N_webcat_id=1
12 Interesting photographs of antique medical vibrators and the claims made on their behalf: www.electrotherapymuseum.com/2005/LindstromSmith/index.htm
13 The Mayo Clinic's assessment of penis-enlargement products: www.mayoclinic.com/health/penis/MC00026

14 A physician's assessment of the medical quackery surrounding cellulite: www.quackwatch.org/01QuackeryRelatedTopics/cellulite.html
15 A review of the life and works of the English mathematician and philosopher W. K. Clifford: http://en.wikipedia.org/wiki/William_Kingdon_Clifford
16 The legal definition of "voir dire": http://dictionary.law.com/Default.aspx?selected=2229
17 A sophisticated discussion of the work of the psychologist and philosopher William James: http://plato.stanford.edu/entries/james/
18 An in-depth discussion of ancient Pyrrhonian skepticism, including Sextus Empiricus: http://plato.stanford.edu/entries/skepticism-ancient/
19 The National Oceanic and Atmospheric Administration's national weather service: www.weather.gov/
20 The complete text of Arthur Conan Doyle's Sherlock Holmes story "A Scandal in Bohemia," first published in *The Strand Magazine* (1891): www.mysterynet.com/holmes/01scandalbohemia/
21 *The Name of the Rose* (1983) trans. William Weaver (New York: Houghton Mifflin Harcourt), p. 399. An overview of Umberto Eco's tour de force novel, *The Name of the Rose*: http://en.wikipedia.org/wiki/The_Name_of_the_Rose
22 A sophisticated account of the ancient Greek philosopher Pythagoras: http://plato.stanford.edu/entries/pythagoras/
23 A short clip from the film *Men in Black* about what people know: www.youtube.com/watch?v=kkCwFkOZoOY
24 The complete episode of *The Simpsons*, season 8, episode 10: The Springfield Files: www.cucirca.com/2010/01/11/the-simpsons-season-8-episode-10-the-springfield-files/
25 A detailed account of Descartes's life and works: http://plato.stanford.edu/entries/descartes-works/
26 Allmovie's synopsis of *The Wizard of Oz*: www.allmovie.com/movie/the-wizard-of-oz-v55014
27 An in-depth discussion of the Chinese philosopher Zhuangzi: http://plato.stanford.edu/entries/zhuangzi/
28 The red pill vs. the blue pill scene from *The Matrix*: www.youtube.com/watch?v=bCUhFZnxoBU
29 An argument that you may in fact be living in a computer simulation: www.simulation-argument.com/
30 The career and thought of the English philosopher G. E. Moore: http://plato.stanford.edu/entries/moore/
31 The official website of the United States Secret Service: www.secretservice.gov/
32 The history of Crane & Co, manufacturer of paper for the Bureau of Printing and Engraving: www.crane.com/history
33 A close analysis and explanation of the fallacy of begging the question: www.fallacyfiles.org/begquest.html

INDEX

Page references relating to figures are given in italics.

This Is Philosophy: An Introduction, First Edition. Steven D. Hales.